RETIRED

D1526365

Essays
in the Numerical Criticism
of Medieval Literature

FIG. 1. *God the Architect uses a compass to assign form and proportion to Creation (mid-thirteenth-century Bible, French: Cod. 2554, fol. iv, Österreichische Nationalbibliothek, Vienna).* By permission of the Österreichische Nationalbibliothek.

Essays in the Numerical Criticism of Medieval Literature

Edited by Caroline D. Eckhardt

Lewisburg
Bucknell University Press
London: Associated University Presses

Associated University Presses, Inc.
Cranbury, New Jersey 08512

Associated University Presses
Magdalen House
136-148 Tooley Street
London SE1 2TT, England

Library of Congress Cataloging in Publication Data

Main entry under title:

Essays in the numerical criticism of medieval literature.

    Bibliography: p.
    Includes index.
    1. Literature, Medieval—History and criticism—Addresses, essays,
lectures. 2. Symbolism of numbers in literature—Addresses, essays, lectures.
I. Eckhardt, Caroline D., 1942-
PN682.N85E84   809'.02   76-55822
ISBN 0-8387-2019-6

PRINTED IN THE UNITED STATES OF AMERICA

129592

for R. B. E.

Contents

Preface

Omnia in mensura et numero et pondere disposuisti.
— Book of Wisdom, 11.21

Euclid alone has looked on Beauty bare.
— Edna St. Vincent Millay, *Collected Sonnets*, 45

Numerical criticism is both old and new. Its basic premise, that the universe and the imitative arts of man are constructed of regularities inherently numerical, is as old as the Book of Wisdom — or as old as Pythagoras, whose followers claimed even that things *are* number. The application of this premise to textual analysis is as old as Augustine, who warned that we "must not despise the science of numbers," which is often of "eminent service" in interpreting Scripture — or as old as Philo Judaeus, who, commenting on the description of Creation in Genesis, explained that the days of God's working are specified as six because six is a "perfect number," and one particularly appropriate to all mortal beings since its factors, two and three, represent materiality and solidity.

Modern analysis of the numbers in medieval literature, however — the new numerical criticism — virtually began with Vincent Hopper's book *Medieval Number Symbolism* (1938) and especially Ernst Robert Curtius's comments on *Zahlenkomposition*, numerical composition, which appeared as an excursus in his book *Europäische Literatur und lateinisches Mittelalter* (1948; English version, *European Literature and the Latin Middle Ages*, 1953). Most numerical studies since are indebted, explicitly or implicitly, to this excursus, in which Curtius went so far as to see in numerical design a medieval alternative to modern concepts of literary coherence and unity.

9

If this viewpoint is correct, then an understanding of the functions of number in medieval literature is clearly of basic importance: number is fundamental form, not superficial decoration.

Since Curtius's work appeared, there has been a veritable treasure hunt for the significant numbers in medieval literature. Two main pathways have been followed. In one, sometimes called *numerological analysis*, the symbolic meanings that the medieval theorists assigned to individual numbers are used as clues to the intentions of the poets. Thus when a medieval poet says that there were five knights at the crossroads or constructs his poem in five-line stanzas, some symbolic meaning conventionally attached to the number five is seen to be part of the intended idea-content of the work. The assumption is that the choice of five (rather than three or four or whatever) was guided by the poet's desire to remind us of a meaning. In the other main pathway, sometimes called *tectonic analysis* or simply *numerical analysis*, a tabulation of the formal units of poetry (lines, stanzas, laisses, fitts, etc.) is seen as a clue to what in general we call *structure*, that is, the arrangement of parts into a whole. Formal tabulations are used, for example, as evidence for the presence of *entrelacement* (interwoven designs) or as a means of solving certain persistent structural puzzles, such as the question of why the stanzas in *Sir Gawain and the Green Knight* or the cantos in Dante's *Commedia* vary in length. The assumption is that the poet's choice of the number of formal units to include and of their position was guided by his desire to create a beautiful and complex (but not necessarily symbolic) pattern. Thus if one stanza contains twenty-four lines and the next twenty-eight, for instance, this variation is thought purposeful rather than accidental. A pattern is there to be seen—if we can see how to see it.

The essays in this collection (two of them previously published, six not so) are attempts to understand medieval aesthetic principles and products, not to champion the numerical approach. In fact, a healthy skepticism is occasionally apparent. Whenever one hunts there is the danger of returning in triumph and in self-delusion, having brought home a prize that is not what one took it to be, or having brought home nothing at all and remaining ignorant of that fact. Certainly the note of caution must be sounded. All the essays share, however, a confidence that when Boethius wrote *Omnia quaecumque a primaeva rerum natura constructa sunt, numerorum videntur ratione formata,* and when Chaucer wrote *alle thynges been ordeyned and nombred,* they were enunciating a philosophical and aesthetic principle of fundamental importance not simply to themselves but probably to the entire thousand-year-long civilization near whose beginning and ending these two writers stand.

This collection begins with Russell A. Peck's "Number as Cosmic Language," an explanation of the relationship of medieval ideas about number to medieval ideas about nature, the arts, beauty, time, and man. Then follows A. Kent Hieatt's assessment of the current state of numerical studies, "Numerical Structures in Verse: Second-Generation Studies Needed (Exemplified in *Sir Gawain* and the *Chanson de Roland*)." After these two largely theoretical essays come six studies of particular texts. The order in which they appear is not chronological; instead, it follows a sequence from the analysis of *explicit* to the analysis of *implicit* numbers or numerical structures. Charles S. Singleton's study of Dante's *Commedia,* "The Poet's Number at the Center," is based upon a count of cantos and *terzine* and lines, each of these units being unmistakably intended as such by the poet; similarly, Elaine Scarry's study of Boethius's *Consolatio,* "The Well-Rounded Sphere: The Metaphysical Structure of the *Consolation of Philosophy,*" is based upon a count of books and the sections demarcated within them. Allan Metcalf's "Gawain's Number," on *Sir Gawain and the Green Knight,* examines the evident line-count numbers in terms of an implied norm against which variation plays. Caroline D. Eckhardt's "The Number of Chaucer's Pilgrims: A Review and Reappraisal" considers textual problems relating to the counting of the Canterbury pilgrims and proposes both a symbolic and an ironic use of number. The collection closes with two structural studies that postulate internal numerical symmetries as formal counterparts for thematic designs. Thomas Elwood Hart, after

12

reviewing the problems of this kind of analysis, describes certain numerical designs in *Beowulf* in "Tectonic Methodology and an Application to *Beowulf*." Finally, in "Patterns of Arithmetical Proportion in the *Nibelungenlied*," Edward G. Fichtner describes two such patterns, each internally symmetrical, with a special symmetry at their point of intersection.

I am grateful to *Modern Language Notes* and to the *Yearbook of English Studies* for their kind permission to reprint "The Poet's Number at the Center," in the first case, and "The Number of Chaucer's Pilgrims," in the second; to the Liberal Arts College Fund for Research at the Pennsylvania State University for its support during the development of this book; to a number of colleagues, particularly Bruce A. Rosenberg of Brown University and Robert W. Frank, Jr., Charles W. Mann, and Henry W. Sams, of Pennsylvania State, for assistance of various kinds; to Susan R. Runk for preparation of the typescript; and to Ronald B. Roth for his editorial guidance.

C.D.E.

University Park, Pennsylvania

Essays
in the Numerical Criticism
of Medieval Literature

Number as Cosmic Language

Russell A. Peck

> Perfection is common to all numbers, for in the progress of our thought from our own plane to that of the gods, they present the first example of perfect abstraction.
> —Macrobius *In Somnium Scipionis*
> To ascend the path towards Wisdom, we discover that numbers transcend our mind and remain unchangeable in their own.
> —Augustine *De Libero Arbitrio*[1]

Because medieval cosmology is thoroughly mathematical in its conception, the rhetoric of numbers permeates all areas of medieval learning. Philosophy and aesthetics, theology and considerations of the soul (what we would call psychology), the various divisions of the quadrivium and creative arts—all become colored with conceptual and procedural similarities through number lore. Whether the end sought be the Oneness of God through the correspondent accidents of the many, the perceiving of likenesses in different modes of human endeavor through analogy, or the exploration of the idiosyncrasies of nature within the generalizations of creation, numerology provides the language shared by all, a common denomination in that most characteristic of medieval mental excursions, the quest to relate particulars to universals. Augustine observes:

If you look at something mutable, you cannot grasp it either with the bodily senses or the consideration of the mind, unless it possesses some numerical form. If this form is removed, the mutable dissolves into nothing; do not, then, doubt that there is some eternal and immutable Form which prevents mutable objects from being destroyed and allows them to complete their temporal course, as it were, by measured movements in a distinct variety of forms. This eternal Form is neither contained nor. . .spread out in space, neither prolonged nor changed by time. Through eternal Form every temporal thing can receive its form, and, in accordance with its kind, can manifest and embody number in space and time.[2]

As long as the Neoplatonic theory of Universal Forms is upheld, this argument of man's participation in the Creator's design, a design without which nothing would exist,[3] is relished with exuberant praise. From the late eleventh century to the early thirteenth, during which period there is an extensive revival of Augustinian study, number theory is the genetrix of most epistemology. Even after Aristotelians, nominalists, and empiricists have seriously challenged the doctrine of universals in the later medieval period, the argument of knowledge through analysis of design continues to be explored, and mathematics maintains its preeminence in epistemology, though in a somewhat altered form. Roger Bacon, for example, may insist that mathematics is a purely descriptive science that must be rid of metaphysical excrescences imposed by tradition. Nevertheless, he relies heartily upon analogical arguments in his discussion of the Trinity and, though a "scientist," is sensitive throughout his writing to the importance of correspondences in the meaning of God's created forms. Even so late a figure as Kepler, though now usually viewed as seminal in the history of our scientific disciplines, was an ardent numerologist.[4]

In my discussion of medieval number theory I shall concentrate on the Neoplatonic tradition and shall consider five interrelated topics: (1) numerology and the theory of correspondent forms; (2) mathematics as basis of all the arts; (3) number and concepts of ethics and mental health; (4) number and the utility of beauty; and (5) number and concentric time. I shall conclude my discussion with a brief excursion into the Middle English poem *Pearl*, a work demonstrating admirably the interrelationship of these topics as understood by the late medieval imagination.

Numerology and the Theory of Correspondent Forms

A revival and proliferation of discussions of a correspondent macrocosm and microcosm occur during the twelfth century. With such discussions came a renewed interest in numerology, particularly as it had been understood and applied by Augustine. Numerology provides a language apart from things. The numbers of creation exist apart from mutability and human error, and are closest to the language of the Creator Himself. As Macrobius had put it, numbers are the primary example of "perfect abstraction."[5] Likewise, Augustine had explained that if a man comprehends number it is not changed; yet if he fails to grasp it, its truth "does not disappear; rather, it remains true and permanent, while man's failure to grasp it is commensurate with the extent of his error."[6] So pure and absolute is number that it was held to exist even before form, time, or space, preexistent in the mind of God.[7]

Because of its purity of abstraction, number offered the cosmic theorist a bridge between the corruptible and the eternal, since in addition to measuring all things it is a language of relationships and proportions. The metaphors most commonly used to explain its utility in cosmological study are *key, guide, motion toward,* and *pathway.* Terms such as *order (ordo), reason (ratio),* and *number (numerus)* are sometimes used interchangeably,[8] for all equate ephemeral realities to the divine, preexistent plan *(forma)* and offer the means of harmonizing the human mind with the Creator and the rest of creation. As a pathway for exploring the *harmonia mundi*, number enables the Christian seeker of wisdom to appreciate created things with no sense of slighting God. Indeed, admiration of the number in things is a form of praise. In discovering form, one exercises the highest of his God-created rights — the grace of participation in divine *ratio*. Number with its eternal language underlies not only such basic medieval concepts as macrocosm and microcosm, form and image, and the explaining through analogy of the relationships of the correspondent parts; it also, as will be shown, correlates morality and mental states with external realities.

The Middle Ages inherited the science of number, whether arithmetical, geometrical, harmonic, or moral, from rich and ancient traditions stretching back through Platonism, Pythagorean lore, and Chaldean astronomy. As a means of conjoining the apparently disparate and of abstracting general principles from nature, numerology differs from modern mathematics in that besides describing analytically it is often seen to have powers of its own derived from creation. Quite simply, things measured by the same numbers were held to be in some way correspondent. Not only do such numbers reveal compatible forms in nature; they also in turn acquire connotations from the comparisons they purvey. Their numerical tie is seen to have meaning in and of itself; there must be a reason behind the ratio, a reason implicit in creation. Thus 7, for example, because of the 7 moving spheres, the 7-day week, the four 7-part phases of the moon, the 7 ages of history, and the 7 tones of the musical scale (all of which are evidently part of God's plan), clearly is a measure of totality, particularly totality in a mutable realm. For so God used the number. Eight, on the other hand, since it is the first number beyond 7, must imply a return to unity, a new beginning, a sign of regeneration and rebirth as in baptism (n.b., the octagonal font), the New Jerusalem (8th age), Easter (*dies octavus*), and Pentecost (a week of weeks and another *dies octavus*: 7 x 7 + 1).

The centrality of number lore to medieval cosmology may best be remembered through specific examples, two of which I shall consider. In his *De Mundo*, Honorius of Autun measures distances between planets by intervals on the musical scale, confident that man as microcosm, whose number is 7 (3 parts soul and 4 parts elements that constitute the body) and who has 7 voices (the 7 tones on the musical scale), reproduces in facsimile the macrocosm's celestial music.[9] His confidence lies in his numbers, which bear out the correspondences.

A fine graphic example may be found in Pol de Limbourg's *Anatomical Man*, which correlates the human body with the macrocosm, in the Duc du Berry's *Très Riches Heures* (Figure 2). Man's miniature universe corresponds to the greater universe, as the 12 signs of the zodiac influence the 12 parts of the body. Yet notice the prominence with which man is depicted, even though he is the microcosm. From mankind's perspective, his nature, replete with the necessary eternal numbers, must be the starting point of his quest for the universals. Pol portrays the central human figure as a twin, a duality, one part of which the mansions influence. The side facing the viewer looks downward, or perhaps inward, in a stance of reflection; the other, the masculine part, looks upward and beyond. The artist uses the 4 corners of his world, that is to say, the page,[10] to delineate the 4 conditions (hot, cold, moist, dry), the 4 humors, and each of the 4 seasons, thereby accounting for another correspondent 12 that, along with the heavenly mansions, frame and at least partly govern man. The dual human figure is surrounded by 7 circles of clouds whose numbered insubstantiality indicates the moving spheres. The mandorla around the fleeting spheres contains the mansions and indicates the eighth sphere of the fixed stars. Its substantial construction indicates its permanence, while its 360-degree circularity implies man's containment within the Universal One (8 being a return to 1). On the flat surface of a single sheet, then, the artist has depicted the whole of the 4-square world with all its oppositions of macrocosm and microcosm symmetrically arranged and, though various, made equable through numbered correspondence. Augustine, commenting on the beauty possible when various meters are set harmoniously against each other, exclaims in *De Musica*: "For what can give the ear more pleasure than being both delighted by variety and uncheated of equality?"[11] If we substitute eye for ear, which even Roger Bacon assures us we may do (for the eye too has its music),[12] Augustine's eulogy provides a fitting comment

FIG. 2. *Pol de Limbourg's Anatomical Man (from the* Très Riches Heures *of the Duc du Berry, fol. 14v).* By permission of Musée Condé, Chantilly.

on Pol de Limbourg's picture. Its variety delights, but the highest pleasure it affords lies in the mathematical equability of its parts. The picture's meaning is its aesthetic unity. There one participates, as did Honorius in his healthful eulogy on the cosmos, in music fitting for both eye and mind.

Mathematics as Foundation of the Arts

In his explanation of the intervals of the spheres, Honorius is not concerned with scientific accuracy as we conceive of it. He is concerned with astronomy, but not astronomy as a separate science. Rather, he views it as an extension of numbering, which brings me to the second main point: for Honorius, all of the sciences are subdivisions of mathematics. His view is not unique; it reflects the most fundamental premise of the medieval curriculum. As Roger Bacon puts it a century later, mathematics is the "gate and key" of all the sciences.[13] He cites Boethius's prologue to De Arithmetica as his authority: "If an inquirer lacks the four parts of mathematics, he has very little ability to discover the truth."[14] The four parts of mathematics are, of course, what Boethius called the quadrivium.[15] In explaining the mathematical foundations of all pursuits, Bacon adheres to the ancient definitions. Arithmetic, the "mother and nurse" of all the arts, is the science of numbers absolute.[16] Bacon notes that it "teaches how all the proportions are investigated in the ratio of numbers."[17] It comes first in the quadrivium since all the rest simply apply in different ways what arithmetic teaches.[18] Moreover, he says, according to Tully (who follows Plato's Meno), arithmetic is the science that man learns most naturally, mathematical knowledge being an innate feature of man's understanding.[19] Geometry comes second. It is the science of quantity at rest, the application of arithmetic to surfaces and planes, angles and volumes. The third science is astronomy, which explores quantity in motion and is the most elaborate of the sciences in the quadrivium. The last is music, the science of numbers in mutual relation; it is the most comprehensive of the sciences.[20] Bacon argues that

even the *trivium* and theology as well rest upon mathematics.
In fact, knowledge of numbers is that which sets man apart
from brutes, "which know neither sacred things nor human."[21]

A glance at the *forma* of medieval university curricula confirms the emphasis Bacon puts upon the prominence of
mathematics in the pursuit of knowledge. Although in the later
Middle Ages study in the arts had become more varied than
Martianus Capella's original outline of a sevenfold curriculum,
the more numerous topics reflect subdivisions of the earlier
scheme. One Oxford *forma* that lists 12 topics of study devotes
7 to aspects of the *quadrivium* (geometry, algorismus
[algebra], meteorics, study of the spheres, arithmetic, computation, and study of heaven and earth),[22] while another
from the early fourteenth century (Merton College) cites 9
items, 5 of which are devoted to mathematical subdivisions, including the study of gematria.[23] These curricula suggest that a
gradual division was taking place between the purely descriptive and analytic side of mathematics (arithmetic, geometry,
and algebra) and its metaphysical side (cosmology and
gematria). Presumably, the division enabled a student to delve
more deeply into all facets of this great and diverse subject. But
in truth, the division ultimately promoted a means of
sloughing off a murky area of study that was more akin to
theology than to pure mathematics. By the end of the medieval
period, the "new math," freed of metaphysical speculation,
became the most serious challenger of the hallowed theory of
universals as it made possible more precise measurements and
calculations, the results of which did not conform to symmetrical patterns.

Of what precisely did a medieval arithmetic text consist?
Nicomachus and Boethius (subsequent versions in both the
Latin and Arab worlds were abridgments of one or the other)[24]
begin with generalizations about the importance of the
language of numbers and its foundation of the sciences. After
defining the categories of number study and various terms,
both concentrate on proportions and sequences of numbers
(e.g., square, quadrangular, pentangular, and hexagonal
numbers). Nicomachus divides numerological analysis into

three categories: the study of limited multitude (i.e., 8 is multitude limited by 8 units); the study of combinations of numbers (6 is a perfect number, 8 is 2 cubed, etc.); and the study of the flow of quantity made up of unities (i.e., 8 holds the fourth position in the flow of even numbers — 2, 4, 6, 8; or the fourth position in the sequence of doubles — 1, 2, 4, 8, etc.). Both Nicomachus and Boethius conclude by considering geometrical and musical harmonies as they relate to arithmetical harmonies.

Some of the arithmetic terms that Nicomachus, Boethius, and their Pythagorean progenitors define must be understood before one can have any clear understanding of the relationship of arithmetic to philosophy and the rest of her entourage of arts. First is the Pythagorean distinction between the *elements* of numbers and numbers themselves. This distinction reflects a principle, typical of Platonic thought, whereby complexity is reduced to simplicity. An element is the simplest factor beyond which there can be no further reduction. The Pythagoreans held that there were two elements of number, *monad* and *dyad*. How the monad is elemental is self-evident; it is the basic unit out of which all other numbers are developed. The dyad's elemental nature is less obvious, for does it not consist of combined monads, rather than being elemental? Nicomachus resolves the problem this way: although the dyad may be understood as a combination of two monads, nonetheless there is a quality of "otherness" about the dyad that the monad cannot possess. That is, the monad is *same*, while the dyad is *other than same*. Thus the dyad is elemental in its own right. All subsequent numbers, the flow from the monad through the dyad, consist of combinations of same and other and are thus not elemental. One (monad) is called the "father of number." Two (dyad) is sometimes thought of as the "mother of number" (cf. male and female numbers, discussed below).

Closely related to the concept of elements is the notion of *real* and *unreal* numbers. The two elements of number, 1 and 2, are classified as unreal numbers, 3 being the first real number. The reasoning here is geometric, where 1 designates

point, 2 designates line, 3 designates space, and 4 designates
volume.[25] In the world that our senses tell us is real, we
perceive reality only as space and volume. That is, we cannot
conceive of point or line except in the abstract (or unreal).
This notion of 3 as the first real number is fundamental to the Christian concept of Trinity (eternity expressed or made real in
temporal-spatial reality).[26] These first four numbers (the
parents of number and the first two real numbers) constitute
the tetrad so important in Pythagorean arithmology.[27]

Another basic distinction the Pythagoreans made is between
odd and *even* numbers. This distinction plays a crucial role in
the discovery of ratios and proportions. In arithmology it provides the basis of *male* and *female* numbers. Male numbers are
odd (i.e., when divided they have a middle part left over) and
were considered strong since they had no even half (fractions
do not count). Female numbers are even and may be split into
even or uneven factors. They are thus called weak. If the
unreal numbers 1 and 2 are called the parents of number, then
3 and 4 become the first real male and female numbers.

Marriage numbers, though not considered in the arithmetics
of the time, were an important part of arithmology and take
their meaning from combinations of male and female numbers.
Five is the first marriage number since it is a combination by
addition of the female 2 and the male 3. Six is the next, being
the product of 2 x 3. Since 5 is associated with Venus and the
senses and is merely a sum, it implies worldliness and
cupidinous marriages, while 6, being a product, is the fruitful
marriage number. Thirty is also a marriage number, being the
product of the first two marriage numbers. Similarly, 7 is
sometimes considered a marriage number since it is the combination of 3 and 4, the first male and female real numbers. As
such it is a worldly marriage number, defining man's marriage
of body (4) and soul (3). By the same logic, 12 is also a marriage number, being the product of the first two male and
female real numbers. Like 6, 12 denotes a more blessed and
fruitful marriage than that produced by mere addition.

The terms *perfect, abundant,* and *deficient* were important
in the arithmetics, however, and like marriage numbers, they

take their meaning from their factors. A *perfect* number is equal to the sum of its factors (aliquot parts). Such numbers are rare. Six is the first, its parts being 1, 2, and 3, which totaled equal the number itself. Twenty-eight is next $(1 + 2 + 4 + 7 + 14 = 28)$, and so on.[28] An *abundant* number is one whose aliquot parts total more than the number itself (e.g., 12, whose parts total $1 + 2 + 3 + 4 + 6 = 16$); a *deficient* number's parts total less than the number itself (e.g., 9, whose parts total $1 + 3 = 4$). This method of calculation was sometimes used to determine the spiritual character of a number, that is, whether it was given to excess or to stinginess.[29] But such metaphysical speculation was for the most part excluded from the arithmetic texts, which stuck rather closely to considerations of proportion, ratio, and factoring.

The geometries of the early medieval period were based on Boethius's redaction of Euclid. Boethius includes all the propositions of Euclid but eliminates most of the proofs. He calls his work a translation, though in fact it is an intelligent abridgment. It was all that the West had until the twelfth century, when Arab geometries, which included the proofs, were translated into Latin. Without the proofs Boethius's work was of limited value, though still important in defining terms such as *point, line, plane,* and *angle*; spatial figures such as *triangle* and *square*; and terms of application such as *truncation* and *bisection*. It also provided simple formulas for measuring area and volume. Boethius concludes his discussion with a short history of the science and its usefulness, which he finds to be threefold: first, for practical matters such as mechanics; second, for matters of health such as medicine; and finally, for matters of the soul, such as philosophy.

Boethius's last point was often heeded by medieval theologians, who used geometry in theological argument. For example, Duns Scotus compares the Trinity and the triangle to demonstrate that although only God knows all things through His essence, man's intellect can be moved by an object to know Him. Then, like Roger Bacon, he holds that knowledge of objects (e.g., a triangle) pertains to the theologian, for to know

that the triangle's three angles are always equal to two right
angles is "a kind of participation of God," since the figure "has
such an order in the universe that it expresses more perfectly as
it were the perfection of God."[30] He adds that this is,
moreover, a more noble way of knowing triangles than simply
thinking of three angles. Another favorite geometric figure
useful to both philosopher and theologian was the circle, which
I shall consider later.

With the rediscovery of Euclid's proofs and the revival of
Roman methods of surveying, the subject of geometry was extended to include some elements of geography, though according to Hugh of St. Victor (*Didascalicon* 2.9) geography had
always been a part of geometry, the science having originated
among the Egyptians who gave it its name ("earth-measurer")
from their surveying of lands along the Nile. Hugh divides the
study of geometry into three parts: *planimetry* (measurement
of surfaces); *altimetry* (measurement of heights and depths);
and *cosmimetry* (measurement of spheres).[31]

Number and Concepts of Ethics and Mental Health

I return now to Honorius and his beautiful analogy between
the measurement of the spheres and the musical scale. The
preceding discussion of medieval theories of correspondence
and the survey of arithmetic and geometry texts show the
characteristic medieval proclivity to extend number study into
the pastures of ethics. When Honorius combines his knowledge
of music and astronomy he is using his mind for its true
"entente." In describing the *harmonia mundi*, he binds his
own mind into harmony with the thoughts of his betters who
lived in former times and who made similar observations; he
also binds his mind to that of the Creator, whose numbers
originally measured and gave form to the great plan. His
numbering is a form of both imitation and meditation that
enables him to achieve the rarified sense of oneness with God,
the world, and men (both past and present) that Augustine
called *caritas* and Boethius *unitas*. And such is usually the goal

of medieval cosmology: the study of the *universe* is a turning toward the One (*unus* and *versus*).

In making his assertions, Honorius works within a long-established tradition that gives medieval man insights into the moral splendor of God's thought as well as the symmetrical workings of creation. Cosmic symmetries and motions teach men such valuable psychological concepts as *wholeness, measure, proportion, harmony, integrity,* and *intention* (goal), all of which are Platonic in origin and essentially mathematical in their approach to ontology. Such terms constitute the basic vocabulary of medieval discussions of mental health. Basic moral concepts such as Augustine's definition of charity ("the *motion* of the soul towards the enjoyment of God for His own sake, and the enjoyment of one's self and of one's neighbor for the sake of God")[32] originate in the fundamentals of number lore, where the term *motion* implies not only direction (what medieval writers were wont to call "entente") but also both rhythm and measure.[33] So, too, Boethius's notion of love as a knitting of chaste marriages and holy bonds between God and creation, where the "nombres proporcionable" draw all together into one participatory understanding.[34] Number underlies medieval concepts of sin and mental sickness as well as their opposites, charity and health. Writing in accordance with Latin Christendom's two greatest numerologists (Augustine and Boethius), John Gower (ca. 1390) defines *sin* as "modor of divisioun" (that is, the fragmentation of one's sense of being and the consequent loss of correspondence),[35] while Chaucer's Parson equates one's psychic sense of Hell with disorder and lack of number.[36] *Atonement*, that is, the return to a condition of oneness, comes for both authors with the release from sin (division) or hellish alienation and a return to a participation and sense of oneness in God's *ratio*. In short, numerology defines not only the bonds and correspondences of nature, but ultimately also a whole way of life.

Plato's mythmaking Timaeus had explained that God gave man vision in order that he might observe the circuits of intelligence in the heavens and adjust his own perturbed revolutions of thought to them. (The idea recurs emphatically throughout Boethius's *Consolatio*.) Hearing, too, like sight, was given to man to enable him to bring the revolutions of his soul into consonance with the divine order, in this case by relating to celestial music. Though the orbits of man's thoughts were deranged at birth, "by learning to know the harmonies and revolutions of the world, he should bring the intelligent part, according to its pristine nature, into the likeness of that which intelligence discerns, and thereby win the fulfillment of the best life set by the gods."[37] Implicit in Plato's argument is a moral obligation to view the universe from such a vantage point that the rhythms of creation might help man measure his own life. Science and morality are thus parts of one and the same discipline. Through number, ethics correspond with created nature.

Augustine and other church fathers (Greek as well as Latin) incorporated Neoplatonic number theory into their Christian writings with no sense of incongruity whatsoever.[38] And such theory is there chiefly because of its ethical value. The symmetrical rhythm between the healthy man and nature that Plato speaks of is emphasized repeatedly by Augustine in such treatises as *De Musica, De Ordine, De Libero Arbitrio, De Quantitate Animae,* and *De Trinitate,* and by Boethius in *De Consolatione Philosophiae.* In the *Consolatio,* for example, Philosophy defines man's sense of freedom and happiness through a numerological perspective. In health, a man comprehends the motions of the heavens, seasons, indeed all creation around him, "by nombres" (1.m.2, Chaucer's translation). The sane man is, in short, a mathematician (a master of the *quadrivium*). When mentally disturbed, man loses his ability to number and "wexeth withoute mesure" (1.m.2). Later in the argument, Philosophy explains the reciprocity of this process in greater detail:

> Ryght so as whan that cleernesse smyteth the eyen and moeveth hem to seen, or ryght so as voys or soun hurteleth to the eres and commoeveth hem to herkne; than is the strengethe of the thought imoeved and excited, and clepith forth to semblable moevyngis the speces that it halt withynne itself, and addeth tho speces to the notes and to the thinges

withoute-forthe, and medleth the ymagis of thinges
withoute-forth to the foormes ihidd withynne hymself.
[5.m.4, Chaucer's translation]

As in *Timaeus*, species are related to universal notes, and images to forms, in which relationship lie man's health and happiness. Aristotle complained that numerology reduces all to
sameness.[39] But to the Platonists, this theological equatability
was its main virtue and the justification of all the arts. The
meaning behind all numerology, the reason for its being, is one
and the same — God. I have already shown how the arithmetics
defined the elements of number as "same" (*unitas*) and "other"
(*alteritas*), sometimes referred to as monad and dyad. The link
between numerology and theology lies in the equation of
monad with God and dyad with creation. In explaining the
likeness, the *Theologumena Arithmeticae* argues:

> [The monad] generates itself and is generated from itself,
> is self-ending, without beginning, without end, and appears
> to be the cause of enduring, as God in the realm of physical
> actualities is in such manner conceived as a preserving and
> guarding agent of nature.[40]

Just as God is the Creator of all nature (the "same" fathering
the "other"), so is the monad creator of all numbers of the
dyad. Photius calls monad the Σπεpmatitus λoyos.[41] All
numbers share in each other through the monad. Without it
they would have no being at all. Thus the numerological
premise whereby God is the measure of all things in
Augustine's definition of *caritas*; so, too, in Boethius's argument that God is One, determining the meaning of all created
ratios. God is the number base of Creation. Through that
number, geometry, music, and astronomy become things of
man, and man attains his universality.

In this way, cosmology becomes the foundation of the most
subtle points in medieval ethics. In the passage cited above,
Boethius relates man's freedom to his ability to number cor-
rectly. Augustine makes the same point: if man misnumbers,

the only unfortunate consequence as far as man is concerned (there is no other consequence) is that he is bound to error and his natural freedom is thus impinged. Augustine explains in *De Libero Arbitrio* that without the preeminent pattern of universals, free choice would be meaningless. If wisdom were not manifest in the guise of numbers, man's choices would be blind and random. Even Augustine's notion of "fate" is thus tied up with number theory. A "fated" person is a weak person who has willfully given up his power of choice. A free person is a strong person who maintains his appreciation of order wholesomely.[42] That is, the fated man, or to put it another way, the sinful man, or to use Boethius's idiom, the exiled man, is a man whose number base is other than One. He is a man whose mental condition throws him out of kilter with the rest of the universe. The circuits are broken: he becomes a nonparticipant. "I turned away from the One and melted away into the many," Augustine laments in his *Confessions*.[43] The consequence of breach of number is misery.

Number and the Utility of Beauty

Number is the surest pathway to wisdom; indeed, Pythagoras is reported to have said that number *is* wisdom.[44] Following Iamblichus, Pythagoras's biographer, Augustine likewise put number and wisdom into the same class, calling both universal and explaining that one commonly manifests itself through the other.[45] Both are "identical" and "immutable," with rules that are "unchangeably present and common to all who see them."[46] But there is another characteristic of equal importance. Because the universe is well numbered, there is a way for man not only to know and participate in wisdom, but also to enjoy his own being. Number offers man access to himself. It affords him both "sentence and solace." Augustine explains that man is so created that he naturally desires beauty. If misdirected, this desire may bring man to grief, yet the desire is always present, a yearning (*cupiditas*) that keeps man vital. "As he gazes attentively at the whole creation," Augustine argues, "he who travels the road to wisdom perceives how delightfully wisdom reveals itself to him on the way, and meets him in all providence. The more beautiful is the road to wisdom towards which he hastens, the more ardently he burns to complete the journey."[47] Boethius dramatically makes a similar point in the *Consolatio*. No reader can help but respond to the exuberance of book 3 when the persona rediscovers his number base and bursts into praise of the Creator. His happiness is beautiful and beauty is his happiness.

Augustine emphasizes the pervasiveness of the universal beauty surrounding man and explains the operation of the seed of desire implanted in man as it urges him to pursue beauty, yet is trained to cooperate with reason.

Wherever you turn, wisdom speaks to you through the imprint it has stamped upon its works. When you begin to slip towards outward things, wisdom calls you back by means of their very forms so that when something delights you in body and entices you through bodily senses, you may see that it has number and may ask whence it comes. Thus you return to yourself: you know that you cannot approve or disapprove of what you touch with the bodily senses, unless you have within you certain laws of beauty to which you refer the beautiful objects that you perceive outside of you.[48]

The beauty of things in nature, even though mutable, has a peculiar importance for man. Their images possess a unique value. "Although the terrestrial sphere is numbered among corruptible things, it keeps as best it can the image of higher things and continually shows them to us as examples and signs."[49] A mutable world predicates change, but it also predicates continuous exemplification. Even the human body, a most corruptible and fragile vessel, instructs the soul and brings pleasure and insight, "for it has a beauty of its own and in this way sets its dignity off to fair advantage in the eyes of the soul."[50] "Look closely at the beauty of the graceful body and you will see that numbers are held in space. Then look closely at the beauty of motion in the body and you will see that numbers are involved in time."[51]

I have dwelt on Augustine's discussion of number's role in aesthetics and of the influence of beauty on man's quest for stability because of its centrality in the aesthetic and psychological theories of subsequent generations throughout the medieval period. The solace of beauty is inseparable from its instruction. As Bonaventure explains:

> Number is the outstanding exemplar in the mind of the Maker, and in things it is the outstanding trace leading to wisdom. Since this is most evident to and closest to God, it leads most directly to God. . . .It causes Him to be known in all corporeal and sensible things while we apprehend the rhythmical, delight in rhythmical proportions, and through laws of rhythmical proportions judge irrefragably.[52]

Apprehension, delight, and *judgment* — these constitute for Bonaventure, as they did for Augustine, the critical steps in aesthetic instruction. Like Augustine, he too insists upon number as the agency for aesthetic perception and participation: "Since. . .all things are beautiful and in some way delightful, and beauty and delight do not exist apart from proportion, and proportion is primarily in number, it needs must be that all things are rhythmical (*numerosa*)."[53]

Bonaventure's qualifying clause that beauty and delight do not exist apart from proportion captures admirably the essence of medieval aesthetic theory. Proportion lies in the relating of the parts to the sequence and the whole. When Geoffrey of Vinsauf exhorts in his discussion of the poet's rhetoric, "Let one and the same thing be covered with many forms. Be various and yet the same,"[54] his premise about art's relationship to truth and delight is in tune with Augustine's notion that the "measured movements" of the Universal are perceived on earth through "a distinct variety of forms."[55] Hugh of St. Victor, in explicating Noah's ark, may see fit to expound four levels of meaning, yet through proportion, they are all the same: "The form is one, though the matter is different."[56] The "artist," as writers such as Augustine, Anselm, Hugh, and Bonaventure so often insist in their discussions of the creative process, is a structurer. He is also an imitator of the idea held firm and wellshaped in his mind. Though he may work with mutable images, the one idea remains true and discernable through the numbers of his varied structures. In the discovery of that idea is the observer's delight.

The virtue of this view of creativity has not been well appreciated by modern man, who has tended to scorn symmetry and the analogical perspective as arbitrary, impersonal, and even inhuman. Allegory, the most glorious of the numbering devices, becomes almost synonymous with dreariness. But so pejorative an approach to the medieval world misses its point altogether. Allegory and analogy were not for the Middle Ages a way of abstracting, but rather a way of internalizing, making personal, and thus humanizing all that was otherwise lost outside them. It was a process of mental incorporation. One should not be disgusted with a commentator such as Pierre Bersuire (1290?-1362), who glosses a classical myth in more ways than an ordinary man might conceive. His point is not "what does the myth mean?" but rather, what *can* it mean? One might do well to take delight in his ingenuity, if not applaud it.[57]

The cosmologists admittedly allowed themselves less fancy than a commentator like Bersuire. Yet I suspect that they would have been most reluctant to give up their stars for modern astronomy, for the losses of such an exchange would outweigh the gain. They loved their metaphors, their plots and analogies, which made a comprehensive sense as opposed to an analytic sense. Their liberal arts not only orient, investigate, and explicate the universe *for man*; they also enable him to play. In reading their arguments, one is struck not only by the elaborateness and symmetry of their hypotheses, but also with the sophistication with which the hypotheses are ventured *as hypotheses*. The great medieval synthesis was very much an acknowledged construct of man's mind, and its principal explicators frequently emphasized, as did "Timaeus," Ptolemy, and Bacon, that they spoke of hypotheses, not facts. When the sciences became separate and literal, much of their beauty was lost. Certainly the play was gone, and with that loss

the fullness of mental engagement required to appreciate the
sciences' domain was considerably diminished. With our lack
of allegorical sense, our carefully indoctrinated inability to
take delight in the play of ideas, and our contentment with seeing no ratio between what is inside ourselves and outside, we
would appear to be the dreary ones.

Number and Concentric Time

A cosmology of 10 concentric circles, 7 of which move and 3
of which are steadfast, combined with a Christian sense of
linear time divided, according to Augustine,[58] into 7 ages with
an eighth (a return to eternity) beyond time, thus bringing the
line full circle (linking alpha and omega), perpetrated for
medieval man a time-sense different from and more complex
than our own. Just as surely as the space around him was
numbered and ordered, so too was time. For the sake of
simplicity, let me suggest that the medieval Christian
understood himself as living in three simultaneous time
schemes, all of which required his attention.[59] His problem was
to coordinate the three in his mind. First, he understood time
as we normally do, that is, as the chronology of an individual
life through all its personal moments from birth to death. His
perspective on personal time would, however, be more contained than ours, largely because of the numbered space around
him. He would not be so aware of a flat span of senseless
decades and centuries; rather, he would have a keen sense of
the cycle of a year, with its numbered seasons and its feasts and
its parade of saints' days through the religious calendar.
Because of the way the prayers and scriptural readings are laid
out in the holy rites, he would also tend to view time in con-
course with the events of Christ's life. If he were educated or
inclined toward astrology, he might also have a sense of his life
in conjunction with astronomical cycles and configurations,
which he might feel had some influence on his personal
behavior. Individual events of his life he would date with
reference to the reigning monarch or some memorable occur-

rence within or near his lifetime. But the main consideration that should be noted is that for the most part his personal sense of time would be contained within the movements of an annual cycle that to him reflected God's plan. That is, his personal life is temporally contained and connected with the ordered world around it.

But in addition to this somewhat ritualized and contained personal sense of time, the medieval Christian would also see himself as part of a continuum of history. Here his perspective would be larger than that to which we are accustomed. For example, in the Augustinian scheme man lives in the 6th Age, the age of the New Testament. It is the penultimate epoch during which the former 5 ages are rehearsed, reinterpreted, and perfected under the new dispensation in preparation for the 7th Age, which will bring the Apocalypse and Judgment. He would be reminded of this linear view of time through sermons and religious training. He would also encounter it in art and in such pageantry as the mystery plays on feast days, especially on Corpus Christi Day. There the whole drama of history would be unfolded before him. Through such instruction he would see that though he lives in the moment, he also participates in the plots of those ancient patriarchs—Adam, Noah, Moses, and Cain too—and comes to know himself through their circumstances, which recur in his own daily life. But though this view of history is linear, its line comes full circle in the Second Adam as the Creator becomes both man's beginning and his end.

Ultimately, the medieval Christian sees himself as living within eternity. This third time-sense is the most difficult of the three to remember and maintain. Augustine, Anselm, the Victorines, and the Franciscans all suggest that one's sense of immortality, so obscured by the Fall, is recovered by a journey inward, eternity being discovered in the heart where the soul resides. With recovery of that center, three-dimensionality resolves itself into eternity. One's triple time-sense is complete, with a sense of being at rest within the concentricities of personal time, historical time, and eternity.

One frequently encounters these three aspects of time

simultaneously in medieval art, where contemporaries of the artist stand side by side with the ancients while a "time line" separates, or better, relates them to the realm of eternity. Unless one knows of this multiple time-sense, medieval art is confusing. Consider, for example, two fourteenth-century tapestries on the Apocalypse, now located in the Château du Roi René at Angers. In the first (Figure 3), John stands at the left in his cubicle contemplating a plain upon which the Beast of the Apocalypse is being destroyed. John's cubicle represents the 4-square world of time and space, the realm of the individual moment. The scrim that forms the background for most of the scene marks the boundary of time and space, setting off the continuum of history that stretches out before him. Beyond the scrim is eternity, represented by a clear blue. In the complex moment of this scene the eternals are piercing the realm of time, from the 7th Age as viewed from the 6th, to bring all time to its conclusion. The tapestry presents all three

FIG. 3. *St. John contemplating a plain upon which the Beast of the Apocalypse is being destroyed (fourteenth-century tapestry, Château du Roi René, Angers).* By permission of the Caisse Nationale des Monuments Historiques, Paris.

time-senses converging in a vision such as man, fragmented in
time, constantly strives for but seldomly realizes. An angel
holds a scroll from which he reads to John the eternal word.
John uses his eyes, ears, and mind to try to comprehend, and,
saint that he is, succeeds.

The second tapestry to consider (see Figure 4) is the final one
in the Apocalypse series. Here Christ himself (the Word) appears through the scrim and speaks directly to John, who
beholds the New Jerusalem as it will appear in the 8th Age.
The vision is so transporting that John has actually stepped out
of his cubicle onto the extended plane and looks directly
toward Christ, his explicator. The water separating him from
the Heavenly city reminds one that John is not himself in the
eternal age when the "sea shall be no more" (Rev. 21:1). Yet
through the convergence of time and eternity, he has his
glimpse, at least.

This complex time-sense dominates much of medieval

FIG. 4. *Christ speaking to St. John, who beholds the New Jerusalem
(fourteenth-century tapestry, Château du Roi René, Angers).* By
permission of the Caisse Nationale des Monuments Historiques,
Paris.

literature also, especially dream-vision literature and the drama, and accounts for much of what philologists at the beginning of the twentieth century regarded as quaint anachronism. In the Towneley *Second Shepherd's Play*, to choose a well-known example, the spectator begins in fourteenth-century northern England, with English shepherds struggling against a miserable winter, and then discovers that he is participating in a second time scheme as well, namely the birth of Christ in his very presence. Ultimately, the players and audience share a glimpse of eternity as all sing with the angels. Time is reborn, perfected, and made complete. The play is designed to help the audience reclaim its own fullness of time.

Piers Plowman offers the most profound treatment of con-centric time in Middle English literature. Will, the restless, wandering persona, sets out toward a goal whose definition keeps shifting, much to his consternation; yet it is a goal for which he senses a great need. All the action is set on a middle ground, that is, on earth, the plane of time and space, where man must discover within himself the links between his existence and a greater reality. For about a third of the poem (in the B — text), Will searches outside himself in a satirical version of fourteenth-century English society. Then, at the outset of the middle third of the poem (Passus 8), a new beginning occurs, as the persona enters into his own mind to encounter such personifications as Thought and Imagination. Finally, in the latter part of the poem, after discovering Anima, who incorporates into one being the various aspects of self he had earlier fragmentally explored, he has a transcendent vision culminating in the Passion itself. In the climax of Will's search, time and the four directions converge on the center of mankind's circle, Christ's Crucifixion and Resurrection. While Will approaches from his fourteenth-century vantage point, he contemplates Abraham and Moses rushing through time from the other direction. They all meet in Christ, that redeeming human aspect of Trinity whereby eternity is realized in time and space.

Time and space are for the medieval metaphysician inseparable concepts. One cannot exist without the other.[60] To explore the soul and its motions the medieval philosopher frequently relies upon geometry and arithmetic, partly because of the peculiar nature of the soul as an eternal entity caught in time. The figure most often used to explain the soul's paradoxical nature is the circle, since it is the only figure mysterious enough to encompass the soul's mysteries.[61] In *De Quantitate Animae* (11.17-12.19), for example, Augustine expounds the perfection of the circle over other geometrical figures. It figures the shape of the soul; and virtue itself is a roundness of life, completely in harmony with its parts, as is a circle with its one undivided line and its circumference of points all equidistant from the center. Boethius too uses the figure to explain one's sense of the soul's containment within a time world. Time is to eternity as "a cercle to the centre," Lady Philosophy explains (*Consolatio* 4.pr.6.142-44, Chaucer's translation). The metaphor suggests that eternity resides within man at that point in his mental composure where space ceases to exist and he slips through toward his "naturel entencioun." To help the lost Boethius find himself, Philosophy uses her craft to weave "a manere wondirful cercle or envirounynge of the simplicite devyne" around his confused sense of being, thus containing by "enclynynge into a compas" those tangential mental vagrancies, "the longe moevynges of his thoughtes" (3.pr.12). In so doing she not only helps the wanderer to locate his center, but also reestablishes for him a viable time-sense. He learns that the further his momentary residence is from the center of his circle the weaker he becomes, the more slow and bound by external temporalities, the more fated. (Cf. Augustine's argument on "fatedness" as weakness, cited above.) The center is necessarily One. The ramifications of this Boethian kernel of wisdom reach far into all corners of medieval thought. Concepts such as *place* or *steadfastness; home, feast, city,* and *New Jerusalem;* and *freedom, happiness,* and *rest* are likely to be understood and explored through this fecund geometrical figure.

Considering the peculiar virtues of the circle, Roger Bacon concluded that the universe must be spherical. Moreover, since a circle can have only one center, he proved that there cannot be more universes than one.[62] His argument touches upon the great mystery of the circle. As long as there is space, there must be a center. The more precisely one defines that center, the more closely one approaches infinity—the second and first dimensions beyond the third. Moreover, beyond the outer reaches of space is also infinity. Between the infinite center and that infinite circumference, which includes all that is, was, and ever shall be, is the realm of time and space. In one's soul-searching, time can be comprehended only by turning simultaneously inward and outward until time and self become both circumscript and uncircumscript by center and circumference.[63]

Before leaving this discussion of time as a number concept, I will return briefly to the discussion of the finite continuum of history. The idea of redeeming time is central to Christian thought, where the New Testament fulfills the Old and in its fulfillment explicates the blind patterns of former time. The pathway to wisdom becomes *imitatio Christi*: just as Christ lived as a second Adam, Noah, Abraham, David, and Daniel (the namesakes of the former epochs), so for men in later time the world becomes a stage for both the participation and the parody of divine and human plots. Parody and participation through analogy are both forms of numbering and are as useful to the soul seeking orientation as are discovering and measuring the circuits of the heavens that in their harmonious patterns help man discover harmony. It is on this principle that a work such as the *Biblia Pauperum* was compiled. Its blockprints exhibit the artistic utility of structural metaphors that convey meaning through number patterns. But they also demonstrate with remarkable clarity the idea of redeeming time by the discovery of its true center, Christ the Creator and Savior. The beauty of the work lies not so much in skillful drawing of human figures, or in the use of color and line, as in the temporal and spatial proportions that become synonymous with the subject of the picture.

Let us consider the print of Christ and Longinus in the 40-leaf Blockbook, ca. 1440 (see Figure 5). The central panel portrays the blind Longinus piercing the crucified Christ's side,

FIG. 5. Christ and Longinus (from the Estergom Blockbook, reproduced in the facsimile edition of Biblia Pauperum, 1967, plate 21). Courtesy of the Corvina Press, Budapest.

thus releasing the Eucharistic blood that trickles down to regenerate earth and the soldier's sight. Five soldiers stand on Christ's left, one of whom holds a pail, while another, the most prominent of the five, points to the cross as if he has seen something he never saw before. Perhaps he represents Joseph of Arimathea, for in his hand he holds a walking stick that looks suspiciously like a cross, and he has turned his saddened face toward the man with the pail (grail?) as if to address him. On Christ's right Longinus kneels, gesturing toward his eyes with one hand and looking up to Christ, whom he now sees for the first time. Behind him stand 2 soldiers, there being 8 soldiers in all.

The left panel (on Christ's right) shows Adam asleep in the Garden while Christ the Creator draws Eve from his side. In the background is a tree bearing 8 fruits. At first one might be dubious about the fruit that is being created from Adam; this division will lead to sin and to the Fall for which Christ must eventually atone through His sacrifice. That is, the ultimate fruit of this action will be the Crucifixion (center panel). But the 8 fruits on the Tree of Life in the background remind us of the ultimate wisdom of Eve's creation, for in the 8th Age Paradise will be restored and the fruits of time fulfilled. The 8 soldiers who witness the advent of the Eucharist in the center panel are likewise new fruit born from Christ's new tree of life, the cross.

The panel on the right (Christ's left) depicts Moses striking water from the rock in the Desert of Sin (Deut. 22:51). Behind him, 5 men of authority look on. In the background stand 10 pine trees. Moses' act is juxtaposed to the centurion's. Both strike upon command of the surrounding multitude. Moses' act brings forth the Waters of Contradiction. The consequence of his blind action is denial of entrance into the Promised Land. Longinus's act, on the other hand, brings forth the Eucharist, which enables the faithful Christian to share in Paradise even though earthbound. The difference between the two actions is Christ's grace, which even Moses will share after Christ pierces Hell, a couple of pages later. The 5 men who surround Moses are probably meant to suggest the Old Law, as do the 10 pines in the background (see Appendix, on 5 and 10 as signs of the Old Law). The trees are pine rather than deciduous to suggest the barrenness of the Law without Christ.[64]

Above the triptych David and Zacharias address the reader. David utters Psalm 68:21, a passage glossed as Christ's voice speaking through David to declare His forthcoming suffering and the reprobation of the Jews. Zacharias likewise speaks a mystery that he himself does not understand. Having declared that a fountain shall flow at a time when prophets shall be confounded and say, "I am no prophet, I am a husbandman: for Adam is my example from my youth," he asserts, "And they shall say to him: What are these wounds in the midst of thy hands? and he shall say: With these I was wounded in the house of them that loved me" (Zach. 13:6). Like the words of David and the action of Moses in the desert, the meaning of this ancient enigma is revealed in Christ's central panel. Until then, the words and acts were but empty parody.

Below the triptych Jeremias and Amos converse. Jeremias recalls that the Lord asked him what he saw and he replied, "I see a rod watching," whereupon the Lord replied, "Thou hast seen well: for I will watch over my word to perform it" (Jer. 1:12). His verse helps to clarify the connection between Moses' rod, Longinus's spear, and the rodlike Eve (n.b., the common *virgo-virga* pun)[65] as she is drawn from Adam's side; but the true import of the rod metaphors lies only in the cross of the center panel. Amos, the 4th corner-figure, tells that it shall come to pass that the Lord shall let down his hook to draw up the fruit and darken the earth as if the sun had set at midday (Amos 8:9). Again, the enigma he speaks cannot be understood until the event of the central panel fulfills time and sense. The hook is the cross.[66]

Without the center panel, the event that inaugurates the 6th Age, none of the earlier events can be truly understood. But through the triangulation of the triptych and four scriptural prefigurations, all the events of the former times acquire full meaning. The panels are arranged like a cross with Christ's panel at the center. The arrangement and interlacing of ideas illustrate admirably this complex time process, where events are understood through meaningful equations with that which is beyond equation. It is impressive that this single blockprint coordinates five of the first six ages (only the 2nd, Noah, is absent), and anticipates the 7th (Judgment) through rod and hook metaphors and the 8th (New Jerusalem) through garden, fruit, husbandman, and "8" metaphors. Its graphic structure is such that even the eye tells the center of time, as all angles, from Adam to our own post-Adventive perspective, point to Christ.

Cognizance of this analogic attitude toward history as well as cosmology is of the greatest importance to a student of the Middle Ages. Little of medieval intellectual history can be understood without it. It means that people living in the 6th Age understood their lives (insofar as they considered history at all) in ways quite different from the modern perspective based on a simple chronological line. Their lives existed within concentric realities. It was not a naive and myopic observation of external reality that convinced the medieval cosmologists that earth must be the center of the universe. Their metaphysics demanded it. Indeed, it is not, in fact, earth that is center of their world; it is man's soul, that immortal point (thus necessarily an image of God, since "point" is beyond time and space) around which man in his temporal environment realizes his being.

Pearl

My discussion of number as cosmic language concludes by briefly examining numerological thought in *Pearl*, a fourteenth-century English dream vision in which Augustinian and Boethian number lore is deeply ingrained. All the topics discussed above — numbering as psychic ordering and as aesthetic principle, circle imagery and concentric time-sense, temporal images orchestrated numerically to reveal a pathway toward universal truth — all are manifest in this tour de force of craftsmanship.

Pearl explores the journey from the many to the One. Its

plot is simple, following the Boethian archetype of the disconsolate seeking consolation.[67] At the outset of the poem the persona, overwhelmed by grief at the loss of his Pearl, throws himself wretchedly over the flowery turf in the arbor where Pearl is buried. The odor of flowers and spices is such, however, that despite his sense of emptiness and great lovelonging a stillness falls over him like music, and he sleeps. He dreams that he is in a wondrous forest, more richly adorned than those in tapestries. So marvelous is the place with its "adubbement" that he is filled with a keen sense of awe and a longing to see more. As he follows the shining stream that passes through the forest, the sheer beauty of the place — its visual music as well as its harmony of singing birds — fills him with bliss, destroys his complaining, and relaxes his discordant tensions ("fordidden my stresse" [1.124]).[68] The glorious images of the scene — "the dubbement dere of doun and dales, / Of wod and water and wlonk [lovely] playnes" (121-22) — function as a psychic restorative, marking the first step of the persona's search for consolation and evincing admirably the utility of beauty to mental health in God's scheme.

As he follows the stream, the persona's desire increases "ay more and more." His mind is moved by a "nwe note" as he approaches a crystal cliff at the foot of which he sees his Pearl. The poet addresses her, lamenting his bad fortune in losing her to death. She, like Lady Philosophy in Boethius's *Consolatio*, immediately begins to uncover his error, the true cause of his unhappiness. He is guilty of misdefining his relationship with temporal things: "Sir, ye have your tale mysetente" (257), she explains. She has not been lost; neither is "wyrde" a thief. The persona has been presumptuous and has confused the earthly with the eternal. She is safely stored with Christ, who has married her, crowned her with bliss, and "sesed" (legally granted) her His whole heritage. The persona is perturbed by this claim: how could she, who on earth was but two years old, be worthy of Christ's marriage? Moreover, has Mary been displaced? At the center of the poem, Pearl explains the nature of grace to the questioning persona. Christ, through the Crucifixion, has supplied worthiness for all. No man merits grace on his own: it comes only from Christ. Moreover, the more who receive His grace, the more happy and blessed are those who have already received. Mary rejoices in Pearl's marriage, for through Christ each shares in each. That One properly defines them all.

The climax to the exposition occurs as Pearl compares heaven to the pearl of great price, an "endeles rounde" (738). That pearl, she explains, Christ has set "inmyddes my brest" (740) as a token of peace. She advises the persona likewise to forsake the world and purchase his "perle maskelles." The persona's response is one of ecstatic admiration and wonder at the beauty of Pearl, her adornment, and her argument, all of which are one and the same:

> "O maskeles perle, in perles pure,
> That beres," quode I, "the perle of prys,
> Quo formed the thy fayre fygure?
> That wroght thy wede, he was fyl wys."   (745-48)

It is his first unprejudiced question — one of complete awe. The forms of her beauty have relieved him of his "surquidrye" so that he can participate more openly and freely than in his grief. In giving himself in open admiration he receives his final instruction, a 120-line hymn of praise (781-900) in which Pearl describes the music of heaven, "a note ful nwe" (879) sung by the "newe fryt," the 144,000 in the company of the lamb. The "new song" that the waking persona at the beginning of the poem had intuited, in the still moment of his grief when he sensed the flowers and spices, has now in his vision been realized. Outer forms have led to inner forms. Time has been sufficiently redeemed that he too, even while dwelling on earth, can contemplate the Heavenly City.

The conclusion to the plot depicts the Holy City. This section of the poem poses special problems to the poet. How can the eternal city be depicted? As other apocalyptic writers have done, the poet relies on the language of mathematics, emphasizing the numbered proportions of the city — its 12-tiered base with 12 foundation stones, its 12-degree elevation, its perfect symmetry ("as longe as brode as hyghe ful faire" [1,024]) with 3 gates on each side, and, at the 12 gates that bear the names of the 12 tribes of Israel, the 12 trees bearing 12 fruits of life 12 times a year, renewing themselves each month, while the 144,000 in the procession of the 7-horned lamb (the fulfiller of time) enter the city of the 8th Age, singing the new song as sonorously as the music of the spheres.[69] To a modern sensibility the description is likely to seem tedious and contrived. But if beauty and delight lie in proportion, as Augustine and Bonaventure insist, then surely this symmetrical structure is the most beautiful of all places. As the lamb passes, his breast wounded "ful wyde and weete" (1,135), the persona is so filled with empathy, that, as "my lyttel quene" (Pearl) joins the company, he too, in a mixture of sorrow and "luf-longyng in gret delyt" (1,152), tries to cross the stream to join the ranks, but awakens to find himself lying upon the little hill. His empathy and desire recall his grief and love-longing at the beginning of the poem. But now, instead of self-pity, his "entente" is Christ. The poem ends with a restored persona holding himself in "trwe entent" (1,191) and, though still earthbound, he participates every day in the grace of Christ's sacrifice through the Eucharist, which "the preste uus shewes" (1,210). His final prayer is to be among the precious pearls of his Prince's pleasure.

This brief sketch of the plot of *Pearl* should be sufficient to illustrate the reordering process as the lost persona rediscovers, through an increasingly symmetrical array of images, the true center of his life. Although he never actually sees Christ face to face (even in his vision he is confined to images), so orderly become the images emanating from the Creator through his grace-filled Creation that he shares in divinity, if only through their rhythm. Like Boethius, he is "enclynynge into a compas" the "long moevynges of his thoughtes" (*Cons.* 3. m.11.5-6). The 8th Age has not yet come; he is still timebound and confined to perception through figures. Like John in the Anger tapestry, he is separated from eternity by a time line (in *Pearl* the stream, in the tapestry the wavy lines). But where John looks directly into the face of Christ, the persona of *Pearl* sees numbers and numbered images.

Milton Stern has suggested a fourfold allegorical reading of

Pearl. On the historical level, the lost Pearl signifies the poet's two-year-old daughter who has died; on the allegorical level, she represents his loss of spiritual peace; on the moral, loss of faith; and on the anagogical, loss of Heaven.[70] Certainly there is truth in all these possibilities, and such an allegorical analysis reveals a characteristic method that medieval readers used in parsing the implications of a plot. As Pico della Mirandola makes clear in his *Heptaplus*,[71] allegory is a form of numbering that originates in the correspondences of Creation itself, where we necessarily, because of the limitations of time and space, understand through parts and enigma. To think of a plot in terms of corresonding levels that address themselves to the reader simultaneously offers delight to the analyst through proportion and symmetrical conjunction. It makes a careful reader of the poem, just as the persona in the poem became a careful reader of the images of reality in his vision. But the rhetorical structure of *Pearl* is so well wrought and subtle that all approaches, even allegorical, leave much out. Though the Pearl is many things, it is also always one. From the beginning the poet emphasizes her roundness, and that, rather than linear analogies, is perhaps the most important quality one should consider, for both Pearl and her poem are indeed round.

At the outset the persona defines her as his "wele." Regardless of whether that "wele" is the persona's faith, heaven, or spiritual peace, she is his sense of roundness without which he has no health or happiness. She is his circle of "suffi-saunce." I have already noted that the persona's confirmation of that roundness, as he contemplates the pearl of great price in the center of Pearl's breast, is what brings him to his final contemplation of the round city. But not only is Pearl round as an idea. The plot of the quest for her is also round. As the persona regains his God-given health, through recognition of Pearl the child fathers the parent. Or, to move closer to the center, his beginning (Christ) becomes his end ("trwe entent"), and in that renewal (that redeeming of time) his end marks his new begining. He is back in the garden where he began, contemplating the mass that here at the end is his means of beginning.

In the process of redeeming time, *Pearl* correlates the three time settings discussed earlier. The waking world of the moment, with the persona suspended above his grave, relates to the second, more complex time-sense, the world of the dream with its elaborate wood extending beyond the moment onto the plane of history, though still this side of the time line. In the vision beyond the stream of Pearl and her city, the former two senses of time are coordinated with eternity. The dream provides the persona with the necessary middle term that enables him to relate eternity to his waking world. It is by means of this third mental dimension of time that he encircles the duality of the moment and eternity within the compass of his mind, to achieve that round sense of wholeness which *Pearl* is about.

The structure of the poem is intricately conceived to enhance this idea of encompassing the glimpse of eternity in temporal forms. Structurally, *Pearl* is an interlacement of circles. The largest circle is the whole poem, beginning with the poet meditating in his garden and ending where he began, albeit with a different sense of garden than when he set out in his dream. The smallest circles are the individual stanzas, each of which has key words repeated in the first and last lines so that the beginning and end form a round. There are 101 such stanzas (even the number count joins beginning and end through the sameness of 1) arranged in 20 fitts. The stanzas in each fitt share the same key words in their last lines and first lines, creating thus larger rounds of the stanzaic epicycles. As one goes from stanza to stanza within the fitt, where last line links with first, one discovers again and again that his ending is his beginning. Moreover, the key words of the last fitt link up with the key words of the first fitt; thus not only is the plot round in its return to the garden where it began, but the overall structure forms a round as well. The structure is, in effect, the mandorla containing all the motions of the plot as one.[72]

Besides the interlacement of circles, *Pearl* is cast in symbolic 12s, the number of Revelation. It has already been noted how elaborately the New Jerusalem is described through that number. But further, the exposition section of the poem preceding the glimpse of the Heavenly City is modulated in 12

fitts (fitts 5-16; see n. 71). And further still, since each of the
101 stanzas consists of 12 lines, the total length of the poem is
1212. It is perhaps worth restating in this context that Pearl's
hymn in praise of her marriage to the lamb (781-900) is 120
lines long (10 x 12) and that her final speech of the poem is 12
lines long (965-76). It is this kind of numerology that is likely to
seem irksome to a modern sensibility. Why write with devices
so obscure that few if any in the audience could catch them, let
alone benefit by them? Charles Singleton has spoken effectively
to the question by comparing such architectonics to obscure
adornments on the top of Chartres Cathedral. For whose eyes
were such carvings intended? Surely not simply those of the
mason who went up on the roof every seventy years or so to
repair a broken shingle.[73]

Although a reader may well conclude that such adornments
are best left to the eyes of God alone, it is not difficult to account for an artist's motives behind such rhetoric. Exegetical
commentators often observed that a writer should write
enigmatically so that his reader would enjoy the sweet kernel of
wisdom all the more after an arduous discovery had whetted
his appetite.[74] Yet such mathematical devices serve the writer
in other ways as well. (1) Numbering is a way of controlling as
well as ordering. In the absence of reams of typing paper, it
helps the craftsman keep track as he holds the work in his mind
during composition. (2) Numbering is a form of imitation. In
view of the numerological basis of cosmology, an artist would
be false to the nature his craft is cousin to if he numbered
carelessly. When *Pearl* is numbered in 12s one should not be
amazed; that is the number in God's plan appropriate to it. (3)
In trying to cope with a complex, perhaps incomprehensible,
subject such as life, history, or God, no one understands the
complexity of valid expression better than the artist or craftsman trying to puzzle out a valid response. Where logic and
reason fail, he may well choose to answer the unanswerable
with an enigma. Such an engima may well be expressed
numerologically, for number defines the pattern and form, if
not the content, of truth. It imitates without prejudice and
thus enables the poem to participate in Creation, if only by the

shape of its being. (4) Finally, number, because of the shape of Creation, is a way to praise. The intricacy of *Pearl*, whether ever fully revealed to the marveling eyes of men, pays tribute to the most wondrous of Creators.

What set medieval Europe apart from other civilizations was the largely successful conjoining of metaphysical and physical universes over a long period of time. The "gate and key" to this success was what medieval men called "mathematics." It enabled them to make reasonable technological advances and at the same time to keep all phases of learning coherent. That its roots reached deep into pagan authority only validated further its glory. Its truths, innate in the internal and external realities of all men, made correspondences perceptible that held for the mind both realities together. "Number teaches us," Hugh of St. Victor reminds us, "the nature of the going out and the return of the soul."[75]

Notes

1. The epigrams are from Macrobius *In Somnium Scipionis (Commentary on the Dream of Scipio)* (trans. William Harris Stahl; New York, 1952) 1.5.4, p. 95; and Augustine *De Libero Arbitrio Voluntatis* (trans. Anna S. Benjamin and L. H. Hackstaff; Indianapolis, Ind., 1964) 2.11.126, p. 64.
2. Augustine *De Libero Arbitrio* (trans. Benjamin-Hackstaff) 2.16.171, p. 76.
3. E.g., see Augustine *De Libero Arbitrio* (trans. Benjamin-Hackstaff) 2.16.164, p. 73: "The sky, the earth, and the sea and. . .whatever in them shines from above or crawls, flies, or swims below," have "form because they have number. Take away these forms and there will be nothing. . . .[They] exist only insofar as they have number." For a vivid restatement of Augustine's thesis, see Isidore of Seville *Etymologiae 3.4.3* (Migne, *PL*, 82.156): "Through number we are instructed in order not to be confounded. Take number from all things, and all things perish." Cf. Macrobius *In Somn. Scip.* 1.5.5 ff. For later medieval views on the interdependence of matter and form, see Avicebron *De Fons Vitae* 4.6 and Robert Grosseteste *Comm. Post Analytica* 2.2.
4. See Bacon *Opus Majus* (trans. Robert Belle Burke; Philadelphia, 1928), pt. 6, where in his plea for experimental science and his exposition of the correct method of scientific approach to solving natural problems Bacon insists on the

importance of mathematics as a purely descriptive science. His eloquent discussion of Trinity and the perfection of 3 occurs in pt. 4 (1:245). For a somewhat discursive discussion of Kepler as numerologist see Gunnar Qvarnström, *Poetry and Numbers* (Lund, 1966), pp. 16-17.

5. Macrobius *In Somn. Scip.* 1.5.4. Or, as Augustine puts it, "The order and truth of numbers have nothing to do with the bodily senses, but are unchangeable and true and common to all rational beings" (*De Libero Arbitrio* [trans. Benjamin-Hackstaff] 2.8.93, p. 50).

6. Augustine *De Libero Arbitrio* (trans. Benjamin-Hackstaff) 2.8.80, p. 54. Cf. Robert Grosseteste's discussion of the superior truth of mathematics beyond the inferiority of mutable natural things (*Comm. Post. Analytica* 1.11).

7. E.g., Plotinus writes: "Number exists before objects which are described by number. A variety of sense objects merely recalls to the soul the notion of number." See Christopher Butler, *Number Symbolism* (New York, 1970), p. xi.

8. *Numerus* is indeed difficult to translate. F. J.Thonnard, *De Musica* (Paris, 1947), pp. 513-14, observes four ways in which the term is used: (1) the ordinary mathematical sense; (2) rhythm; (3) harmony among parts in movement or harmony among sensible, intellectual, or moral activities; and (4) the unity of God, source of mathematical law, beauty, rhythm, and the sympathetic activities of nature and man. Cf. D. W. Robertson, Jr., *A Preface to Chaucer* (Princeton, N.J., 1962), p. 114.

9. Honorius *De Imagine Mundi Libri Tres* 2.59 and 1.80-82 (Migne, *PL*, 172.154, 140). Cf. Isidore *Etymologiae* 3.23.2. The relating of the music of the spheres to the tones of the scale is a Pythagorean notion, of course. Cf. Aristotle's account in *De Caelo* 2.9.

10. On the world as a book, recall Hugh of St. Victor: "The world can be likened to books written by the hand of the Lord (that is, through the power and wisdom of the Lord), and each creature is like a word in those books, showing the power and wisdom of the Lord. The unwise looks only at its outward beauty and the comeliness of the beautiful creation, and clings to it with love. But he who is wise sees through the beauty of the exterior and beholds the wisdom of the Lord." See Miloslav Bohatec, *Illuminated Manuscripts* (Prague, 1970), p. 61. On the relation of "mansions" to parts of the human anatomy, see Robertus Anglicus *Comm. in De Sphaera*, Lec. 6, in *The Sphere of Sacrobosco*, ed. Lynn Thorndike (Chicago, 1949), p. 219.

11. Augustine *De Musica* (trans. Robert C. Taliaferro) 2.9.16, in *The Fathers of the Church*, ed. R. J. Deferrari et al. (New York, 1947), 4:225.

12. "Whatever can be conformed to sound in similar movements and in corresponding formations, so that our delight may be made complete not only by hearing, but [also] by seeing, belongs to music" (Bacon *Opus Majus* [trans. Burke], 1: 260). Cf. Boethius *De Musica* 1.32 (Migne, *PL*, 63. col. 1194), who notes that the ear is affected by sounds in the same way as the eye is by optical impressions.

13. Bacon *Opus Majus* 4.1 (trans. Burke), 1: 116.

14. Ibid., p. 117. Boethius's *De Arithmetica* was the standard arithmetic in the schools of Western Europe until well beyond the medieval period. Boethius is

following Nicomachus *Introductio Arithmetica* 1.3.3-5, who in turn is following Plato *Laws* 13 and puts the matter this way: "Every diagram, system of numbers, every scheme of harmony, and every law of movement of the stars, ought to appear one to him who studies rightly; and what we say will properly appear if one studies all things looking to one principle, for there will be seen to be one bond for all things, and if any one attempts philosophy in any other way he must call on Fortune to assist him. For there is never a path without these" (Nicomachus *Introductio Arithmetica* [trans. Martin D'Ooge in his *Introduction to Arithmetic*; Ann Arbor, Mich., 1938] 1.3.3-5, p. 186). Cf. D'Ooge, *Introduction*, p. 185 n. 3.

15. Although the term *quadrivium* is from Boethius, the fourfold classification is ancient. Plato, Aristotle, Theophrastus, Nicomachus, Cicero, Macrobius, Boethius, Cassiodorus, and Martianus Capella all wrote on all four as being part of one greater mathematical science.

16. Nicomachus *Intro. Arith.* (trans. D'Ooge) 1.5.3 and 1.3.1. Cf. Bacon *Opus Majus* (trans. Burke), 1: 198, where Bacon gives the credit to Cassiodorus, who in fact gets the idea from Boethius's translation of Nicomachus. Cf. Hugh of St. Victor *Didascalicon* (trans. Jerome Taylor; New York, 1961) 2.15.

17. Bacon *Opus Majus* (trans. Burke), 1: 245.

18. Again the idea goes back to Nicomachus, who eloquently explains arithmetic's preeminence "not solely because. . .it existed before all the others in the mind of the creating God like some universal and exemplary plan, relying upon which as a design and archetypal example the creator of the universe sets in order his material creations and makes them attain to their proper ends; but also because it is naturally prior in birth, in that it abolishes other sciences with itself, but is not abolished together with them" (*Intro. Arith.* [trans. D'Ooge]1.4, p. 187). Hugh of St. Victor (*Didascalicon* 2.7) also treats the idea through etymology, deriving the term from *ares* ("power") and *numerus* to mean the "power of number," noting that "all things have been found in its likeness" (trans. Taylor, p. 67).

19. Bacon *Opus Majus* (trans. Burke), 1:121. Bacon is alluding to Socrates' discussion with a peasant youth who is shown to know innately complex mathematical theorems. Tully's source is Plato's *Meno*.

20. Nicomachus gives the first clear statement of the classifications and definitions (*Intro. Arith.* [trans. D'Ooge] 1.3.1-7); unless otherwise noted, I have followed his definitions here. The classification was standard, however. Cf. Hugh of St. Victor *Didascalicon* (trans. Taylor) 2.6, which follows Boethius's translation of Nicomachus *De Arithmetica* 1.1. On the comprehensiveness of music, see *Didascalicon* 2.12.

21. Bacon *Opus Majus* (trans. Burke), 1: 243. Cf. Boethius *De Arithmetica* 1.1 (Migne, *PL*, 63.1082) and Boethius *Interpretatio Euclidis Geometriae 2* (Migne, *PL*, 63.1360).

22. Hastings Rashdall, *The Universities of Europe in the Middle Ages*, ed. F. M. Powicke and A. B. Emden (Oxford, 1936), 3: 480-81.

23. Ibid., p. 482. See the Appendix for a brief discussion of *gematria*.

24. For a diagram of the interrelationship of Greek and Latin arithmetic texts, see

Frank Egleston Robbins, "The Tradition of Greek Arithmology," *Classical Philology* 16 (1921): 123.

25. Professor John E. Hankins (personal communication) reminds me here of a dual tradition regarding the progression. Ficino's commentary on *Timaeus* elaborates upon the 1-2-3-4 (point-line-space-volume) theory of Plato. But in *Somnium Scipionis* Macrobius modifies Plato, saying that there are two progressions from the One, signifying the solid and the nonsolid respectively. The solid is produced by the progression 1-2-4-8 (point-line-square-cube), which represents the visible and tangible world, while the intangible, i.e., the soul, is represented by 1-3-9-27, in stages corresponding to those of the solid. Thus, odd numbers are masculine and divine, even numbers feminine and of the visible world. Whereas Plato seemed to think of the point as being extended in a new line at each stage, Macrobius thinks of the line as extended to make a four-point surface and the surface as being moved to form an eight-point solid. "In my opinion," Hankins observes, "later writers followed Macrobius' interpretation, signalized by the frequent use of 'square' in reference to the solid world. In Plato's progression toward solidity, there is no square, only triangle and pyramid. In both authors the 4 is a part of solidity or the progression thereto, so it could be used with reference to the visible world, though it was stage 4 with Plato and only stage 3 with Macrobius. One has to watch with care since Latin *quadrangulus* could mean either 'square' or 'four-cornered'; Thomas Aquinas uses it once to describe a pyramid."

26. E.g., Bonaventure *Sententiae*, dist. 31, art. 3, qu. 2. The notion is implicit in all arguments that see the 3d Person as the bond or product of the first 2 Persons or of 3 containing 1 essence. Cf. Augustine *De Trinitate*, passim; Anselm *Monologion* 49-63, 78-79; Alanus de Insulis *Regulae Caelestis Juris*, reg. 1; Peter of Poictiers *Sententiae* (Migne, *PL*, 211.926); Albertus Magnus *De Caelo et mundi, ab initio;* Bacon *Opus Majus* (trans. Burke), 1: 245.

27. On the importance of the tetrad and the tetrachtys as pyramid of justice, see Butler, *Number Symbolism*, pp. 8 ff.

28. Nicomachus *Intro. Arith.* 1.16 explains a foolproof method for calculating perfect numbers, whereby he adds 496 and 8,128 to the known list.

29. E.g., Nicomachus observes: "It comes about that even as fair and excellent things are few and easily enumerated, while ugly and evil ones are widespread, so also the superabundant and deficient numbers are found in great multitude and irregularly placed—for the method of their discovery is irregular—but the perfect numbers are easily enumerated and arranged with suitable order; for only one is found among the units, 6, only one among the tens, 28, and a third in the rank of the hundreds, 496 alone, and a fourth within the limits of the thousands, 8,128" (*Intro. Arith.* [trans. D'Ooge] 1.16, p. 209). The moral virtue of perfect numbers was a favorite topic with Augustine.

30. Duns Scotus *Concerning Human Knowledge*, trans. Allan Wolter, in *Duns Scotus: Philosophical Writings* (Indianapolis, Ind. 1962), p. 138. Cf. Bacon's discussion of geometry as tool of the theologian in *Opus Majus* (trans. Burke), 1: 245).

31. Hugh of St. Victor *Didascalicon* (trans. Taylor) 2.13, p. 70.

32. Augustine *De Doctrina Christiana* (trans. D. W. Robertson, Jr.; Indianapolis, Ind., 1958) 3.10.16, p. 88.

33. Macrobius, in fact, goes so far as to define *soul* as "a number moving itself" (*In Somn. Scip.* [trans. Stahl] 1.6.6, p. 100).

34. Boethius *Consolatio* (trans. Geoffrey Chaucer, in *The Works of Geoffrey Chaucer*, ed. F. N. Robinson [Cambridge, Mass., 1957]) 3.m.9.18-19, p. 350. All quotations from Boethius's *Consolation* will be from this translation and will be indicated by book, section, and line number in Robinson's edition.

35. John Gower *Confessio Amantis*, Prologue 1030, in *The English Works of John Gower*, ed. G. C. Macaulay (Oxford, 1900), 1: 33. See Prol. 967-1,052 for a broader discussion of the horrible effect of division on all aspects of society.

36. *Parson's Tale*, ll 218-19, in *Works of Geoffrey Chaucer*, ed. Robinson, p. 233.

37. Plato *Timaeus* (trans. Francis M. Cornford; Indianapolis, Ind., 1959) 90d, p. 114. See also *Timaeus* 47c-e, pp. 45 ff. Plato's observations on planetary and spiritual motions did not go unappreciated in the later medieval period. William of Conches (12th century), in his *Commentary on Timaeus*, writes of these passages: "God gave man eyes so that when man saw that there are two motions in the heavens and two in himself, and that the Divine Wisdom makes the erratic planets follow the rational motion of the firmament, man would subject the erratic movements of his flesh to the rational motion of his spirit, a matter for practical philosophy" (see Taylor, ed., *Didascalicon*, p. 224, n. 22).

38. Augustine allows that not only did the ancients benefit by study of the correspondent patterns of creation open to all observers, thereby arriving at a partial understanding of God's plan, but also that Plato must have had at least indirect contact with the writings of Jeremiah and Moses (*De civ. Dei* 8.11-12). Besides, "it is perfectly clear to the most stupid person that the science of numbers was not instituted by man but rather investigated and discovered" (*De Doct. Christ.* (trans. Robertson) 2.38.26, p. 72.

39. Aristotle *Metaphysica* 1093a1. See Christopher Butler's discussion of Aristotle and the Pythagoreans in "Numerical Thought," in *Silent Poetry*, ed. Alastair Fowler (London, 1970), p. 10, and in *Number Symbolism*, pp. 1-7.

40. *Theologumena Arithmeticae*, ed. Ast, as cited by Frank Egleston Robbins, "The Philosophy of Nicomachus," in *Introduction to Arithmetic*, trans. D'Ooge, p. 96. Cf. Macrobius *In Somn. Scip.* (trans. Stahl) 5.6.7-8. On the transmission of arithmological lore into 12th- and 13th-century Europe, see Taylor, ed., *Didascalicon* (New York, 1961), pp. 198-99, n. 25; p. 200, n. 29; and esp. in 41, p. 202, where Professor Taylor cites Thierry of Chartres *De sex Dierum operibus* 43: "Just as all things derive their existence from the One, so from the One Equal to the One [the divine Mind or Wisdom] proceed the form, mode, and measure of each thing. . . .Therefore, as the One Equal to the One contains within himself and generates from himself the ideas of all things, so does he contain within himself and bring forth from himself the very forms of all things. . . [together with] all proportions and inequalities. And all things resolve themselves into him."

41. Robbins, "The Philosophy of Nicomachus," p. 96.

42. Augustine *De civ. Dei* 5.9.

43. Augustine *Confessiones* 2.1.

44. Iamblichus *Life of Pythagoras* (trans. Thomas Taylor; London, 1926) 18, p. 43.

45. E.g., Augustine *De Libero Arbitrio* 2.9.108, 2.11.123, 2.11.127. Cf. Iamblichus *Life of Pythagoras* (trans. Taylor) 18, pp. 43-44).

46. Augustine *De Libero Arbitrio* 2.10.3-2.11.127.

47. Ibid. (trans. Benjamin-Hackstaff) 2.17.174, p. 76.

48. Ibid. 2.16.163, p. 73. Chaucer's *Book of the Duchess* offers a superb example of the higher truth of measure and number through the beauty of the "goode faire White." For further discussion of the point, see my "Theme and Number in Chaucer's *Book of the Duchess*," in *Silent Poetry*, ed. Fowler, pp. 73-115.

49. Augustine *De Libero Arbitrio* (trans. Benjamin-Hackstaff) 3.9.100, p. 109.

50. Augustine *De Musica* (trans. Taliaferro) 6.4.7, in *Fathers of the Church*, ed. Deferrari, 4:332.

51. Augustine *De Libero Arbitrio* 2.16.166, p. 74. Roger Bacon picks up the point in *Opus Majus* (trans. Burke), 1:260, to explain that dancing is thus a category of music (i.e., number in motion).

52. Bonaventure *Itinerarum Mentis ad Deum* (trans. George Boas; Indianapolis, Ind., 1953) 2.10, p. 70.

53. Ibid. I have made a similar point, using these examples from Bonaventure in a somewhat different context, in "Numerology and Chaucer's *Troilus and Criseyde*," *Mosaic* 5 (1972): 4-5.

54. Geoffrey of Vinsauf *Poetria Nova* 223-25, in *Les Arts Poétiques du XIIe et du XIIIe Siècle*, ed. Edmond Faral (Paris, 1924), p. 204: "repone / Pluribus in clausis unum; multiplice forma / Dissimuletur idem; varius sis et tamen idem."

55. Augustine *De Libero Arbitrio* (trans. Benjamine-Hackstaff) 2.16.171, p. 76.

56. Hugh of St. Victor *De Arca Noe Morali* 1.11, in *Hugh of St. Victor: Selected Spiritual Writings*, trans. a religious of C.S.M.V. (London, 1962), p. 60.

57. I have elaborated upon the ideas here and in the next section in my essay "Public Dreams and Private Myths: Perspectives in Middle English Literature," *PMLA* 90 (1975): 461-68.

58. E.g., *De Trin.* 4.4.7; *Ennarrationes in Psalmos 6;* and *De Civ. Dei* 11.31, 15.22, 17.4.

59. For a Jungian view of number, space, and the psychology of time, see part 5: "Number and the Parapsychological Aspects of the Principle of Syncronicity," in Marie-Louise von Franz, *Number and Time: Reflections Leading toward a Unification of Depth Psychology and Physics*, trans. Andrea Dykes (Evanston, Ill., 1974).

60. E.g., Augustine *De civ. Dei* 11.6 argues that time and space must have been created simultaneously, for one could not exist without the other. Cf. *De civ. Dei* 12.15, and *Confessiones*, 11.30.31.

61. The other favorite geometrical figure was the equilateral triangle, which suggested unity in space (the first geometrical figure) and Trinity (see n. 30 above and accompanying text). The triangle and circle share metaphysical qualities because of the ideas of center, point, and 3 as the first real number. In seeking

the center one moves from 3 (unity expressed) to 1 (point), 1 being the number base. Trinity is the spatial expression of that number base. Christ, the alpha and omega, completes the circle of time, thus providing the circumference to the circle; He is also the Creator and thus the center of the circle.

62. Bacon *Opus Majus* 4, 4th distinction (trans. Burke), 1: 176, 185-86.

63. See the last stanza of Chaucer's *Troilus and Criseyde*, where Chaucer plays with the paradox. (Cf. Dante *Paradiso* 14. 28-30.) See my "Numerology and Chaucer's *Troilus and Criseyde*," pp. 20-21.

64. The pine, because of its lack of fruit, is associated by Bernard (Migne, *PL* 183. 378-79) with the sterility of the old law, and in the *Romance of the Rose*, for example, it is the tree of the fleshy garden as opposed to the inner garden or Shepherd's Park (trans. H. Robbins, pp. 29, 434-35). Cf. Hugh of St. Victor *De Fructibus Carnis et Spiritus* (Migne, *PL* 175).

65. Aaron's rod that bloomed (Numbers 17:8) was commonly glossed as a figure for the Virgin, whose bloom was Christ. See plate b (second plate) of the 40-Leaf Blockbook.

66. The Cross is the supreme love-hook of Christ the fisherman. (Cf. the folk etymology of *amor* from *amus* in Andreas Capellanus *De Amore* 1.3). Recall the capturing of Leviathan by a hook (Cross) in the *Hortus deliciarum* illustration reproduced in Emile Mâle, *The Gothic Image* (New York, 1958), p. 380.

67. See my discussion of the genre of consolation in *Confessio Amantis*, ed. Russell A. Peck (New York, 1968), pp. xi ff. Besides *Pearl*, fine examples of this genre in English medieval literature may be seen in Chaucer's *Book of the Duchess*, and, less exactly, in the *Canterbury Tales*; Gower's *Confessio Amantis*; the short English romance *Sir Orfeo*; and, in a complex variation, in *Piers Plowman*. In Italian literature Dante's *Divina Commedia* affords the best example, and, in French, *Le Roman de la Rose*, through parody.

68. All references to *Pearl* are taken from *Pearl*, ed. E. V. Gordon (Oxford, 1953), and will hereafter be identified by line reference only.

69. *Twelve* is commonly glossed as the spreading of Trinity throughout space. (E.g., St. Thomas Aquinas *Expositio in Apocalypsim* 4; St. Gregory I *Moralia in Job* 1.12; and Augustine *On the Gospel of St. John*, tractates 27.10 and 49.8.) Here it suggests the revelation of divinity to all.

70. Milton R. Stern, "An Approach to *The Pearl*," *Journal of English and Germanic Philology* 54 (1955): 684-92.

71. After explaining that the tabernacle of Moses was a model of the world, Pico considers the creation of the elements and relates them to God's primal unity (Same). In doing so, he shows how the world is a tabernacle: "Celestial or even earthly names are often given to divine things, which are presented figuratively now as stars, now as wheels and animals, now as elements; hence also, heavenly names are often given to earthly things. Bound by the chains of concord, all these worlds exchange natures as well as names with mutual liberality. From this principle. . .flows the science of all allegorical interpretation" (*Heptaplus*, trans. Douglas Carmichael [Indianapolis, Ind., 1965], pp. 78-79). The early Fathers could not properly represent some things by the images of others unless trained in the hidden alliances and affinities of

all nature.

72. There are other epicycles within the larger structure of *Pearl* that add to the incremental roundness of the poem. Fitts 1-4 function as a unit, moving the plot from its inception with the enigmatic description of Pearl to the dreamer's discovery and description of her in his dream. Fitts 1 and 4 share "Perle" as their key words. Then the next 12 fitts, which constitute the exposition of the poem, form the next round. The last four fitts form the final unity given over to the description of "Jerusalem so nwe" and the return to the garden in waking.

73. Charles Singleton, "The Poet's Number at the Center," *Modern Language Notes* 80 (1965): 10 (and reprinted in this vol.). For an even more exact parallel Professor Singleton might have noted number structures within cathedrals — e.g., the measuring of the nave of the Great Church at Cluny (Cluny III), which was laid out according to perfect numbers (1 + 6 + 28 + 496 = 531). See Kenneth John Conant, "Mediaeval Academy Excavations at Cluny," *Speculum* 38 (1963): 33.

74. For defenses of allegory on grounds of the pleasure of mystery-solving see Augustine *De Doct. Christ.* 2.6.8, *De civ. Dei* 11.19; Hugh of St. Victor *Didascalicon* 5.2; Alanus de Insulis *De Planctu Naturae*, pr. 4; Richard de Bury *Philobiblon* 13; Boccaccio *De Genealogia Deorum Gentilium* 14.12.

75. Hugh of St. Victor *Didascalicon* (trans. Taylor) 2.4 p. 64.

Appendix

The Noble Art of Glossing Numbers

By the twelfth century the glossing of numbers, particularly the numbers in the Holy Scriptures, had become an elaborate science. Hugh of St. Victor in *Exegetica de Scripturis et Scripturibus Sacris 15* (Migne, PL 175. 22-23), sets down nine guidelines for discovering numerological significance:

1. *Secundum ordinem positionis*, where numbers generally become more imperfect as they recede from unity. Two, which recedes from One, signifies sin, which has deviated from the One Good.

2. *Secundum qualitatem compositionis*, where 2 can be divided and thus signifies corruptibility and transitoriness. Three cannot be divided and thus designates the indissolvable and incorruptible.

3. *Secundum modum porrectionis*, where 7 after 6 equals rest after work; 8 beyond 7 equals eternity after mutability; 9 before 10 suggests defect amid perfection; 11 beyond 10 denotes transgression outside of measure.

4. *Secundum formam dispositionis*, where 10, which has length, signifies rectitude in faith; 100, which expands in width, signifies amplitude of charity; 1,000, which rises in height, signifies the altitude of hope.

5. *Secundum computationem*, where 10 signifies perfection because by extension it is the end of computation.

6. *Secundum multiplicationem*, where 12 is a sign of universality because it is composed of 3 and 4 by multiplication, 4 being the corporeal, 3 the spiritual form.

7. *Secundum partium aggregationem*, where 6 is a perfect number, 12 abundant, and so on.

8. *Secundum multitudinem partium*, where 2 signifies 2 unities, the love of God and neighbor; 3 (3 unities) the Trinity; 4 (4 parts) the 4 seasons or 4 quarters of the world; 5, the 5 senses; and 7, the 7 sins.

9. *Secundum exaggerationem*, where the 7 penalties of Lev. 26 signify multiplicity of penalties.

The following index lists some of the more typical glosses bestowed on 1-12.

ONE: Monad: self-generating, self-generated; without beginning, without end (*Theo. Arith.*) Father of number: unity, both male and female, source of all numbers though not number itself (Macrobius *In Somn. Scip.* 1.6). The unity of God is repeatedly emphasized by the Church Fathers (e.g., Aug. *De Trin.* 4.7. 11 and *De civ. Dei* 11.10; Boethius *Cons.* 3. pr. 9, pr. 11-12). Correlative metaphors: circle, Divine Simplicity, center, point, Wisdom, Truth, Order, fulfilled entente, goal, *summum bonum*, atonement, steadfastness, home, harmony, tranquility, peace of mind, virtue.

TWO: Dyad: other, the many; shadows as opposed to reality; corruptibility, mutability, division, disintegration, flux; divided mind, cupidity, self-pity; extension of point, motion. The 2d day of Creation was not pronounced "good" by God; 2 is an unclean number and a breaker of unity (Jerome *Adv. Jov.* 1.16). The Devil is duplicity (Aug. *De civ. Dei*11.13-16). 2 is a sign of a devil as opposed to the simplicity of a Christian. Correlative metaphors: duplicity, effeminacy, exile, isolation, alienation, illusion, Fortune. However, 2 can also have positive connotations, though more rarely: the 2d Person of the Trinity; the 2 new commandments of love, 2 as conjoiner, the marriage bond as 2 made 1. 20 (an extension of 2) is an unlucky number (*Adv. Jov.* 1.22, or the expression "a twenty devil way").

THREE: The first real number (male); the expressive form of unity.

The first figure in plane geometry; elemental form (Timaeus's atoms). Completeness, all, or the whole. Like One and circle, a sign of perfection: the sum of monad and dyad, that is, of all its elements (Bacon *Opus Majus*). The number of soul insofar as man is image of God (Trinity). (See Aug. *De Trin.* and *De civ. Dei* 11.24-28; Anselm *Monologion*; Bonaventure *Itinerarum Mentis ad Deum*). 3 is the realized form of unity just as the soul is the perceptible emanation of imperceptible God (Plotinus *Enneads* 5.1.10; cf. Alanus de Insulis *Regulae de Sacra Theologia* [Migne, *PL*, 210.623]; Peter of Poictier *Sententiae* [Migne, *PL* 211.926]; Aquinas on substance, form, & Word, in *Summa Theo.* 1 qu.45.art.7, and see also 1.qu.208, qu. 290-91). 30 (an extension of 3) is the active life, a marriage number, the beginning of Christ's ministry, the number of books in the Bible (22 O.T. + 8 N.T.: Hugh of St. Victor *De Sacramentis*, prologue, ch. 7, and *De Arca Noe Morali* 1.14).

FOUR: The second real number (female). The first figure in solid geometry (volume); the first square number (Justice). The tetrad (the sum of its integers is 10); it forms the base and sides of the pyramid of justice (tetrachtys). Body, carnality, earth: 4 elements, 4 humors, 4 conditions (hot, cold, moist, dry), 4 directions (see Macrobius *In Somn. Scip.* 1.24-33, or Hugh of St. Victor *De Arca Noe Morali* 1.16). Because of the world's 4ness, then, there are 4 evangelists with 4 signs spreading the Good News (4 gospels) to all ends (4 quarters) of the earth; 4 virtues (Justice, Prudence, Fortitude, Chastity); the *quadrivium*; 4 branches of knowledge to assist the soul (theoretical, practical, mechanical, and logical). Correlative metaphors: earthliness, time, space, fortune, mutability, time-weariness, contrariety; balanced opposition, harmony. 40 represents a period of exile or trial.

FIVE: Quintessence (Plutarch *Moralia* 389f-390). The created world, because of Euclid's 5 solid forms (*Elements* 13); there are 5 zones of the world, 5 species of living creatures (man, quadrupeds, fish, reptiles, and birds), and 5 senses (Honorius *De Imagine Mundi* 1.6). Thus, worldliness and animality: Philo says that God began creating animals on the 5th day since "there was no one thing so akin to another as the number 5 was to animals" (*De Mundi Opificio* 15-16). The 5 senses is the most common gloss for biblical 5s. 5 is also a sign of the Old Law (Pentateuch), of spiritual blindness, of rigidity (cf. Aug. *On John*, tr. 24.6.1-14; *Glossa Ord.* [Migne, *PL* 114.373]; and *Catena Aurea* [trans. J.H.N.] 2.536, 3.123-24, 4.145, 4.309). In answer to 5's worldliness and blindness there are Christ's 5 wounds and Mary's 5 sorrows and 5 joys. 5 is a love number: Venus and Mars (because of the spheres), the carnal marriage number (as the sum of the first two numbers of the dyad, $2 + 3$), Solomon's star, and the endless love knot. 5 is a circular number because of the pentangle and the arithmetic fact that in multiplication it repeats itself in the last digit. It is the Pythagorean sign of Justice because it is the middle point in the decade. (See my "Numerology and Chaucer's *Troilus and Criseyde*," *Mosaic* 5 [1972]: 7-11).

SIX: A perfect number ($1 + 2 + 3 = 6$). The completion of Creation on the 6th day. 6 is the fruitful marriage number ($2\text{x}3 = 6$).

SEVEN: Totality, because of the 7 moving spheres, 7-day week, and 7 ages of the world. A uniquely strong number because it is indivisible and is a factor of no other number in the decad. 7 is a sign of the mutable world since no other number so thoroughly measures the world: every physical object is determined by 7 in that it has 3 dimensions (length, breadth, and depth) and 4 boundaries (point, line, surface, and volume); there are 7 motions (up, down, left, right, front, back, and circular); 7 things seen (body, distance, shape, magnitude, color, motion, and tranquility); and 7 musical notes. Man reflects the cosmic 7s; he consists of 4 (body) + 3 (soul); his body has 7 visible parts (head, chest, belly, 2 arms, and 2 legs) and 7 invisible parts (stomach, heart, liver, lungs, spleen, and 2 kidneys); his head, the most prominent part, has 7 orifices (2 eyes, 2 nostrils, 2 ears, the mouth) and 7 voice changes (acute, grave, contracted, aspirated, tone, and long and short sounds) to accompany the 7 notes. The body secretes 7 fluids (tears, snot, saliva, sweat, 2 kinds of excrement, and generative secretion). Children receive life in the womb at 7 months; diseases and fevers reach a climax on the 7th day. Man's life is measured by 7s: at 7 he gets adult teeth; at 14 he reaches puberty; at 21 he grows a beard; at 28 he is at the fullness of manly strength; at 35 he reaches the season of marriage, at 42 maturity of understanding; at 49 he enjoys his most rapid improvement of intellect and reason; at 56 his reason and intellect are perfected; at 63 the passions assume mildness; at 70 desirable life comes to an end (Cf. Philo *De Opificio Mundi* 33-43; and Macrobius *In Somn. Scip.* 1.6). Hippocrates measures life by 7 stages (infancy, childhood, boyhood, youth, manhood, middle age, old age). Woman's menstrual cycle is measured by 7s, as is the month. Augustine says that 7 stands for all numbers together (*De civ. Dei* 11.31). 7 marks apprenticeship, steps toward perfection, a period of trial. The 7 virtues and 7 vices equal all virtues and vices.

EIGHT: Eternity: the sphere of the fixed stars. 8 is a return to 1 or a new beginning after 7; 8 survive the Deluge to begin again. 8 is the sign of circumcision as purification and the sign of baptism. *Dies octavus* (8th day) is Easter or Pentecost (a week of weeks + *dies octavus*). The 8th Age is the New Jerusalem. As the only cube in the decad, 8 is a sign of justice (Macrobius *In Somn. Scip.* 1.5.17). Correlative metaphors: home, regeneration, redemption, felicity, harmony, transformation, new beginning.

NINE: An in-between number, defective if understood as short of 10, but also suggesting nearness to perfection: 9 is the number of hierarchies of angels surrounding God's throne, obtaining their perfection in His One. 9 is Dante's number for Beatrice. Like 5, 9 is a potent number and a circular number because it reproduces itself in multiplication (2x9 = 18, 1 + 8 = 9; 3x9 = 27, 2 + 7 = 9; 4x9 = 36, 3 + 6 = 9; 5x9 = 45, 4 + 5 = 9; etc.).

TEN: Unity, perfection, all-inclusiveness; ONE extended to include all numbers. The 10 spheres; the Old Law because of the decalogue; justice because of the tetrachtys (the Pythagorean pyramid of justice, 1 + 2 + 3 + 4 forming an equilateral triangle).

ELEVEN: Sin: in excess of 10, deficient of 12.

TWELVE: Fullness, totality. There are 12 mansions, 12 months, 12 tribes of Israel, 12 apostles. Revelation: the spreading of the Trinity (3) to the 4 corners of earth (Aug. *On John*, tr. 29; a very common gloss). Because of its cosmic implications, 12 is a sign of the Apocalypse.

Glosses of this sort were particularly useful in scriptural exegesis, but they pertain to all the arts as well since the basis of the glosses lies mainly in the numbers of Creation and, as Hugh of St. Victor points out, "the products of artificers, while not nature, imitate nature, and, in the design by which they imitate, they express the form of their exemplar, which is nature" (*Didascalicon* [trans. Taylor] 1.4, p. 51).

In addition to numerical glossing based upon correspondences in nature, the twelfth century witnessed the revival of gematric study. *Gematria* is the art of equating numbers with letters so that words can be expressed by numerical equivalents. Gematria had flourished among Greek and Hebrew scholars at the beginning of the Christian era simply because for a considerable period of time it had been the standard Greek method of arithmetical notation (see Louis Charles

Karpinski, "Greek Arithmetic Notation," in *Introduction to Arithmetic*, trans. D'Ooge, chap. 4). To the 24 letters of the Greek alphabet 3 were added (*digamma, koppa,* and *sampi*) so that the 27 letters could provide signs for numbers up through the 3d decimal place, whereafter accent marks were added to extend the notation system to higher numbers:

α	β	γ	δ	ε	ϝ	ζ	η	θ
1	2	3	4	5	6	7	8	9
ι	k	λ	μ	ν	ξ	o	π	ϙ
10	20	30	40	50	60	70	80	90
ϱ	σ	τ	υ	φ	χ	ψ	ω	ϡ
100	200	300	400	500	600	700	800	900

This system of notation prevailed in Greece from the time of Plato into New Testament times and is reflected in New Testament writings and commentaries, especially in the Alexandrian school. Gematria is stressed in the *Theologumena Arithmeticae*, a work once attributed to Iamblichus (probably a translation of a lost work by Nicomachus). As an example of its application in scriptural exegesis, consider Augustine's explication of John 2:19-21: " 'Destroy this temple, and in three days I will raise it up.' Then said the Jews, forty and six years was this temple in building, and wilt thou rear it up in three days? But he spake of the temple of the body." Augustine explains that 46 means ADAM, since by gematria a = 1, d = 4, a = 1, and m = 40, the sum being 46. The passage says, then, that the Jews will destroy the body (ADAM) by crucifying Christ (the 2d Adam), but that Christ on the 3d day will restore the temple through the Resurrection.

Gematria flourished along with cabalistic studies into the seventeenth century. Knowledge of the art was spread throughout Europe by Franciscan preachers such as Jacobus de Fiore. A curriculum *forma* at Oxford in the fourteenth century, for example, indicates that 12 days were devoted to its study. Because of the occult nature of gematria, it is impossible to know with much certainty whether it was used extensively for purposes other than scriptural explication. A few gematric numbers were well known and crop up in literature as symbols. I have argued for a possible gematric puzzle in the Middle English poem *St. Erkenwald* ("Number Structure in *St. Erkenwald,*" *Annuale Mediavale* 14 [1973]: 18-21), where the phrases "whan aghtene wonted" and "threnen aghte" (i.e., 888) might be understood as riddles on the names of Jesus, 18 being the first two letters of His name, 888 the whole name: I (10) + η (8) + σ (200) + o (70) + u (400) + s (200) = $I\eta\sigma ous$ (888). There are also examples of riddles in Middle English based upon gematric use of the English alphabet. Magdalene College, Cambridge, Pepys MS 1236 and Bodleian MS Douce 257 contain versions of the following riddle:

In 8 is alle my loue $\left.\right\}$
& 9 be y-sette byfore $\quad$ IHC
So 8 be y-closyd aboue
Thane 3 is good therefore

(See Rossell Hope Robbins, *Secular Lyrics of the XIVth and XVth Centuries* [Oxford, 1955], p. 80). A variant that spells out the full name JHESUS occurs in Balliol College, Oxford, MS 354:

8 is my trew love;
do beffore 9;
put þerto 5,
so it wil beseme;
18 twyse told,
20 betwen.

The author goes on to explain: "this goth by the letters of the abse as þe letters stond in nombre" (Robbins, *Secular Lyrics,* p. 253).

Numerical Structures in Verse: Second-Generation Studies Needed (Exemplified in *Sir Gawain* and the *Chanson de Roland*)

A. Kent Hieatt

In looking at the present status of studies of numerically controlled structures in medieval verse, one sees the following situation. (1) The believers insist, and their opponents do not deny, that number possessed numinosity and for most medieval thinkers was a prominently recognized aspect of all *realia*, and indeed of all reification, so that number was considered an essential aspect of divinely created time and space, of human thought, and of human artifact, particularly the divinely inspired kind. (2) However, for the artifact called *verse* there is in the Middle Ages not even a single clear recipe for the kinds of complex structures that modern numerical structuralists impute to medieval verse — no single recipe, for example, like the clear recipes for numerically defined metrical schemes and rhyme schemes in the fifteenth-century *Arts de seconde rhétorique*. (3) Nevertheless, believers are able to point to, and their opponents concede, a body of obviously numerically structured medieval Latin and vernacular verse, most of it also "numerological" (i.e., having symbolic values attached to the numbers); and there is now a large body of secondary literature in the classical Latin and Renaissance fields — studied carefully by the specialists in these fields — that imputes numerical structure, at least, to much Latin and Renaissance verse.

Notwithstanding the positive achievements referred to, however, much of the now large body (in both German and English) of numerical studies of *medieval* verse still suffers from fantasticality; from results conditioned not so much by the object of the researcher's study as by his own angle of approach and by that of his research community (e.g., his German- or English-speaking academic community); from a hydroptic desire for achieved patterns; and from a neglect of adverse evidence. Partly as a consequence of these faults, and partly as a consequence of the opposing camp's grumbling conservatism, the yield of such research is not yet highly regarded in most circles outside the immediate ones in which the research is produced. I do not know, in fact, where in the medieval field (certainly not in my own work) there is to be found a numerical-structuralist study that has gained the degree of general acceptance elicited by my seventeen-year-old discovery of the numerical structure of the Renaissance poet Spenser's *Epithalamion* (*Short Time's Endless Monument* [New York, 1960]; now reprinted by Kennikat). One of the directions that those interested in this medieval field should follow, I believe, is that of second-generation studies — studies that need not always and exclusively be critiques of what has already been done, but that proceed more temperately in the light of what can now be seen as the mistakes of the past.

One such second-generation study[1] in part attacks (temperately and judiciously in my opinion) and in part radically revises the results of my own study of the structure of *Sir Gawain and the Green Knight* — my first numerical work, completed (as I remember) in the middle 1950s although not first published until 1968.[2] I shall pay less attention here to this second-generation study of Hans Käsmann's than to my own critique (which appears in a different and much more detailed form elsewhere[3]) of the results of Professor Eleanor Bulatkin's numerological study of the Oxford manuscript of the *Chanson de Roland*.[4] A set of what I think are generally applicable, rule-of-thumb caveats will eventuate, and some bibliographical leads are laid out in the notes.

Käsmann starts by accepting two of my overall numerological proposals for *Gawain* (having to do with the total number of lines) but then, in the matter of the editorial third fitt of the poem, rejects my numerological conclusions based on *stanza*-units in favor of nonnumerological (i.e., simply numerical-structural) conclusions based on *line*-units and having the solely aesthetic validity of numerical symmetry and arithmetical proportion.

He seems, then, initially impressed by the following of my conclusions: in the 101st, and final, stanza of the companion poem *Pearl*, the line that echoes the first line of the poem is number 1,212; and 12 is probably the significant numerical symbol in the poem — the massed twelves and the 144,000 derived from Revelation having everything to do with the bridegroom who is the Lamb and with his bride Pearl (as Russell Peck points out in another way in his essay for the present collection). Although the total of 1,212 lines in *Pearl* follows necessarily from its 101 stanzas, each of 12 lines, no such necessity attends a total in *Sir Gawain*'s corresponding sum of 101 stanzas, in the same manuscript and no doubt by the same hand, since these stanzas *vary* in length. Yet the line in the last stanza that echoes the first line of the poem is number 2,525, and 25 is surely a most important symbolic number in the poem, for Gawain with his pentangle has, we are told, 5 x 5 excellences, all duly listed and responsible for his apparent physical and moral invulnerability.

However, where I had seen in the third fitt a structure corresponding to the events of the three days of the Temptation of Gawain in Bercilak's castle, namely a series of three eleven-stanza units plus one supernumerary stanza (corresponding to a "supernumerary" 101), Käsmann finds that he can accept nothing, and directs at my theory a criticism in part truly withering and in part dependent upon an orientation of research that I should say belongs to a German school of numerical-structural analysis; it has appeared in the English-speaking world exclusively, I believe, in the proportional "modules" of Professor Thom Hart's analyses of *Beowulf* and of other Old English poetry.[5]

Käsmann notices a set of features of which the significance
had escaped me, namely, that if the sequence within each narrative of the three successive days is divided up under certain
convincing and consistent rubrics (A, the beginning of the
hunt; B, the temptation scene in the castle; C, the completion
of the hunt; D, the end of the day in the castle), then some
striking, but nonsymbolic, symmetries and proportions
emerge. On the first day A and C are of the same length, and
on the second day A & C differ in length by only one line, as
has formerly been noticed. However, Käsmann also points out
that on the first day the total (139 lines) of A, C and D differs
by only one line from that of B (the temptation scene, 140);
and that the total (186 lines) of A and B is exactly twice the
total of C and D (93). On the second day the total (184 lines) of
A, C, and D is exactly twice that of B (92). On the third day
the total of A, C, and D is 140, nearly corresponding to the 139
lines of the equivalent scenes on the first day, and exactly corresponding to the 140 lines of the first temptation scene of the
first day. But (he points out with commendable restraint) only
if the last 7 lines of fitt 3, lines apparently merely transitional,
are included do we reach a total of 74 for D, which is only one
line more than A plus C and which produces a nearly exact
(206: 104) ratio of 2 to 1 of the total lines of A plus B to the
total lines of C plus D.

His conclusion is that in fitt 3 the poet was not concerned
with symbolic numbers "as Hieatt suggested," although he
seems to favor the symbolic significance of the overall line
count to the echoing line. "The poet's purpose was primarily
aesthetic. He aimed at giving the narrative of Fitt III a compositional symmetry based on simple numerical proportions."

I believe that much can be said for this conclusion, but also
that something can still be said for some of my original ones.
However, I do not wish to pursue this matter further here. The
point is that Käsmann has followed with much good sense a notion of aesthetic symmetries often pursued in Germany in investigating medieval romance and epic[6] (in which, incidentally, interest must usually be directed at the numbers of lines
rather than the numbers of stanzas, since most of the works

studied are not in stanzaic form). However, from a contrary point of view my fellow researcher in the Renaissance Alastair Fowler has recently contended that numerical symmetries are unconvincing *unless* they can be identified with numerical symbolic values. In this matter we can as yet say only that while we recognize the habitual association of a specific number with a specific symbolic value (sometimes one value, sometimes another value) in the Middle Ages, we must recognize as well the appearance in medieval art of proportion and symmetry solely for their own sake. For the "modulists," the Celtic and Primitive Germanic interlace design forms a *Lieblingsthema* here, for this interlace seems to embody a play of proportions and symmetries in which there is no ideational content whatever. The contradiction between the two schools of research will sooner or later have to be brought to the stage of conscious confrontation and perhaps, as usual, some *modus vivendi* will be found in the wide pastures of compromise.

One kind of research that involves partly aesthetic and also partly symbolic symmetries, and that I should like to bring to the attention of more students of the subject, is represented by the claims for bilateral symmetry in lyric verse made by J. A. Huisman in *Neue Wege zur dicterischen und musikalischen Technik Walthers von der Vogelweide, mit einem Exkurs über die symmetrische Zahlenkomposition im Mittelalter* (Utrecht, 1950; Studia Litteraria Rheno-Traiectina 1). The results seem to me robustly trustworthy. A parallel effort has been made by Constance Hieatt and myself in the field of Middle English literature; specifically, we endeavored to set forth a bilaterally symmetrical numerical structure consisting of two "wings" surrounding a center—the analogy with the Gothic triptych is intentional—in the fourteenth-century moral poem "The Bird with Four Feathers."[7] (In connection with this a reader might perform the experiment of looking for a pattern before consulting the proposed one. The Bodley 596 version of the poem is no. 121 in Carleton Brown's *Religious Lyrics of the XIVth Century.*)

The next division of the subject can be broached by looking incidentally at a small item of faultiness in Käsmann's analysis.

It will be remembered that of his four units for the first day of the temptation, A, C, and D are approximately equal in length (46 or 47 lines each), while B, the temptation scene itself, amounts to 140 lines. Käsmann points out that if one adds together A, C, and D, one gets almost the same total as for B, and that, on the other hand, A and B totaled give exactly twice as many lines as C and D totaled. This is true, but in fact one of these conclusions entails the other: they are not separate arithmetical felicities. If the value of either A or C or D (all approximately equal) is x, and the value of B is y, and if $3x = y$, as in the first of these conclusions, then it necessarily follows that $y + x = 2 \times 2x$, or, otherwise expressed, that $y + x = 4x$, which is the second of these conclusions. The poet may have had both of these felicities in mind, but it is requisite to say that he may have had only one (in this case probably the first, which establishes a closer analogy with the narrative of the second day), since either necessitates the other.

A very good rule, then (although less important than others that I shall come to) is not to exclaim over arithmetical felicities that follow automatically from other such felicities. Professor Bulatkin's chief proposed numerical structure in the *Roland* consists of a series of modules, or units, of 66 laisses that start at three separate points (namely, laisses 1, 18, and 44) and go leapfrogging over each other through part of the poem. She says (p. 32) "It is rather startling that the numbers of laisses at each narrative point (i.e., at the beginning or end of each module, 18, 44, 66, 84, 110, 132, 150, 176) are all divisible either by eleven, or by six, or by eleven and six." Certainly there is nothing surprising about this. The number 66, the module-unit, is divisible by 11 and 6; the point, laisse 18, at which the second set of modules begins gives us a number divisible by 6; and the point at which the third set begins—laisse 44—gives us a number divisible by 11. What would be really startling would be for any of the ensuing sums *not* to be divisible by 11 or 6. Examples of this particular procedural error could be multiplied in Bulatkin's book and in other similar research.

Another and more important rule is to think about what is entailed physically and chronologically in the origin and survival of any numerical scheme that one proposes. C. A. Robson,[8] for instance, has shown that the recurrence of certain units of lines in designated manuscripts of French romances had to do with no more than the numbers of lines ruled per page. Considerable difficulty arises with Professor Bulatkin's theory with respect to the physical embodiment of the *Roland*. To credit this theory one must suppose (and it seems to me reasonable to suppose) that the poem was a product of written composition, even though many continue to believe that the *chansons de geste* were orally composed. Bulatkin premises an initial system of three series of units of 66 laisses, the third of which, through two steps, arrives at laisse 176: obviously, if this is accepted, a written document was required. But then, she says (in accordance with a familiar theory) that the Baligant material, after the martyrdom of Roncevaux, was added by another hand (and the more usual form of the theory is that this addition was made as much as a century later). This new hand worked with three series of 91 laisses (not 66) beginning with laisses 18, 44, and 85; the third series ends with a second step in laisse 267. What is required here is that the second writer, after a considerable lapse of time, worked from a version of the first poet's work in which at least the original number and arrangement of the first poet's laisses were *perfectly* preserved, even though other jongleurs were reciting many other forms of the story of Roncevaux, perhaps often on the basis of the first poet's work.

This is a real although not insuperable difficulty. Is one to suppose that a second writer of sufficient numerical sophistication gravitated to a sophisticated center where a uniquely veritable manuscript was preserved? Or that a number of properly ordered manuscripts were in existence—of which one found the man of the hour who discerned and wished to continue the hidden numerical pattern?

I am not trying to destroy Professor Bulatkin's theory with ironic aspersions. Indeed, the first part of the theory seems to me to have much likelihood, and I shall continue to credit the 66-modulist until I am shown why I should not, for the points of articulation proposed for these modules in the narrative seem to me in large part decisive ones. It also seems to me, however, that the physical aspect of the problem that I have raised should have been taken into account, particularly since the modules proposed for the second poet seem rather less convincing than those for the first.[9]

A third and even more general rule is that one must think out carefully all of the internal consequences of the pattern that one imputes to a work. Professor Bulatkin presupposes two poets, with the second of whom the 91-module is a completely new and independent device. Yet of the three series of such modules, the first step of the first series and the first step of the second series are completely within the run of laisses ascribed to the first poet! Does Bulatkin mean that the continuator interpolated the required details for his scheme within the original laisses 109 and 135? Possibly in 109, but scarcely in 135, for 133 and 134 give an asymptotic approach to the necessary fact of Ganelon's treachery in 135: these laisses would not exist except for the discussion of this treachery. At no point, I believe, does Bulatkin show a consciousness of this difficulty, although an explanation of it would have been easy: she could have proposed that the continuator did not invent the 91-module but found *ex post facto* significance in this originally unintentional interval, just as the numerological symbolism of church architecture sometimes seems not to have been built into an edifice but to have been invented after the edifice's erection.

Perhaps the most vexed rule of all, which brings me back to Käsmann's objections to one of my theories, has to do with the assignment of a symbolic value to a particular number: the value assigned should seem not arbitrarily chosen but mandated by all available evidence. Bulatkin finds in the divisibility of the 66-module by 11, and in the fact that 66 is the sum of the sequence of the numbers 1 through 11, the sinister significance of the number 11: transgression, going one beyond proper measure in exceeding the perfect ten — Commandments and so on (an interpretation of 11 shared by Professor Peck[10]). The number 6, the corresponding factor of 66, may signify, she says, sin, for example as the number of Venus and perhaps as the 666 of the beast of Revelation (here Peck tends not to follow her). There is considerably more of this kind of citation, not touched on here. In the 91-series, 13 is a factor of 91, and can, she says, be connected with leadership of the twelve peers and of the twelve apostles. For 7, the other factor of 91, she chooses the meaning "completeness" (cf. Peck's material on approximately the same meaning). "The major function of the 91 pattern was to link the tragedy of Roncevaux, in which Charlemagne's role was one of rather lethargic nonparticipation, with the vigorous and positive acts by Charles to avenge the defeat" (p. 47). Further, "the dominant number 13 would most certainly signify Charlemagne, the leader of Christendom, while the number 7 would symbolize the completeness of Charles. . ., the earthly representative of his Creator" (p. 51).

It is true that the factors of a number are sometimes taken in biblical exegesis to explain a significance of that number, so that 11 and 6 *might* be of significance in explaining a 66-module that, it must be remembered, itself remains putative. For 11, indeed, the significance of *démesure*, as that fault is often ascribed to Roland, may be supposed to explain the disaster to himself and to Charlemagne's army, which is often recognized as the great point of the first part of the poem. This significance for 11 is recognizably traditional, as Peck confirms. But what of 6? If, indeed, Martianus Capella called it the number of Venus, and if one Carolingian poet confused 6 with sex, and finally if a bad association of 6 might be thought to stem (on what evidence, though?) from the 666 of the Beast of Revelation, how does this accurately express the sinfulness of Roland in his overconfidence, or even that of Ganelon? The kinds of sinfulness the evidence associates with 6 seem aesthetically and logically a perplexing choice, arbitrary and in need of further explanation, as compared, for instance, with 11 or with nonnumerical features of the author's art. Why would the poet have chosen it?

Perhaps, says Bulatkin (p. 37), in a surprising reversal, this was *not* what the poet meant. Perhaps he chose an entirely different meaning for 6 (the one documented by Peck): the perfection of God's creation, in which case the perfection of

Roland multiplied by his *démesure* produced the disaster.

The difficulty with this kind of speculation is that it builds on what is assumed to be the ironclad certainty of the 66-module, whereas in reality the degree of its certainty is not great. Unless a symbolic significance of 6 can by its precise appropriateness increase the likelihood of the module itself, the investigator may be said to be building upon a defective premise and to be trying to identify *ignotum per ignotius*.

With the factors of the 91-module, one is in even worse difficulties. How much of a tradition can be found for the association of 13 with the leaders of the 12 peers and of the 12 apostles? Speaking generally of the Middle Ages, probably none; but speaking specifically, Charlemagne is mentioned as the thirteenth, as taking a thirteenth seat, in the *Pèlerinage de Charlemagne*. Of course this *may* be the explanation, but there is some flimsiness in the evidence for a choice of 13, which, Bulatkin says, would have had to seem, to an author and to his audience, plainly motivated. The mere speculation that a leader of 12 *must* be considered to be a thirteenth is really not of any further help. The unlucky aspect of 13, emphasized by Hopper, is another difficulty. For 7 the multitude of associations was plainly good, but a generalized, vague goodness is of little help in giving support to the initially doubtful 91-module. The choice of "completeness" fits nicely in terms of Bulatkin's theory, though somewhat less satisfactorily in terms of the transcendental, divine completeness that seems in accord with Peck's evidence. Here, however, the great difficulty is the extremely large number of meanings that medieval writers found in this number. Unless one is sure that the creator of the Baligant material *chose* 91 and the factor 7 (and I am not), it seems arbitrary to narrow the significance of 7 so drastically to suit the convenience of a doubtful theory.

What is wrong with this aspect of the first-generation study that I have been discussing (in the hope of making a second-generation advance) is that it gives no satisfying sense of a confluence of evidence. Similarly with all too many numerological, as contrasted with numerical-structural, conclusions: the ascribed mystical meanings seem arbitrary because they are picked from a grab bag of miscellaneous available meanings, and even when thus selected to meet the theorist's convenience, they often seem perplexingly astray from what the poet seems (even to the theorist himself) to be saying.

A fifth and obvious rule is to try to find confirmation of a suggested numerical pattern in the subject matter of the work being analyzed. Probably, it is true, there are cases in which the numerical structure of a lyric (like, at times, a lyric's metrical or musical structure) cuts across its meaning-structure as an independent second voice (cf. Huisman in *Neue Wege*). But in her analysis Bulatkin accepts the premise of numerical articulation by means of subject matter. By and large she seems to me to have been successful in working out the consequences of this premise in the material of the *Chanson* through the Roncevaux episode. In the Baligant material I believe that she has not been thus successful.

For this part of the poem, she posits three series of 91-laisse modules. We have already pointed out that the first modules of the first and second of these series are completed within the runs of laisses ascribed to the originator of the poem, not to its continuator. For the third series, the narrative incidents at the juncture points are (1) an instance of Roland's *démesure* (the last of the three laisses in which Roland refuses to blow the Olifant), (2) the death of Roland, and (3) the burial of the heroes (including Roland: one of several circumstances in laisse 267). Here one wonders why the last among the three successive cases of horn-blowing was chosen by the poet, although it hangs together well with Roland's death. But the case of the burial is so unsatisfactory as to elicit from Bulatkin the theory that the continuator was straitjacketed by his own clumsily chosen module into introducing the burial abruptly (6 lines) in a laisse (30 lines) filled with other circumstances for which he could find no room elsewhere. Yet he could easily have made this laisse, and others, longer. It is nearly impossible to believe that, motivated by the scheme ascribed to him, he would not have done so. The second 91-series is even less satisfactory: perhaps (1) Ganelon's description of his plan coheres with (2) the intimation to Charles of this treachery, but (3) Charles's prayer for vengeance is a sad anticlimax for this group. Finally, of the first 91-series it can be said that the poet has let Bulatkin down badly if his intention was really as she says, to conjoin (1) Olivier's prediction of *démesure*, (2) the author's comment on the betrayal of Ganelon and advance notice of his trial in accordance with which vengeance will be executed on him, (3) Baligant's oath of vengeance on Charles for Marsile's loss of his right hand in battle, and (4) the end of the poem. In context these really cohere on no important basis; yet they form Bulatkin's only basis for believing in the existence of modules of 91 laisses in her third series.

A sixth, and somewhat personal, rule is (where possible) to avoid proposing short structural systems arbitrarily located within the body of a larger work. The sudden apparent illumination that there is numerological significance in a clump of 7 or 11 or 33 or 100 lines of verse beginning and ending almost anywhere in a work of, say, 20,000 lines is to be distrusted initially, because one lacks the rigorous cross-checking procedures available when one has proposed a closed system for an entire work. The situation here is rather like that of Ferdinand de Saussure's *anagrammes* and *hypogrammes* in Greek and Latin poetry: his discovery that a key word near the beginning of a work seems to distribute its syllables through the neighboring lines of verse. The embarrassing subsequent discovery of such a superfluity of *anagrammes* in the most unlikely places made it seem probable that they arise by some factor below the level of conscious choice, or conceivably, that they arise by chance.[11] No example of a medievalist's breaking this rule comes to mind, but the well-known practices of Maren-Sophie Röstvig in her study of Milton's work have sometimes been taxed with what amounts to doing just this.

A final point is an injunction, not a rule: let us talk, or continue to talk, with mathematicians specializing in probability theory or statistical analysis. The ones with whom I have talked say that without an initial assumption on the basis of a known degree of probability in analogous areas, no statement of likelihood can be made about any given claim that there is authorial intent behind a newly discovered numerical structure in a literary document. One day, however, I hope that we may find an interested party who combines literary and statistical specialties in such a way as to do something more useful in this direction. I have seen nothing of much help in the secondary literature. Even the fact that two or more of us see the same pattern in a work may not be finally signficant. We may be psychologically conditioned to see it. Of course, the same holds for any other literary-critical conclusion. If we can get some kind of mathematical confirmation, it will be a help; but we may have to do without it.

Notes

1. Hans Käsmann, "Numerical Structure in Fitt III of *Sir Gawain and the Green Knight*," in *Chaucer and Middle English Studies in Honour of Rossell Hope Robbins*, ed. Beryl Rowland (London, 1974), pp. 131-39.

2. A. Kent Hieatt, "*Sir Gawain*: Pentangle, Luf-Lace, Numerical Structure," *Papers on Language & Literature* 4 (1968): 339-59; reprinted in *Silent Poetry, Essays in Numerological Analysis*, ed. Alastair Fowler (London, 1970), pp. 116-40. See also my "Symbolic and Narrative Patterns in *Pearl, Cleanness, Patience*, and *Gawain*," *English Studies in Canada* 2 (1976): 125-43.

3. A. Kent Hieatt, "Arithmetic Metaphor in the *Roland*," *Medium AEvum* 43 (1974): 37-41.

4. Eleanor Bulatkin, *Structural Arithmetic Metaphor in the Oxford "Roland"* (Columbus, Ohio, 1972).

5. Thomas Elwood Hart, "*Ellen*: Some Tectonic Relationships in *Beowulf* and their Formal Resemblance to Anglo-Saxon Art," *Papers on Language & Literature* 6 (1970): 263-90; idem, "Tectonic Design, Formulaic Craft, and Literary Execution; the Episodes of Finn and Ingeld in 'Beowulf,'" in *Amsterdammer Beiträge zur älteren Germanistik*, ed. Cola Minis (Sonderdruck, 1972 Bd. 2); idem, "Tectonic Methodology and an Application to *Beowulf*," below.

6. Probably the best introductory essay on numerical structure for medievalists in general, and not just for specialists in German, is Michael S. Batts, "Numerical Structure in Medieval Literature," in *Formal Aspects of Medieval German Poetry, a Symposium*, ed. Stanley N. Werbow (Austin, Tex., 1969), pp. 93-119. On the Germans the concluding bibliography in this piece is very satisfactory, and a more general short bibliography precedes it. The bibliography of German works may be supplemented by the fuller but more difficult-to-use one in Wolfgang Haubrichs, *Ordo als Form. Strukturstudien zur Zahlenkomposition bei Otfrid von Weissenburg und in karolingischer Literatur* (Tübingen, 1969).

7. "'The Bird with Four Feathers': Numerical Analysis of a Fourteenth-Century Poem," *Papers on Language and Literature* 6 (1970): 18-38. *Ordo als Form*, cited above, contains many examples of analyses on the same principle.

8. C. A. Robson, "The Technique of Symmetrical Composition in Medieval Narrative Poetry," in *Studies in Medieval French Presented to Alfred Ewert*, ed. E. A. Francis (Oxford, 1961), pp. 26-75.

9. See my "Arithmetic Metaphor."

10. See the Appendix to Professor Peck's essay on this collection.

11. See the review of Jean Starobinski, *Les Mots sur les mots*, in the *Times Literary Supplement*, January 21, 1972, pp. 67-68.

The Poet's Number at the Center*

Charles S. Singleton

In memory of
Adolf Katzenellenbogen

The central canto of the *Commedia* is, of course, the seventeenth of the *Purgatorio*, the central *cantica*. Nor is that canto the central unit of the whole structure merely in numerical terms; for, as every thoughtful reader of the poem knows, *Purgatorio* 17 can rightly be said to contain the central argument that is basic to the whole moral order, that is, the general exposition of Love, which is shown to be the all-embracing and all-motivating force of creatures and Creator:

"Nè creator nè creatura mai,"
  cominciò el, "figliuol, fu sanza amore,
  o naturale o d'animo, e tu 'l sai."

These verses, marking the beginning of that treatment of the great theme, constitute, in fact, the thirty-first *terzina* of the central canto, and they bear the numbers 91, 92, and 93 (which fact may finally not seem devoid of meaning within a context we have now to consider). Thus Love, as the central concern and argument, is seen to inform both God's world and the poet's world, there at the center of both — and this we shall hardly view as an accident.

*This essay first appeared in *Modern Language Notes* 80 (1965):1-10; permission to reprint has been granted.

However, canto 17 does not in itself contain the entire treatment of love, as such a foundation and motivating force, since
Virgil continues to expatiate on that subject well into canto 18.
Freewill, moreover, is clearly an integral part of the central
concern of the poem, and that comes into the argument with
Marco Lombardo in canto 16, so that we pass from *libero arbitrio* to Love through this central area, and come to see that
both themes are really one, which extends out from center, so
to speak, out from the exact center of canto 17 into the two adjacent cantos, thus marking off three cantos at the center of
the structure—a number that (there is scarcely any need to
observe) is seldom without meaning in Dante's work.

Of all this we have long been aware in our reading of the
Commedia. But it may be of some interest to note what is less
commonly observed (if at all), to wit, that if we count to either
side of the central canto 17, and if we count *terzine*, we come
to see that the central argument, which treats of freewill and
Love, extends into exactly 50 *terzine* that are equally balanced,
as 25, on either side of this central canto. This we note,
perhaps, first of all, because Virgil's general discourse on the
theme of Love ends with the *terzina*

La nobile virtù Beatrice intende
    per lo libero arbitrio, e però guarda
    che l'abbi a mente s'a parlar ten prende[1]

which couples her name with the key term *libero arbitrio* in the
central verse of this the 25th *terzina*, counting from the end of
canto 17. Then, encouraged by this fact, we may also count
terzine back from the beginning of canto 17 to find that we
come, in the 25th, not to the beginning of Marco's discourse, to
be sure, but to the *terzina* in which the term *libero arbitrio*
makes its first appearance in his disquisition:

Se così fosse, in voi fora distrutto
    libero arbitrio, e non fora giustizia
    per ben letizia, e per male aver lutto.[2]

The number 25, thus arrived at and clearly visible in this balance of *terzine* to either side of center, will prove to be not without significance as we proceed in our considerations of patterns at the center, if we remember to follow an established practice and add the numbers that make it up. The number 25, in this sense, displays a number 7, the sum of its two digits, equally balanced on either side of the central canto. And we may now add to this the fact that the central verse of canto 17 of the *Purgatorio*, and thus the central verse of the entire *Commedia*, bears the number 70.

If we turn our thoughts to the journey now rather than to numbers of cantos and verses, we will be reminded that, with canto 17, the wayfarer Dante has come to the center of the seven-terraced area of Purgatory proper, and that the very method of Virgil's exposition of Love there is, first, to look back over the three terraces already traversed and thus speak of the sins that are purged there as one kind of *malo amor* that may be called *triform*; and then to look ahead and speak of the three terraces yet to be traversed as those on which another kind of Love is purged, and it too is *triform*. Thus, out from a central terrace the pilgrim's attention (and ours) is directed to either side of center, to areas that balance out in the architecture of this second realm, even as, in number of *terzine*, the argument in a broader sense contains the central discourse (as noted). All of which is also fairly clear to most readers of the poem and needs no more than a passing reference to bring it to mind—all, that is, except perhaps the point of there being 25 *terzine* in the balance to either side of center.

Now it was precisely this feature that came to my attention for the first time when I had come to consider how a somewhat broader "center" of the poem might possibly be marked out in the numerical composition of the cantos; and the matter of the 25 *terzine* to either side would, perhaps, not seem particularly significant to me now, had I not, in the pursuit of such an inquiry, hit upon a pattern of numbers at the center of the *Commedia* that, to my knowledge, has not been noticed before, an equal balance of numbers to either side of center that is far more wondrous.

We may remind ourselves that the one variable in the component parts of this poem, as the poet has conceived it, is the length of the cantos. In each the number of verses will vary (within a maximum range of 45 verses, apparently, since the shortest canto has 115 verses and the longest 160), but that number will also be one that is always evenly divisible by 3, if the number 1 be first subtracted from its total, because the poet has chosen to end each canto with a verse that exceeds the last *terzina*. Clearly such a device is carrying out, in miniature, the number of the whole, so to speak, since each of the cantiche, *Inferno, Purgatorio, Paradiso*, is made up of 33 cantos, a number that could not be more evidently a multiple of 3, thus giving 99 cantos, to which must be added a first "prologue" canto of the poem, which completes the perfect number 100.

Here then, in the matter of the length of the cantos, is a great *variable*, as I have termed it, which (as occurred to me for the first time not very long ago) might perhaps be found to contain some significant numerical pattern, if one were to list those numbers in a table that would present the entire picture. Such a picture is very easy to come by, if one turns to any modern edition of the poem, for all have the verses numbered and the totals of the cantos plainly displayed at the end of each. And it would seem right, to any reader who undertook such a listing, to arrange the numbers in three columns, according to their respective *cantica*, and to set the first prologue canto above the whole, thus counting canto 2 of the *Inferno* as the first, properly speaking, of that *cantica*.

What met my eye at once, after drawing up such a table, will meet the eye of any reader who takes the trouble to scan it. For there, at the center I saw (to my not inconsiderable excitement, I may say) a cluster of numbers, a little figure, a constellation of seven numbers, which, to my knowledge, has not been noticed before (but if such is not the case and if it has been seen before, no matter: what matters is that we see it *now*).

Canto 17 of the *Purgatorio* contains 139 verses; and though these numbers, taken separately, are apt to be significant in any medieval work (even as they are in God's created universe), they are not, as the number of a canto length, unique in their occurrence here at the exact center of the poem, as a scrutiny of the adjoined table will show. But when such numbers (and in that particular sequence, of course) are framed to either side by the numerical pattern 145, 145, 151, we are bound to see that it can only be by deliberate design that 139 is framed thus at the center. And only such a canto length, moreover, could yield a verse numbered 70 at the precise midpoint of the whole poem. Indeed, it is the presence of the number 7 here at the center that is most impressive, possibly because we tend to take 1 and 3 and 9 much more for granted. Clearly the framing number in that central pattern is 151, which, to one side and the other of center, marks off 7 cantos there, with canto 17 of the *Purgatorio* in the middle. And that pattern is so clearly terminated by 151 at equal distance on either side that no one can fail to see it so.

Now, as every student of numerology knows, one is always expected to add up the digits composing such numbers to see if their sums may not prove important. Accordingly, part of my own excitement over the pattern at the center (as the reader may have guessed) came from my having noticed already that exactly 25 *terzine* could be seen to frame the "center" of the poem in another way, as explained above. Here, then, are framing canto numbers (151) whose sum is 7, here are framing *terzine* (25 to either side) the sum of whose number is 7, and here finally at the exact center of the poem is a verse whose number is 70, the sum of which is 7!

Between the central number 139 (not particularly important in the sum of its digits, apparently, though something could obviously be made of the number 13) and the framing numbers of 151 to either side, there is the number 145, twice repeated, the sum of its digits being clearly significant as the perfect number 10. Thus, in this central nucleus appear the numbers 1, 3, 7, and 9, to restate them in an ordinary sequence, and they are indeed nothing less than the great odd numbers below 10, as a tradition reaching back to Pythagoras would have it; and note also the number 10 expressed thus 4 times in the

TABLE OF CANTO LENGTHS

Inferno		Purgatory		Paradise	
Canto	lines	Canto	lines	Canto	lines
1	136				
2	142	1	136	1	142
3	136	2	133	2	148
4	151	3	145	3	130
5	142	4	139	4	142
6	115	5	136	5	139
7	130	6	151	6	142
8	130	7	136	7	148
9	133	8	139	8	148
10	136	9	145	9	142
11	115	10	139	10	148
12	139	11	142	11	139
13	151	12	136	12	145
14	142	13	154	13	142
15	124	14	151	14	139
16	136	15	145	15	148
17	136	16	145	16	154
18	136	17	139	17	142
19	133	18	145	18	136
20	130	19	145	19	148
21	139	20	151	20	148
22	151	21	136	21	142
23	148	22	154	22	154
24	151	23	133	23	139
25	151	24	154	24	154
26	142	25	139	25	139
27	136	26	148	26	142
28	142	27	142	27	148
29	139	28	148	28	139
30	148	29	154	29	145
31	145	30	145	30	148
32	139	31	145	31	142
33	157	32	160	32	151
34	139	33	145	33	145

frame. Yet none among them commands attention so much as the number 7. For 7 is the framing number (151), 7 is the number of the cantos that are framed, and 7 is the number of the central verse of the central canto 17. Of course one may also view the pattern thus disclosed in terms of 3 + 1 + 3, for this corresponds to the 7 terraces of Purgatory, in the way noted, and to the strategy of the exposition there.

Now if the poet has so deliberately framed these 7 cantos at the center in this way, we should not fail (this poet being Dante) to inquire if they may not hold in themselves perhaps a "center" of the action and argument of the poem in some sense. They do not cover the area of the 7 terraces, of course, but they do contain the exposition of their arrangement in an upper and a lower Purgatory; and clearly they do, as 7 cantos, point to a broader center than is marked by the 25 *terzine* extending to either side. What, then, is it that is so centrally framed by these cantos?

The answer is quite plain in the structure of the poem: it is that what is thus framed amounts to nothing less than the central pivot of the whole poem in terms of the action, in terms, that is, of what happens to the wayfarer Dante as he "passes through the center." I may not, in a brief article that is aimed primarily at pointing out this numerical figure at the center that has so lately swum into our ken (and with a wild surmise), undertake to explore this point in any depth or detail, but can only suggest what every reader may test in his own reading —namely, that the area of these 7 cantos holds the experience of a "conversion" at the center, a great turning about, which is variously presented in explicit statement and in imagery. It begins in the question that arises concerning certain words spoken by Guido del Duca,[3] words that perplex the pilgrim and leave him with a problem; and these words come precisely in canto 14. The question they lead to[4] concerns the radical difference between possessing earthly goods and possessing heavenly goods. This heaven-bound pilgrim is being told, over and over again through this center, that he must learn to "look up," and understand how things are up there, where lies his proper goal, that he must adjust the eyes of his

mind to a polarity of difference between cupidity of material
things (which means looking down at them) and the charity of
Heaven, where possession of spiritual goods increases by shar-
ing. This argument, which passes then through the matter of
free will and Love, will be seen to continue to its completion as
the central, pivotal issue of the poem in canto 20, where an
avaricious pope lies face down for having fixed his eyes so exclusively on earthly goods, and where the entire mountain
trembles then because a soul has liberated itself from such a
position and is free to move on upward to its heavenly reward.
This central argument and action in the broader focus at the
center every thoughtful reader will have sensed in some way.
And now we see that the poet has framed it for us, in his canto
length at the center, marking off its area as beginning in canto
14 and ending in canto 20. And we come thus to see that the
number pattern at the center is no mere surface ornament, but
that it reaches deep into the movement of the poem; and this will
come to us as no great surprise, but rather as the expected thing,
for we do not forget that the same was true of the number pattern
of the *Vita Nuova*.[5]

Nor is there space here to undertake an examination of the
symbolic significance of the number 7 that is thus so emphatically present at the center. Every student of number symbolism, particularly as it reaches through medieval thought
and imagination, will have some awareness of the vast
bibliography that awaits and invites close study in this regard,
and it seems certain that a small volume can easily be written
on the possible meaning or meanings of such a number at the
center of the *Comedy*. I may make the barest suggestion here
of what appears to me at the present moment to be the primary
symbolic import of that fact, in the intention of the poet—for
this number 7 is the poet's number and must be viewed as *his* in
a poem where so many of the numbers are God's. His number 7
here is comparable to his triple rhyme throughout the poem;
these are *his* numbers, which imitate God's, in analogy.

Now 7 is the number of creation, for reasons that will puzzle
no reader of Genesis. And it is interesting to note that most
medieval manuscripts that deal with cosmology, if they bear il-

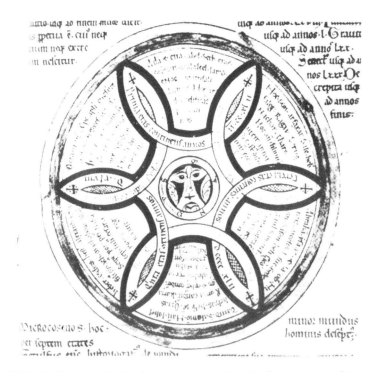

FIG. 6. *Cosmological schema representing 7, the number of Creation, as 1 surrounded by 6* (Liber Floridus, MS Voss. Lat. fol. 81, Leyden University).

luminations at all, testify abundantly to the significance of that number in this respect by displaying, over and over again, just such schemata as are represented by the accompanying illustration (Figure 6)[6]. Nor is the reader expected to be able to make out the writing in this diagram, for there is not time to dwell on it. Suffice it to say that the whole figure and the writing within it symbolize and explicate the essential structure of the Creation and of created Time in its manifold facets; and one may attend to the general design of the schema in itself, in which a central medallion (which will sometimes contain a representation of Adam or his name, and sometimes of the hand of God, or of God setting His compass upon the world) is surrounded by the figure of 6. Thus God's Creation, His macrocosm, bears the number 7 centrally imprinted upon it, in this sense, even as a poet's analogical world, his microcosm, may be seen to bear that same number at its center. And once more we have the essential glimpse of the principle that can guide a poet's hand as he imitates in his work the best of all possible models, which is God's universe. This has lately been referred to as the *discarded* Model, the great Image that a Renaissance finally did away with.[7] And discarded it surely is. Yet some readers of Dante's poem will, it is hoped, learn ever better to recover that *model* by an exercise of the historical imagination, as they meet up with it in Dante, as nowhere else; and they will continue to explore the world of the great poem he left as the *speculum* it is, and (hopefully) to make new discoveries in its amazing structure.

One such discovery (?) I have wished to point out here ever so briefly. Clearly it demands a far more searching treatment. We must understand the full import of this pattern at the center, so deliberately hidden away there, as we are tempted to say. But we may think a little, finally, about just that point, and wonder how "hidden" the poet would have thought it to be. It was a simple matter, as noted, to draw up a table of canto lengths from a modern edition, which has the verses numbered. But the manuscripts do not have the verses numbered. We must conceive, therefore, that a reader of the poem, before the invention of printing and the numbering of the lines, would be obliged, if he wished to get the whole picture of the canto lengths before him, to count the verses of each of the 100 cantos for himself, a job that some editor or printer does today and that all take for granted. However, that might be a work of love and is hardly any great or extremely laborious feat. But why *would* he ever count and list the verses of 100 cantos in this way? And are we to think that the poet expected his poem to find a reader, or readers, with *that* kind of curiosity? And if he did not expect this, why would he bother to construct such a pattern of numbers at the center of his structure, as we now see that he did? For we have certainly to face the fact that the poet had to have the plan of that design in mind *from the first canto to the last*, and never lose sight of it; for might it not fall out, simply happen, in part and quite accidentally, somewhere in the 100 canto lengths, and thus obscure the clear outline of it at the center? Only through a vigilant control of canto lengths can such a design be made to shine forth at the center of the whole; which brings us back to the question: did Dante expect his reader to see it within the whole? Which can only mean, did he expect him to draw up such a table as we have been examining, for only so can the number pattern at the center become visible?

One may perhaps suggest the answer to such a question by turning it another way, by directing it, say, to Chartres Cathedral, to some sculptured and finely finished detail in the stone work on the roof of that great edifice, a detail as carefully wrought as any on the façade itself, but which, being where it is, might never be seen again by human eye, once the roof was finished and the workmen had withdrawn — unless someone should climb up to repair that roof and happen to take notice of it. But may we think that any such consideration even occurred to the master who designed that detail or to the stonemason who fashioned it with loving care? We may not, for we know that such an edifice was not addressed to human sight alone, indeed not primarily to human sight at all. He who sees all things and so marvelously created the world in number, weight, and measure would see that design, no matter where its place in the structure; and would surely see it as a sign that the human architect had indeed imitated that created Universe which the Divine architect had wrought for His own contemplation, first of all, and for that of angels and of men.

Even so, though He who sees all things has seen it there these several centuries, we may perhaps think that Dante would not be displeased, could he know that the analogical figure he so carefully built into the center of his cosmos, the figure of Creation itself, has presented itself to our *human* view for the first time since the poet placed it there, and this on the occasion of a centennial of his birth, which happens to bear the number 7.

Notes

1. Dante *Purgatorio* 17.73-75.
2. Dante *Purgatorio* 16.70-72.
3. Dante *Purgatorio* 14.86-87.
4. Dante *Purgatorio* 15.44-75.
5. See my *Essay on the Vita Nuova* (Cambridge, Mass., 1949; rpt. Baltimore, Md., 1977), pp. 78-79 and passim.
6. I wish to acknowledge here the kindness of Professor Harry Bober of New York University in supplying me with this reproduction, from ms. Voss. Lat. (fol. 81) of Leyden University, the *Liber Floridus*; and for many other examples of this kind of schemata, on which he is the great authority, as well as many stimulating and helpful suggestions toward a more thorough exploration of the whole matter as it may connect with Dante. The reader may consult with great profit, in the matter of such schemata, two articles by Dr. Bober: "In Principio. Creation Before Time," in *De Artibus Opuscula XL, Essays in Honor of Erwin Panofsky* (New York, 1961), pp. 65-97; and "An Illustrated School-Book of Bede's 'De Natura Rerum,'" *Journal of the Walters Art Gallery* 19-20 (1956-57):65-97. In the latter article the author refers to such diagrams as schemata of Microcosmic-Macrocosmic Harmony, and points to their frequent occurrence in medieval manuscripts that deal with cosmology.
7. I refer to the posthumous volume of C. S. Lewis, *The Discarded Image* (Cambridge, 1964).

The Well-Rounded Sphere: The Metaphysical Structure of the *Consolation of Philosophy*

Elaine Scarry

I saw on the horizon where plain, sea, and mountain meet, a few low stars, not to be confused with the fires men light at night or that go alight alone . . . .

It is as though you were looking at the squalid earth and the heavens in turn; by the very law of sight you seem to be in the midst now of mud, now of stars . . . .

I say unto you: One must have chaos within to give birth to a dancing star. I say unto you: You still have chaos within.

— Beckett, Boethius, Nietzsche

The possibilities of the human soul manifest themselves along a vertical axis: at the lower terminus is the phenomenon of chaos; at the higher, a dancing star. Although master of his movement along this axis, man often deludes himself into the belief that he is chained to the nether pole. Recognizing his capacity for destruction, he despairs. Despairing, he relinquishes his control over his moral and psychic energies. The dance of a star, still latent within him, is forgotten. Man

91

forfeits his most cherished possibility.

Boethius refused the forfeit. His *Consolation* is an attempt to release man from his nether bondage into a sphere where he can participate in the realization of the human spirit. A large body of personal testimony suggests that there was, in fact, a time when the effect of the *Consolation* coincided with its author's intention. Today its consoling power has diminished: St. Jerome's momentary cry, "Deus Absconditus," has become modern man's first principle of despair, from which he derives his countless axioms of irrationality. Perhaps it is the twentieth-century love of paradox that allows an Absence to exist as a solid barrier separating the medieval author from his modern reader. At any rate, *absconditus*, Deus has deprived the *Consolation* of an appeal based on objective truth. If today the *Consolation* is to console, our sensitivity to its power must originate in a reverence not for God but for the attempt of a passionate intelligence to reckon with the mud lest it eclipse the stars. While the validity of the *Consolation's* argument has diminished, the honesty of its underlying impulse has not. The intensity of that moral impulse is made visible in the aesthetic excellence of the work; however, that aesthetic excellence itself, though visible, is often unseen.

The specific aesthetic structure of the *Consolation* has until recently been ignored. Earlier commentary on its structure tended to stress the generic influence of such classical forms as "consolation literature" (Cicero, Seneca), "incentives to philosophy" (Aristotle, Cicero), and "Menippean satire." Emphasis on these genres has inevitably carried with it the implication that a hard center of thought and feeling must be made palatable by presentation in a leisurely style. Even E. K. Rand's admiring consideration of the *Consolation* occasionally threatens to slip into the diminutive: "To vary the presentation, to break the flow of dialogue, a number of little poems are interspersed — thirty-nine in all — which now sum up the argument of the preceding prose section, and now themselves carry it on."[1] While the leisurely element of the work should be recognized, the words of Boethius in *Quomodo Substantia* should be remembered: "[I] would rather bury my speculations in my own memory than share them with any of those pert and frivolous persons who will not tolerate an argument unless it is made amusing."[2] The "leisure" of the *Consolation* might be more accurately described as the grace with which Boethius presents a rigorously premeditated structure. It is in part by understanding the logic of that structure, its aesthetic integrity, that the passion of the author's conviction and the power of his *Consolation* are made accessible to the contemporary reader.

As this essay will show, the structure of the work reflects and sustains the idea of the work. The circular relation of form and content is immediately suggested by the title "consolation of philosophy": *Philosophy* originally *consoles* Boethius (book 1) so that he will be receptive to *philosophy*, by means of which he may eventually attain *philosophy* and so be *consoled* (book 5). Philosophy is the cause of its own consummation; philosophy is the cause of the consummation of consolation; consolation is the cause of its own consummation; consolation is the cause of the consummation of philosophy. Knowledge and happiness are one in the co-incidence of form (cause) and idea (end). The consistency with which form recapitulates idea will be shown after first suggesting Boethius's attitude toward this circularity.

Certainly Boethius did not intend this identification of form and content as a gratuitous act of craftsmanship. On the contrary: the structure of the *Consolation* mirrors his conception of the first and final cause of the universe. For Boethius, God's perfection, His divine simplicity, consists in the coincidence of substance, *id quod est*, and form, *esse* (*Quomodo Substantia*). In book 3, prose 10, Lady Philosophy demonstrates the unity of end, origin, and cause (*summa, cardo, causa*) in the coterminous realities of God, Happiness, and Goodness. A crucial "corollarium" — a word that denotes both "corollary" and "gratuitous gift" — then follows (1.83): man becomes happy by acquiring happiness; happiness is divinity; therefore, man becomes happy by acquiring divinity. The identification of form and content in the *Consolation* is, then, an aesthetic corollary to the metaphysical reality of God: it is Boethius's attempt to attain the gift of godlikeness by participating in a simple unity of form and substance.

Further assurance that the author deliberately intended his

work to have this identification of form and content is found in book 3, prose 12. Both Boethius and Philosophy attempt to define the nature of God's government. Predictably, the first fails and the second succeeds. But, as Boethius himself realizes, what differentiates the two contestants is less the content of their respective explanations than the form, the mode of argument and articulation (ll. 65-68). Boethius's beloved Plato had argued in the *Theaetetus* that one approaches knowledge only when the content of belief is attended by *logos*, the verbal image, rational explanation, and differentiating principle of the idea (208 C,D; see also *Timaeus* 29 B). Appropriately, book 3, prose 12 concludes: "You have no cause to marvel at what you have learned from Plato's teaching, that language must be cognate with the subject about which one is speaking." Throughout the *Consolation* Lady Philosophy explicitly links her mode of presentation with that which is presented: "'It cannot be doubted that there is some solid and perfect [*solidam perfectamque*] happiness.' 'Thou hast,' quoth I, 'concluded most firmly and most truly [*Firmissime, verrissime*]'" (3.pr.10. 20-23); "'Then taking as it were a new beginning [*alio orsa principio*] she discussed [*disseruit*, both "to argue" and "to plant"] in this manner, 'The generation [*generatio*] . . .' " (4.pr.6.21, 22); "You bind [*astringas*] me to the word necessity [*necessitatis*]" (5.pr.6.97, 98). It is important to stress, however, that Philosophy's insistence on the necessity of a form cognate with the idea becomes most explicit and self-conscious at that point where the idea itself is the identification of God's form and substance (3.pr.10-12).

This identification in the *Consolation* is visible not only in isolated sentences and passages but also in the work as a whole. As a result there emerges the degree of emphasis on aesthetic form found in Plato's dialogues such as the *Republic, Symposium,* or *Phaedrus,* in which the philosophical argument is carried as much by subtleties of structure as by overt statement. But while Plato is Boethius's earthly model and teacher, God is his ultimate model and teacher. As suggested above, Boethius conceives of the *Consolation's* structure as a potential vehicle to godlikeness: the extent to which structure coincides with substance is the extent to which he, as author, approximates divine simplicity and participates in the happiness of God's goodness. His success will be demonstrated here by first summarizing the central idea of the *Consolation* and then showing the ways in which that idea manifests itself in the formal structure of the work.

The central idea of the *Consolation* is the definition of man as knower. If Boethius is to regain his humanity, if he is to become man, he must by definition know man, for man's being resides in man's knowing man's being: "Such is the condition of human nature that it surpasses other classes only when it knows itself, but is reduced to a rank lower than beasts when it ceases to know itself" (2.pr.5. 85-88). Book 5 clarifies the nature of man as knower by presenting the hierarchy of cognitive faculties in both its human and cosmic manifestations. That hierarchy, articulated in the final three prose sections of the work, can be summarized as follows:

	COGNITIVE FACULTY	MANIFESTATION WITHIN CREATION	PROPER OBJECT OF EACH FACULTY
(Passive)	1. Sense	Lower Animals: animals without motion (e.g., sea slug)	Material Particular
	2. Imagination	Higher Animals: animals with motion	Immaterial Particular
	3. Reason	Man	Immaterial Universal
	4. Insight	God	Simple idea: all aspects simultaneously seen

(Active)
Here cognition
and will are
identical.

All moral and metaphysical questions are ultimately answered
with reference to these hierarchies. As is clear from the opening of the *Consolation*, the exile grasps both the concept of
universal order and the concept of man as a rational animal:
his difficulty originates in his inability to comprehend their
relation (1. m.5, pr.6). Consequently, the *Consolation* attempts to articulate this relation between the hierarchy of
cognitive faculties within man and the hierarchy of cognitive
faculties without man, a relation that in its final formulation
entails the two apparently antinomous terms, *man's will*
(knowledge and motion) and *God's foreknowledge* (knowledge
and stillness).

It is this concept of graduated cognitive levels that determines the structure of the *Consolation*. The idea of the hierarchy generates three distinct patterns. The first is linear and
static: the four faculties are reflected in those technical
elements of structure, such as the dual media of prose and
verse, which are common to all five books. The second pattern
is linear and dynamic: there is a steady upward progression
from the realm of sense in book 1 to the realm of Insight in
book 5. The third pattern is geometric: book 3, verse 9, the
physical center of the *Consolation*, is the center of a circle
whose circumference is defined by the remainder of book 3,
and book 3 is the center of a sphere whose circumference is
defined by books 1, 2, 4, and 5. After each of the three patterns has been examined in isolation, the final and single shape
of the *Consolation* will begin to emerge.

Technical Elements of the Consolation's *Structure: Personification, Verse, Prose, Book Divisions*

Because man is knower, the answer to the question "What is
man?" requires an answer to the question "What is
knowledge?" Here knowledge itself becomes an object of
knowledge. Consequently, like any other object of cognition, it
is knowable in four aspects: the sensitive or material particular,
the imaginative or immaterial particular, the rational or im-

material universal, and the Simple Idea or all aspects simultaneously seen. If the concept of knowledge is not first made knowable in its limited aspects, it can never be known in its ultimate form; for, as Boethius repeatedly asserts, "it is from particulars that all our comprehension of universals is taken" (*Contra Eutychen*, 3.35,36). Boethius attempts to accommodate the four aspects of knowledge in his selection of the *Consolation's* basic structural elements: knowledge is given (a) "sensitive" representation in its personification as Lady Philosophy, (b) "imaginative" representation in its manifestation as poetry, (c) "rational" representation in its manifestation as prose, and (d) representation as "all aspects grasped simultaneously" in that structural element which grasps all structural elements simultaneously, the *Consolation* as a single entity — an entity whose "singularity" and "simultaneity" are made visible in the work's internal bonding: the division into five books, and the multiple bonds by which they are bound.

This section of this essay will examine each of these four elements as aspects of knowledge or modes of thought irrespective of particular subject matter. Here, for example, it will be irrelevant that one verse has for its subject the realm of sense (e.g., 1.m.1) and another, the realm of Insight (3.m.9): both are poetic articulations of their subjects; consequently, it will be argued, both here represent the imaginative mode of thought. What matters is the fact of personification rather than what that persona says in any given instance, the fact of the verse medium, prose medium, or book divisions rather than the content of a particular verse, prose section, or book.

Personification: knowledge as material particular. Certainly Lady Philosophy is not without literary antecedents: Homer, Plato, Cicero, Lucretius, Seneca, Augustine, Symmachus, Claudian, and Prudentius have all been credited with contributing to her portrait.[3] Recognition of her participation in a tradition, however, should not deflect attention from her specific function in the structure of the *Consolation*. She is not simply a mechanical response to the author's prolonged immersion in the classics. Although Boethius was sensitive to the antique charm of personification, he was equally sensitive to its inherent epistemological significance.

Heretical interpretations of Christ's *nature* and *person* had provoked the writing of *Contra Eutychen*, Boethius's attempt to provide clearly articulated definitions of the two terms. There *person* is defined as "the individual substance of a rational nature" (3. 45): Boethius argues that the term can be applied only to the particular Cicero or Plato and not to the universal species of rational animal, an argument familiar from the traditional distinction between the particular person, Socrates, and the universal quality, wisdom. Sanction to infer the author's concept of "personification" in the *Consolation* from his definition of "person" in a theological treatise is provided by his explication of that definition. He locates the origin of the term in the *persona* of ancient comedy and tragedy; he explains its etymology as "mask," "sound," and, in combination, "the larger sound necessarily produced through a hollow mask"; and he concludes that the dramatic meaning of *persona* is consonant with his theological definition (*CE* 3. 6-25). Even in this theological treatise, then, the concept of person has an aesthetic referent.

Boethius and the reader are not at the opening of the *Consolation* immediately confronted with philosophy; rather, they are confronted with Lady Philosophy. The persona of philosophy is the materialization of philosophy, the "individual substance of a rational nature." By her bodily presence in the prisoner's cell, Lady Philosophy is knowledge as it manifests itself in the material particular, the concept of knowledge made accessible to the senses. When she first enters (1.pr.1), the author emphasizes her physical immediacy: she is neither specter nor apparition but *mulier*, a woman. If he deprives her of tear glands and blood beneath the flesh, he endows her with burning or passionate eyes (1.4, *oculis ardentibus*) and coloring that is "fresh and suggestive of inexhaustible vigor" (1.6). Her acts are physical: she sits by the prisoner's bed (1.pr.1.48), wipes his eyes with her robe (1.pr.2.15), and lays her hand upon his breast (1.pr.2.13). Her relation to the prisoner is physical: he is a sick man with white hair and sagging skin

(1.m.1); she is his nurse, his physician (1 passim). Her idiom is physical: she will ascertain the source of his difficulty by "touching" and "stroking" his mind (*tuae mentis attingere atque temptare* [1.pr.6.1]).
Certainly this initial emphasis on the physicality of the persona diminishes as the work progresses. As the prisoner graduates to higher modes of cognition, he approaches the abstract form of knowledge that is only symbolized or materialized in the *mulier*, Lady Philosophy. The function of physical nurse, for example, is transferred from Philosophy in book 1 to Fortune in book 2, where Philosophy herself becomes the spiritual nurse, "the nurse of all virtue" (2.pr.2.9-13; pr.4.1). The artistry with which Boethius charts the details of this progression will be studied in a later section of this essay. For now, it is important to stress that the persona remains an element of structure throughout the *Consolation*. While references to Lady Philosophy's material aspect are concentrated in the opening book, there is nothing to suggest that she gradually grows frail and finally evaporates out of the prison cell. Since higher modes of cognition apprehend objects of sense without using the faculty of sense (5.pr.5), higher books in the *Consolation* need no longer stress the presence of the persona. That her physical appearance is the *sensory* manifestation of knowledge clarifies what might in the later books seem some unphilosophic, if ladylike, moments of behavior. Despite, for example, her continual injunction "Look skyward!", she is seen "for a while looking steadfastly at the ground" (3.pr.2. 1). Repeatedly the author's love for his subject is betrayed in the care with which he selects such details. One instance is the detail chosen for the final reference to Philosophy's physical countenance: it is the slight smile on her lips as she confesses the impossibility of apprehending Simple Unity through a perspective grounded in temporal multiplicity (4.pr.6.5). It is the archaic smile, the smile on the face of the sphinx, calmly acknowledging the inevitable discrepancy between what is and what can be known.

The meters: knowledge as immaterial particular. The *Consola-*

tion is written in alternating sections of verse and prose. It is
the poems, or meters, that represent the imaginative mode of
cognition. Perhaps this assertion requires no evidence, since for
Boethius, as for his twentieth-century reader, there is a natural
association between art and the imagination. In his attempt to
differentiate imaginative forms from intellectual forms in *De
Trinitate*, Boethius illustrates the former by first alluding to a
piece of sculpture before extending the sphere of reference to
include nonaesthetic examples (2.19-28). The Latin language
itself reflects the association. In the *Consolation*, for example,
the concept "paintings" is designated by the word *imagines*
(1.pr.1.16). While there is for Boethius an assumed intimacy
between art and the imagination, it will be helpful to make the
nature of that intimacy explicit by specifying what he meant by
that sometimes equivocal term *imagination*, and then showing
how the songs conform to that definition.

While the sensitive faculty apprehends the matter of the
material particular, the imaginative faculty apprehends its
form (5.pr.4). Here a linguistic ambiguity arises, for the higher
cognitive powers, reason and Insight, also have form as their
object. In *De Trinitate*, the author insists on the importance of
avoiding the ambiguity: "We misname the entities that reside
in bodies when we call them forms [*formas*]; they are mere images [*imagines*]" (2.53, 54). Consistently throughout the
Theological Treatises and the *Consolation*, form as the imagination perceives it in the particular is designated by the
words *figura, imago,* or *forma* qualified and specified by the
context, such as *forma corporis, forma materia, forma im-
aginis.*

The imagination is intermediate between sense and reason.
Like sense, and unlike reason, its object is the particular rather
than the universal; like reason, and unlike sense, its object is
form rather than matter. While sense is passive, acting only as
the recipient of a sensory stimulus, the imagination is active,
able to sustain the figure or image of the particular after the
sensory stimulus is no longer present (5.pr.6.111-15). It is from
the imaginative retention of particular figures that reason
derives the form of the universal (5.m.4). The primary func-

tion of the imagination is, then, its active mediation between the material world of the senses and the immaterial world of reason, a function celebrated in the penultimate meter of the *Consolation*.

Boethius's conception of the imagination can be summarized as follows. First, its object is the immaterial particular, the "figure" of the material particular. Second, it is an active power: in the hierarchy of creation, imagination first manifests itself in animals capable of external and internal movement, capable of motion and emotion (5.pr.5). Third, its function is to mediate between sense and reason. That structural element of the *Consolation* which represents the imaginative mode of cognition must accommodate these three defining characteristics.

The two basic elements of poetic language, imagery and rhythm, are identical with the first two characteristics of the imagination, its connections with the realm of the immaterial particular and with the capacity for mood and movement. Poetic images or figures belong to the realm of the immaterial particular: as Aristotle explains in *De Anima*, "Images are like sensuous contents except in that they contain no matter" (3. 8).[4] While the images in the songs depict particulars rather than abstract concepts, they themselves are immaterial — they are not, as Lady Philosophy is, physically present in the prisoner's cell. The way in which the songs fulfill the second criterion of the imagination is also immediatley apparent: rhythm and meter are as essential to song as movement and mood are to the imagination. So intimately related are music and motion that in *De Institutione Musica* Boethius can argue that a music of the spheres, although inaudible, must necessarily exist, since those spheres undergo constant and rapid rotation: "How indeed could the swift mechanism of the sky move silently in its course? And although this sound does not reach our ears (as must for many reasons be the case) the extremely rapid motion of such great bodies could not be altogether without sound" (1. 2). Just as music is caused by motion, so it in turn causes motion, motion within the soul of the listener. *De Musica* opens with a chapter devoted to the effects of music on mood and moral growth. Throughout the *Consola-tion*, the changes in the prisoner's psychological disposition are repeatedly attributed to the meters: they have the power to mollify and make calm (1.pr.5.38-44), to refresh weary minds (3. pr.1. 4-6), to inspire delight (4. pr.6.17-20), and to excite (4. pr.2.2,3).

The first two defining characteristics of the imagination — its connections with the realm of the immaterial particular and its capacity for mood and movement — are, then, visible in the imagery and rhythm so essential to the meters. The third characteristic of the imagination, its function as a mediating power between the faculties of sense and reason, is identical with Boethius's conception of the function of song: "What human music is, anyone may understand by examining his own nature. For it is that which unites the incorporeal activity of reason with the body" (*De Musica* 1. 2).[5] In the *Consolation*, the importance of music's mediating function is visible in the apparent ambivalence of Lady Philosophy's attitude toward music. The first words she utters are an angry dismissal of the prisoner's poetic muses, his "seducing mummers" (1. pr.1,30). The next words she utters are in verse (1.m.2). Her apparent inconsistency is instead a coherent distinction between songs that "do kill the fruitful crop of reason" (1.pr.1.33) and songs that serve philosophy (1.pr.1.40, 41; 2. pr.1.23) — between the music that grounds the individual in the sensitive realm and the music that leads the individual out of the sensitive into the rational realm. The distinction is a classical one: it occurs throughout Plato (e.g., *Timaeus* 28 A, B; 47 D; *Republic* 401 D); it appears again in Augustine, who is plagued by the fear that he has allowed the sensory beauty of music to become an end in itself rather than a vehicle to God (*Confessions* 10.33); and it emerges once more in Dante, whose Cato chastises the pilgrims when, entranced by song, they linger to rest rather than continuing their upward climb (*Purgatorio* 2.115-23). Boethius's treatment of the meters in the *Consolation* reflects his emphasis on the mediating function of music and the imagination. It is clear why the meters are placed between prose sections, mediating between one argument and the next. It is also clear why each of the final meters in the five books contains a warning to look not toward the ground but toward the sky.[6] Finally, it is clear why the fifth book does not, like the previous four, end with a meter: music, the exponent of the imagination, is not an end in itself but a vehicle to a higher faculty, a faculty that in the *Consolation* is represented by the medium of prose.

Prose: knowledge as immaterial universal. Nowhere in the *Consolation, De Musica, Tractates,* or *De Arithmetica* does Boethius explicitly designate prose the proper medium of rational thought. Nor does Plato, Aristotle, Cicero, or Augustine provide any explicit assurance that Boethius would have associated the two. Nor is there any authority in Whitehead's tardy assertion that prose makes possible the "rationally coordinated" verbal system through which the suggestive resonance of poetry becomes the self-evident truth of philosophy.[7] Assurance that Boethius intended the prose of the *Consolation* to represent the rational manifestation of knowledge is, however, visible in the way he presented that prose. In addition to the obvious and crucial fact that the rational arguments occur in the prose sections, several other factors encourage the identification of reason and prose.[8]

That prose stands for the rational mode of cognition is suggested by the fact that it is presented as a higher, more demanding medium than poetry. At the opening of book 3, the prisoner who has just experienced the refreshing and comforting power of music (pr. 1, 3-6) but whose eyes are clouded with *imagines* (19) is told that he is ready for remedies that are "bitter to the taste, but being inwardly received wax sweet" (13, 14). At a later point Philosophy explains, "Time is short . . . but if the sweetness of verse delight thee, thou must forbear this pleasure for a while, until I propose unto thee some few arguments" (4. pr.6.14-20). The superior power of prose, acknowledged in Lady Philosophy's explicit comments, is also visible in the spatial relations of the media. While there is a continual alternation of poetry and prose throughout the entire work, the ratio of poetry to prose gradually diminishes as one progresses to the higher books: in book 1 the ratio is approximately one to two; in book 5, one to five.

The nature of the relationship between poetry and prose is also suggested by the etymologies of the two words. *Prosa* is derived from *prorsus*, a compound of *pro* and *vorsus*. It is, then, like *versus*, derived from the root *verto* or *vorto*. Verse or *versus* is so named because it entails turning: it requires of its writer and reader the repeated act of turning back to begin a new line.[9] This requirement dissolves when the prefix *pro* is added: while *versus* means "turning," *prorsus* means "forward" or "straight ahead." One begins to wonder whether it is only coincidental that just as verse denotes a continual alternation between forward and backward movement, so the imagination must continually move back and forth between the material world of the senses and the immaterial world of reason; that just as prose denotes a free and forward movement, so "there can be no reasonable nature, unless it be endowed with free will" (5. pr.2.5,6). The other Latin terms for prose also denote the ideas of straightforward movement (*oratio recte*) and freedom from metrical restraint (*oratio soluta, verba soluta*), a freedom whose importance is stressed by Aristotle's *Rhetoric*, which argues that meter destroys the reader's trust and diverts his attention (3.8). Prose is, then, the higher medium: its movement is straightforward rather than back and forth; its flow is directed by logical connectives rather than restricted by meter; its content describes mental acts rather than material objects; its words are the immaterial universals of abstract definition rather than the immaterial particulars of images. Prose makes possible the semantic conception of truth that is inaccessible to poetry.

The identification of prose with reason is evident not only in its ability to accommodate those aspects of knowledge inaccessible to poetry but also in its inability to accommodate that aspect of knowledge which belongs to the sphere of Insight. The point in the *Consolation* where the subject becomes the simplicity and simultaneity of the divine presence is also the point where the final inadequacy of prose is acknowledged: "The cause of which obscurity is that the motion of human

discourse cannot attain to the simplicity of divine knowledge"
(5. pr.4.6-9). Just as reason is able to move relentlessly forward
through deductive arguments without turning back to the
material universe, so the great strength of prose is its ability to
move relentlessly forward. But its strength is also its weakness.
Its multiple truths can be presented only sequentially, not
simultaneously. Like reason and unlike Insight, it tries to approximate by moving the plenitude it cannot comprehend by
staying (5. pr.6.54,55).

Book divisions: knowledge as Insight. The highest power of
cognition, that which God alone possesses, is Insight. It is that
faculty which subsumes all other faculties, comprehends all
but is comprehended by none, contains but is itself uncontain-
ed (5. pr.4.92-101; 5. pr.5.55,56). Accordingly, in the *Consolation* it is represented by that which contains all the
previously examined structural elements, that which binds but
is itself "enclosed within no bounds" (5. pr.5. 55-56), the work
as a whole.

The *Consolation* approximates the simplicity and
simultaneity of Insight through the book divisions and the
multiple bonds by which they are bound. It will not be possible
to demonstrate the nature of this binding until the final section
of this discussion. For the moment, however, Insight can, on a
much more elementary plane, be understood to be represented
by each individual book—each a single entity containing persona, verse, and prose, each a single unity comprehending the
sensory, imaginative, and rational manifestations of
knowledge.

The preceding discussion has shown the way in which
Boethius's selection of the *Consolation*'s basic structural
elements accommodates the four cognitive faculties. This first
manifestation of the cognitive hierarchy is a static one: persona, verse, prose, and book divisions are all consistently present throughout the entire work. The following section will
focus on the second manifestation of the hierarchy, the steady
upward progression from the realm of sense in book 1 to the

realm of Insight in book 5. While the first pattern was static, the second is dynamic. An understanding of the way in which the work simultaneously accommodates both the static and the dynamic requires a recognition of the internal complexity characterizing Boethius's use of the technical elements.

As has been shown, persona is the sensitive manifestation of knowledge; poetry the imaginative manifestation; prose the rational; and each book, Insight. But each of these technical elements represents not simply *knowledge* as it manifests itself in one particular aspect, but *each aspect of knowledge* as it manifests itself in that one particular aspect. Lady Philosophy is not simply the sensitive manifestation of knowledge, but the sensitive manifestation of the sensitive, imaginative, and rational aspects of knowledge. Boethius's initial presentation of his persona proceeds according to this hierarchy. He first describes her physical vitality and great age (1. pr.1.1-9)—the sensitive aspect of knowledge as it manifests itself in the material particular. He then moves to the imaginative aspect of knowledge as it manifests itself in the material particular: he describes her stature (the *figura* or form of the material particular and, therefore, its immaterial particular), which alternates between the height of humanity and the height of heaven, mediating between the material and immaterial realms. He then presents the rational manifestation of knowledge as it manifests itself in the material particular, her robe with its indissoluble weave and its abstract symbols. Significantly, of these three aspects, it is only the first—her health and age, the sensitive manifestation of the sensitive aspect of knowledge—that is wholly intelligible to the prisoner. His lengthy first sentence of description (1-9) sustains a tone of conviction until the final phrase, *statura discretionis ambiguae*, her stature uncertain and ambiguous; the sensitive manifestation of the imaginative aspect of knowledge eludes his grasp. It is only in the poetry that he will comprehend the imaginative aspect of knowledge: the imagination's intimacy with the realm of the immaterial particular, unintelligible when presented in the persona's figura, becomes intelligible in the imagery of the meters; the imagination's mediation between the material and immaterial spheres, unintelligible when presented in the persona's changes in height, will become intelligible in the mediating power of the meters. Similarly, the sensitive manifestation of the rational aspect of knowledge is equally inaccessible to the prisoner: the weave of the persona's robe is both torn and darkened, obscured by duskiness like pictures in a smoky room (16, 17). It is only in the prose that he will comprehend the rational aspect of knowledge: reason's intimacy with the sphere of the immaterial universal, unintelligible when presented in the obscured abstract symbols on the persona's robe, becomes intelligible when presented as the vocabulary of logical definition in the prose; the indivisibility of universals, unintelligible when presented in the weave of the persona's robe (*texuerat, intextum* [16, 19]) becomes intelligible as the "weave" of rational arguments (*contexo rationes* [4. pr.6.20]; *inextricabilem labyrinthum rationibus texens* [3. pr.12.83]) in the prose. While, then, the persona represents the sensitive manifestation of the sensitive, imaginative, and rational aspects of knowledge, it is only the sensitive manifestation of the sensitive aspect that can be fully comprehended here, for "the superior force of comprehending embraceth the inferior but the inferior can by no means attain to the superior" (5. pr.4. 91-93).

Just as the persona represents the sensitive manifestation of the various levels of the cognitive hierarchy, so the poetry represents the imaginative manifestation of those various levels: which level is represented at any given moment depends upon the content and meter of a given verse. So, too, the different prose sections, through their changes in content, represent the rational manifestation of the different cognitive levels. The controlled complexity of the *Consolation*'s structure begins to emerge. While, for example, the stature of the persona is the sensitive manifestation of the imaginative aspect of knowledge, the opening meter — in which the prisoner-philosopher describes the physical effects of his illness and old age — is the imaginative manifestation of the sensitive aspect of knowledge. Again, while Lady Philosophy's robe is the sensitive manifestation of the rational aspect of knowledge, that prose section devoted to her physical description (1. pr.1) is the rational manifestation of the sensitive aspect of knowledge. It is this internal complexity of the technical elements that makes possible the progression through the work, for while each book represents Insight, the content of a given book determines which level of the cognitive hierarchy is there perceived by Insight. As the following section will suggest, the books of the *Consolation* move from Insight's grasp of the realm of sense in book 1 to Insight's grasp of the realm of Insight in book 5.

The Five Books of the Consolation: Progression through the Cognitive Hierarchy

The *Consolation* contains two explicit definitions of man. The first is given by Boethius in the opening book; it is the inadequacy of this definition that alerts Lady Philosophy to the seriousness of her patient's sickness. The second and correct definition is enunciated by Lady Philosophy in the final book. The two definitions are as follows:

Man is an animal rational and mortal. [1. pr.6.36, 37]

Man is an animal rational and biped. [5. pr.4.108]

There is, of course, a logical basis for Philosophy's quarrel with her student's definition: the fact that man dies does not differentiate his species from other species while the fact that he is biped does. But the displacement of the first definition by the second has metaphorical significance that goes beyond its logical validity. In the transition from the first to the second, man is stripped of his mortality and endowed with two feet, changes that stress his capacity for a journey toward immortality.

The *Consolation*, like so much of the medieval literature that would follow it, has as its central focus a journey or pilgrimage, a sustained movement toward immortality. While this movement is partially conveyed through metaphors of physical movement, it is primarily a mental journey, a journey toward understanding and philosophical insight. The progression does not evolve from changes in subject matter, for in its subject matter the *Consolation* is very repetitious. The same questions — what are good, evil, fate, and free will? — are reiterated throughout the entire work. The progression evolves instead from the changing perspectives through which that subject matter is viewed. As Philosophy herself counsels, "All that is known is not comprehended according to the force which it hath in itself, but rather according to the faculty of them which know it" (5. pr.4.75-77). As will be shown, the five books of the *Consolation* progress through successive levels of the cognitive hierarchy. Those issues that are viewed through the faculty of sense in the opening book are in the final book viewed through the faculty of Insight.

This section of this essay will show the progression of the cognitive faculties from sense in book 1 to imagination in book 2, reason in book 4, and Insight in book 5. But before demonstrating that progression, it is first necessary to explain the relation of book 3 — missing in the sequence just given — to this structural progression. While the other four books follow one another through successive levels of the cognitive hierarchy, through successive levels of the created material world, the central book of the *Consolation* is lifted out of and above the material world of creation. The relation of book 3 to the other four books can be represented visually as follows (Figure 7).[10]

Book 3 is divided into two parts of almost equal length: the two differ by about one hundred lines. Sections 1 through 9 recall all that has been said in books 1 and 2; sections 10 through 12 anticipate all that will be said in books 4 and 5. Sections 1 through 9, like books 1 and 2, deal with and ultimately dismiss the false forms of happiness, while sections 10 through 12, like books 4 and 5, deal with the true form of happiness. Implicit in this distinction between the false forms and the true form is the distinction between finite diversity and divine unity, a distinction reflected in the differing treatments of the false and true

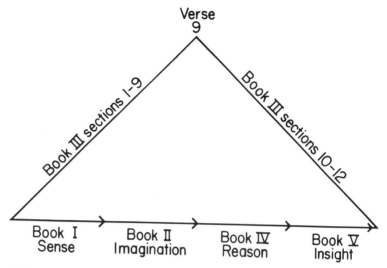

FIG. 7. *Relationship of book 3 of Boethius's* Consolation *to books 1, 2, 4, and 5.*

forms. In the first half of the *Consolation*, each of the false forms of happiness — sufficiency, power, respect, fame, and pleasure — is examined in isolation despite the fact that in each case the argument given is almost identical to the others. In the second half, an argument about one form is considered necessarily valid with reference to all forms: if, for example, Philosophy arrives at a truth about sufficiency or power, she will then simply say, "And we may conjecture the same of respect, fame, and pleasure" (3. pr.10.122,123; see 3. pr.10.102 and 3. pr.11.14). Eventually, however, even these individual terms are completely displaced by single and all-embracing terms for happiness, goodness, unity. This distinction between diversity in the first half of the *Consolation* and unity in the second half is, in turn, reflected in the numerical divisions of book 3: the first half is comprised of nine sections and the second half of three; the second is, then, the square root of the first.

While book 3 thus recapitulates and anticipates the contents

of the other four books, it does so in a way that distinguishes it
from those four books. The central book is raised out of and
above the progression[11] by the perfection of its reasoning, by
the "inextricable labyrinth of arguments" with which
Philosophy creates a "wonderful circle of divine simplicity"
(pr.12.82-86). Sections 1 through 9 proceed inductively; a conclusion — unity is good, division evil — is reached in prose 9; this
conclusion then becomes the first premise in 10 through 12,
where the reasoning becomes deductive. The perfection of
Philosophy's weave of arguments is matched by the perfection
of Boethius's ability to assimilate those arguments. Not once
here does he falter, protest, or backslide as he occasionally will
even in book 4 (4. pr.1.1-19; 4. pr.4.1-5, 31-33, 91-94; 4.
pr.5.3-22; 4. pr.7.12-16); here he becomes *o alumne laetor* in
whom his teacher rejoices (3. pr.11.17,18).

The central book, then, is a retreat from the world into the
"most secret seat of the mind" (3. pr.2.1,2), where Philosophy
and her student attain the sight of God, after which they
return to earth (books 4 and 5) to confront with new vision the
apparent paradoxes of the mortal realm: their journey "Now
lifts its head to highest things,/ Now down to lowest falls
again,/ Now turning back unto itself/ False things with true
things overthrows" (5.m.4.22-25; see also ll. 35-40 and
m.3.28-31). As one reads the books sequentially, the central
and perfect book is flanked on both sides by books that, even at
their height, are capable of only a lesser perfection, flawed by
their participation in the created world. This arrangement
reflects the picture of the universe celebrated in the *Consolation*'s central and climactic meter (book 3, verse 9), the picture
of the created encircling the uncreated, Plotinus's "dance of
the imperfect around the perfect."[12] The relationship between
books 1, 2, 4, and 5 and book 3 is analogous to the relationship
between time and eternity; for just as time is a moving image of
eternity (5. pr.6.29-31), so books 1, 2, 4, and 5 provide a moving or sequential image of all that is contained in stillness and
simultaneity in book 3. It is well that Boethius placed this book
at the center rather than at the end of the *Consolation*. Dante
took his pilgrim to heaven but did not, at the end of the *Com-

media, bring him back to earth again. Boethius did. That he did, assures us that the final vision of the *Consolation* is one attainable by mortals on earth.

One additional aspect of book 3's relation to the other four books, implicit in the visual illustration above, concerns the bonds between book 1's verse 1, book 3's verse 9, and book 5's conclusion, prose 6 — the three vertices of the triangle. Book 3, verse 9, the pinnacle, is a direct inversion of book 1, verse 1, the lowest point in the *Consolation*, the point where Boethius bitterly protests Death's deafness to his pleas for life to end. Book 3, verse 9, in contrast, is a prayer, not a complaint; its preoccupation is not Death, the personification of man's mortality, but God, the realization of man's potential immortality. The bond between book 3, verse 9, and the conclusion of book 5, prose 6 — the second, though different climax of the *Consolation* — is equally important. Book 3, verse 9, a hymn to God, a prayer to discover "the source of the supreme good" (3. pr.9.102), is uttered in order to prepare a "proper foundation" for the endeavor: this answered prayer makes possible all subsequent understandings attained in books 3, 4, and 5. These understandings, in turn, climax in the final understanding of book 5, prose 6, the final understanding of the *Consolation*, the understanding that the relationship between man and God is one that carries the assurance that prayer is not vain. The relation between book 3, verse 9 and the end of book 5, prose 6 is, then, circular: the prayer to see ultimately enables Boethius to see that prayer, immediate communication with God, is meaningful.

This, then, is the nature of the structural relationship between book 3 and the four books that surround it. It now remains to show the progression through the cognitive hierarchy in books 1, 2, 4, and 5, a progression that begins when Boethius's teacher converts his plea of political innocence into the charge of philosophical ignorance. Some evidence of this progression has already been encountered in the examination of the *Consolation*'s technical elements in the first part of this essay: the reference to the physical countenance of Philosophy, Boethius, and their surroundings grow far less frequent as one

progresses to the higher books; so too the ratio of poetry, the
exponent of the imagination, to prose, the exponent of reason,
diminishes. These two details are symptomatic of the sustained
and coherent movement from one faculty to the next as one
moves through successive books.

As was noted earlier, the different prose sections, through
their changes in content, represent the rational manifestation
of the four cognitive levels. Their changing content and the
resulting progression are immediately visible in the changing
remedies or modes of argument used by Lady Philosophy.
Book 1 represents Sense, for here Philosophy's higher talents
are diverted by the necessity of chasing mummers, chastising
and comforting the prisoner, and making the diagnosis of his
illness that will allow her to go on to higher remedies. In book
2, the mode of argument is Imaginative: here Philosophy's two
remedies are what she herself repeatedly designates as "music
and rhetoric" (2. pr.1.21,23; pr.3.5,6; 3. pr.1.5). The bond
between music and the imagination has already been shown.
The bond between rhetoric and the imagination is equally
strong. Rhetoric is credited for its "power of sweet persuasion"
(2. pr.1.21,22), its ability to give arguments a "fair form" (2.
pr.3.4,5), and its power to comfort (3. pr.1.6); but it is explicitly differentiated at the opening of book 3 from inward
arguments, arguments addressed exclusively to the rational
faculty (3. pr.1.1-14). Like the imagination and like music,
rhetoric mediates between the material realm of the body and
the immaterial realm of reason, for it is by appealing to the
emotions that it leads its listener to the truth of its argument.[13]

The arguments in book 4, by contrast, are devoid of emotional appeal. In fact, Boethius is here not always immediately
able to assimilate Philosophy's teachings; here he is like the
young Socrates in *Parmenides* who is not wholly willing to accept the "necessary conclusion" to which the logic of the argument relentlessly leads (4. pr.4.33-39, 91-110). Philosophy's
mode of argument, now far more demanding, has moved from
the Imaginative to the Rational, from rhetoric to reason.
While the rational mode is superior to the imaginative, it is still
necessarily flawed by its participation in the temporal world.

Philosophy acknowledges the difficulty of attaining a vision of unity through the perspective of temporal multiplicity. She explains that their investigation of good and evil requires that they follow two separate paths, moving back and forth between them (4. pr.2.1-11; pr.3.32 ff.); at another point she confesses that their subjects of inquiry are multiple, and, because they cannot all be pursued simultaneously, as soon as "one doubt has been removed, countless others spring up in its place, like the Hydra's head" (4. pr.6.7-9). However, the problems of multiplicity and temporality dissolve in the transition from book 4 to book 5, for now Reason yields to Insight as the mode of argument graduates from the logical to the analogical. In the early part of the *Consolation*, analogical movement between the temporal and the eternal is considered impossible: Philosophy cautions her student that "limited things can be compared among themselves but the infinite in no way admits comparison with the limited" (2. pr.7. 57-60). The infinite does begin to admit comparison with the limited, however, as one progresses through the books. Analogies appear and become more frequent until, by the final book, analogy resides at the very heart of Philosophy's discourse.[14] Man's temporal existence now becomes the metaphorical ground for the exploration of eternity. Philosophy presents to her student the description of the cognitive hierarchy and shows him how an understanding of the relations among the three lowest faculties makes possible an understanding of the relation between those finite three and the infinite fourth. In this fifth book, Philosophy has exhorted Boethius, "Let us raise ourselves to that height where reason will perceive what it can't itself perceive" (5. pr.5. 50-53)—let us see the unseeable. Analogy bestows visiblity on the invisible by permitting that mental leap from the created world to the uncreated mind of God.

The intimacy between Insight and analogy can be seen by contrasting the analogical mode of argument here with the deductive logic that dominates book 4. Deduction belongs to the temporal world in which events necessarily follow one another *sequentially*:

A is B.
B is C.
∴ C is A.

While the final term is built on the first two, it *follows* from and replaces them in our attention. In contrast, analogy—

A:B::C:D

—is like Insight; for just as Insight grasps all aspects of knowledge simultaneously (5.pr.4.100-104), so the analogical phrase grasps all its terms simultaneously, requires that all terms be simultaneously present in the mind. Analogy, reenacting the simultaneity of Insight by illuminating things in the immediacy of their identification with other things, affirms the consistent repetition of a single pattern throughout the created and uncreated worlds, affirms the unity of divine consciousness.

While analogy is the dominant manifestation of Insight in book 5, four additional factors signal the transition to a perspective characterized by simultaneity. First, the deductive "It follows," which recurs throughout book 4 (e.g., 4. pr.2.35,68; pr.4.73,74,88,127; pr.7.1) is almost totally absent in book 5, where it is usually displaced by the definitive "It is" (5. pr.4, p.6 passim). The sequential future has become the assertive present. Second, simultaneity is on several occasions explicitly attributed to the ideas or actions of Philosophy or Boethius:

"There is no fear [that I will not be able to finish the direct journey]," quoth I, "for it will be a great ease to me to understand those things in which I take great delight, and *simultaneously*, when thy disputation is fenced in on every side with sure conviction, there can be no doubt made of anything thou shalt infer." "I will," quoth she, "do as thou wouldst me have," and *simultaneously* began in this manner. [5.pr.1.13-18; italics mine]

Significantly, the single other time that the adverb *simul* is used

in the *Consolation* to describe the actions of Philosophy occurs at the physical midpoint of the work, in the transition
from book 3, prose 9, to the climactic verse 9. The aura of having escaped the confines of the temporal is further reinforced
by Philosophy's apparent foreknowledge of her student's
thoughts; for like Beatrice in the *Paradiso*, Philosophy toward
the end of book 5 anticipates Boethius's questions and objections. The reader repeatedly encounters phrases such as "Here
if thou sayest . . . I will grant . . . but I will answer" (5.
pr.6.95,98,100), "But thou wilt say . . ." (pr.6.136), and "But
yet thou wilt inquire" (pr.6.145)—phrases that create the impression that what is time-future to Boethius and the reader is
time-present to our teacher. Finally, simultaneity is visible in
the concluding affirmation of prayer, for prayer not only confirms the immediacy of the relation between man and God but
also allows man to participate in God's everlasting present and
thereby indirectly participate in his own future. The transition
from Reason in book 4 to Insight in book 5 is, then, primarily
visible in the displacement of the sequential by the
simultaneous, a displacement signaled by the presence of
analogy, assertion, anticipation, and prayer.

The progression through the cognitive hierarchy in books 1,
2, 4, and 5, visible in Lady Philosophy's changing remedies, is
also visible in her patient's changing condition. In book 1,
Philosophy's mode of argument is grounded in the sensory
because her patient is grounded in the sensory. There are
repeated allusions to the fact that his senses are impaired: he is
tongue-tied and dumb (1 pr.2.20; pr.4.131); his sight is blind-
ed by tears (1. pr.2.15-18; m.2.1-3; pr.1.44,45); his hearing,
too, is affected (Philosophy asks him if he is an "ass deaf to the
lyre" [1. pr.4.5]). As one progresses to subsequent books,
Boethius's difficulties are no longer located in the sensory mode
of cognition. His growth can be seen by focusing on the concept of blindness. In the opening book the cause of his blindness is physical; his vision is obstructed by tears (pr.1.44,45;
pr.2.15-18; m.2.1-3). In book 2, the cause of blindness is no
longer the material particular but the immaterial particular,
for Boethius's vision is said to have been dimmed by *imagines*

(3. pr.1.21). In book 4 it is the nature of reason itself that limits vision, for man is "penned in by the narrow space of time" (pr.6.16), confined to a perspective that converts the singular and simultaneous into the multiple and sequential. In the final book Philosophy demands that Boethius transcend his mortality, the ultimate source of blindness (5. m.3.8), and let reason "see what she can not behold in herself" (5. pr.5.52,53), that is, God's "providence or 'looking forth'" (5. pr.6.70-72). The *Consolation*, then, moves from the physical cause of Boethius's blindness in book 1 to the beneficent reality of God's vision in book 5.

The progression visible in the concept of blindness is again visible in the concept of movement. Sense, the reader is told in book 5, is the faculty of animals incapable of movement.[15] Accordingly, at the opening of book 1 Boethius is described in images of inertia. He complains that "life drags out its wearying delays" (1. m.1.20); he is surrounded by images of chains (m.2.25; m.4.18; m.7.29-31), lethargy (pr.3.12), weight (m.2.26), and men lying prostrate on the ground (pr.4.169, 170; m.5.32.33). Imagination, explains Philosophy in book 5, first manifests itself in animals capable of movement. The imagery of inertia in book 1, consequently, gives way to the imagery of movement in book 2. But it is not yet the controlled, self-willed, rational movement that will be found in book 4; here it is precarious and erratic. While the idea of erratic movement finds its primary manifestation in the image of Lady Fortune (book 2 passim), it is also present in many other images describing movement dictated not by man's will but by an external and arbitrary force (2. pr.1.55, 56; m.1; m.2 passim), as well as in Philosophy's exhortations to hold firm, to seek stability (pr.4.30-36; m.4.14-22). In the transition from book 2 to book 4, the concept of movement changes not only from the erratic to the controlled but also from the physical to the mental (4.pr.1.35-38; m.1): what was previously the physical course of a journey now becomes the mental paths of the argument (4. pr.2.9-11,71-73) and the ethical "paths of high example" (m.7.33-35). When images of physical movement do occur, their function is no longer descriptive, as in book 2, but analytic. For example, when attempting to convince her student that the good are more powerful than the wicked, Philosophy demonstrates the superiority of natural over unnatural acts by comparing walking on one's feet to walking on one's hands (4. pr.2.55-62); shortly afterward, the image of running a race is used analogically to clarify the nature of reward and punishment (4. pr.3.4-8). While in book 5 there again appear images of physical movement that function analytically,[16] as well as images of mental movement that function descriptively, the dominant manifestation of movement is almost wholly divorced from any imagistic content or capacity. Just as the imagery of vision ultimately climaxes in the investigation of "pro-vidence," so the imagery of movement ultimately climaxes in the second great issue of book 5, the metaphysical correlative of physical and mental movement, free will. The concept of movement, then, progresses from images of inertia in book 1, to images of erratic movement in book 2, to images of mental and controlled movement in book 4, to an exploration of the metaphysical and moral reality of man's capacity for free will in book 5.

Finally, the changing cognitive perspectives, visible in Philosophy's changing remedies and in the imagery surrounding Boethius's changing condition, are also visible in the progression in subject matter. While the same questions are reiterated throughout the *Consolation*, the nature of any given subject changes as the perspective through which it is viewed changes. One subject is the nature of man. As was suggested at the opening of this section, a comparison of the two explicit definitions of man (1. pr.6.36,37; 5. pr.4.108) reveals that he begins in book 1 as a mortal creature and ends in book 5 as an immortal being. The distance between these two definitions is mediated by a more gradual progression in the conception of man as one moves through the cognitive hierarchy.

In the final books Philosophy explains that "Man himself is beheld in different ways by sense-perception, imagination, reason, and intelligence" (5. pr.4.84, 85; see also ll. 85-91). Accordingly, man is beheld in different ways in the four books. In the opening book, man is seen through the sensitive faculty, as he manifests himself in the material particular — not man the species but the particular person Boethius. The movement through subsequent books is a movement away from the particular toward the universal. This progression was implicit in the preceding discussion of the imagery: images of blindness and movement, initially introduced as expressions of Boethius's condition, are increasingly divorced from him in the higher books.

A second manifestation of this progression is the decreasing emphasis on biography. The dominant interest of book 1 is in Boethius's present circumstances and their immediate cause. While one again encounters biography in the first half of book 2, the nature of the biographical allusions has changed. While book 1 focused almost entirely on Boethius's present, now that focus expands to include his past; while in book 1 his prosperity was measured solely by his own isolated successes and failures, now his identity becomes partially contingent on his participation in a larger humanity, for Philosophy demands that he measure his prosperity not only by his own successes and failures but also by those of his wife, his sons, and his father-in-law. By the middle of book 2 the biographical allusions begin to dissolve (pr.4.41 ff.). Because Philosophy no longer addresses herself exclusively to her student, the antecedent of "you" ceases to be Boethius and becomes "you mortal men" (2.pr.4.72), "you creatures of the earth" (2. pr.6.14, 15). With the exception of one oblique reference to Boethius's exile (4.pr.5.4-7), books 4 and 5 are completely devoid of biographical allusion.[17]

Perhaps the most important manifestation of the evolving conception of man is its movement through different planes of existence. The opening book is dominated by references to Boethius's physical well-being. The physical is displaced by the psychological in book 2, which examines the multiple sources of mortal pleasure and pain. The psychological, in turn, yields to the moral in book 4, where man's capacity for good and evil is explored. Finally, in book 5 the dialogue transcends moral categories and becomes metaphysical, examining man in the immediacy of his relation with God.

The sequence of stages through which this conception of man evolves — from the physical through the psychological and moral to the metaphysical — is equally descriptive of other subjects in the *Consolation*. While, for example, Philosophy proves that evil has no existence (3. pr.12.80,81,96,97), in each book there emerges an apparent evil that must be dealt with and dismissed. In the central book, book 3, the essential definition of goodness is given: goodness is unity. Its opposite, evil, is division or disjunction (pr.9.45-49). In each of the other four books, a particular form of disunity appears. In the opening book the apparent evil is physical. It is the distance between Boethius's illness and desired health, the distance between his place of exile and his home:

> "Doth the cruelty of fortune's rage need further declaration, or doth it not sufficiently appear in itself? Doth not the very countenance of this place move thee? Is this the library which thou thyself hadst chosen to sit in at my house. . . . Had I this attire or countenance when I searched the secrets of nature with thee?" [pr.4. 7-15]

In book 2 the apparent evil is psychological: it is the emotional pain that results from the perception of change, the perception of the discrepancy between what fortune gives at one moment and what she gives at the next (2. pr.1.3-6, 15-18). It is in the fourth book that evil becomes explicitly moral: this is the only book of the four in which the term *evil* consistently recurs, for it has become a rationally articulated category. Furthermore, man is here not only a potential victim of evil, as in books 1 and 2, but also a potential agent. The "chiefest cause of [Boethius's] sorrow" (pr.1.9,10), however, and therefore the major source of apparent evil, is not the existence of wicked men but the discrepancy between vice and virtue on the one hand and punishment and reward on the other (pr.1.9-19). In the fifth book the disjunction is metaphysical or epistemological, for there is an apparent "enmity between two truths" (m.4.2,3), the truth of God's Providence and the truth of man's free will.

A third instance of the progression in subject matter is the evolving conception of the coincidence of knowledge and power. In book 1 the idea is given sensitive representation in the objects carried by Philosophy, her books (knowledge) and her scepter (power). In book 2 the idea is given imaginative representation in the imitation or impersonation of Fortune (power) by Philosophy (knowledge). The idea is given rational representation in book 4 where, through reasoned discourse, Philosophy proves the truth of Plato's words in the *Gorgias* "that only wise men can do that which they desire" (4. pr.2.140-42; see also pr.3.15,29-32). Finally, the coincidence of knowledge and power is represented in the fifth book by the climactic recognition that God's foreknowledge and man's free will are harmonious truths.

But the single most crucial progression in subject matter is the changing conception of cosmic order. Throughout the *Consolation* recur the problematic terms *chance, fortune, fate,* and *Providence.* Certainly these concepts are not unrelated. Repeatedly a discussion focusing on one of the terms will, without explanation or hesitation, slide over to focus on a second term. In the midst of a passage investigating the nature of chance, for example, Boethius suddenly asks, "Is there nothing that can rightly be called chance or fortune?" (5. pr.1.33,34). The relation implied by this repeated act of cross-reference is made explicit in three passages at the close of book 4 and the opening of book 5, where the dialogue openly addresses itself to the relation between fate and Providence (4. pr.6.21-101), fortune and Providence (4. pr.7.1-55), and, finally, chance and Providence (5. pr.1.4-57). Only in the first of these passages is the precise nature of the relationship articulated: what Insight in the purity of its vision sees as Providence, reason in the limitation of its temporality and multiplicity sees as fate (4. pr.6.78-82). While the next two passages are less explicit, there is a clear implication[18] that just as fate is Providence viewed from below, so fortune is fate viewed from below, and chance is fortune viewed from below. That is, just as fate is Providence as it manifests itself to the rational faculty, so fortune is Providence as it manifests itself to the imaginative faculty, and chance, Providence as it manifests itself to the sensitive faculty. That this hierarchical conception of cosmic order corresponds to the four cognitive faculties is suggested by the disposition of the four terms in the *Consolation*. The term *chance* occurs most frequently in book 1,[19] *fortune* in book 2, *fate* in book 4, and *Providence* in book 5. More important, the correspondence is suggested by the nature of the faculties themselves. The faculty of sense is capable only of perceiving the material particular: unlike the imagination, it is incapable of sustaining the image of the particular after the particular is no longer materially present. It is an atemporal faculty. Throughout book 1 Boethius is so overwhelmed by his immediate present (literally, "prae-sens," that which is before the senses) that he suffers from the loss of memory (1. pr.2.13,14; pr.3.31-34; pr.6.25,26,34,42,46,47). Because the sensitive faculty, capable of perceiving only a series of unrelated moments each eclipsed by its successor, is incapable of perceiving time, it is also incapable of perceiving cause. It becomes, therefore, a victim of chance, a word that denotes the absence of causation, the absence of any principle of cosmic order.[20] The perception of time originates with the imaginative mode of cognition, for the power to sustain the image of the particular after the particular is no longer materially present is the power of memory. Accordingly, it is in book 2, the book that represents the imaginative faculty, that Boethius learns "It is not sufficient to behold that which we have before our eyes" (pr.1.45,46) and begins to regain his memory (pr.1.9-12; pr.3.14-44; pr.4.3,4). The power of memory, in turn, makes possible the perception of cause, the perception of a connection between anterior and posterior events. Unlike reason, however, the imagination expresses its perception of agency not in the language of abstract universals but in the language of the immaterial particular, not in the vocabulary of causal sequence but in a *figura*, the figure of Lady Fortune.

The progression through the four conceptions of cosmic order is, finally, accompanied by a progression in imagery. The sensitive faculty, incapable of perceiving pattern, sees only chance, the absence of pattern. Consequently, the concept of

chance is unaccompanied by any single, coherent image in the
Consolation. The imagination is capable of perceiving pattern:
its conception of cosmic order is represented by an imaginative
object, Fortune's wheel. In the transition from imagination to
reason, from fortune to fate, the image of the wheel is displaced by the image of multiple and moving concentric circles (4.
pr.6.65-78). While both Fortune's wheel and this new image
involve the idea of a circle, the displacement of the first by the
second represents a progression from a material object to an
abstract geometric figure, as well as a progression from a
dependence on the precarious reversibility of "up" and "down"
(2. pr.2.31-33) to a dependence on the predictable measure of
distance between "center" and "circumference" (4.
pr.6.73-76). In the transition from fate to Providence, such
distinctions as *up* and *down* and *center* and *circumference*
dissolve and are replaced by absolute unity and consistency,
"for such is the form of the Divine substance that it is neither
divided into outward things, nor receiveth any such into itself"
(3. pr.12. 102-4). While the idea of the circle residing in the
image of fortune and in the image of fate is carried forward into the image of Providence, the multiplicity, motion, and two-
dimensionality of "the multiple and moving circles of fate" are
replaced by the singularity, the stillness, and the three-
dimensionality of that shape considered by Parmenides and
Plato to be of all shapes the most perfect: "a sphere well rounded on all sides" (3. pr.12.106). As the concluding section of this
discussion will show, the final shape of the *Consolation* is also
"a sphere well rounded on all sides."

Before examining that final shape, it will be helpful to summarize and clarify the relation between the two manifestations
of the cognitive hierarchy already examined, the hierarchy visible in the technical elements and the hierarchy visible in the
progression of content from book 1 to book 5. Both the
similarity and the difference between the two can be articulated in terms of time. As this section of the discussion has
suggested, the progression through the cognitive hierarchy in
books 1, 2, 4, and 5[21] is accompanied by a progression in tem-

poral perspective. Book 1 represents the limited atemporal, for it is grounded in the present; book 2 represents the recovery of the past, the power of memory; book 4 represents sequential time—past, present, and future; and book 5 represents the simultaneity of the eternal present. There is a parallel progression within the technical elements: *persona*, the concept of knowledge made immediately accessible to the senses, is atemporal; *verse* represents the emergence of the retentive faculty, for in its imagery it reflects and sustains the content of the previous prose sections;[22] *prose* represents sequential time, the free and forward movement from past to present to future; and each *book*, containing persona, verse, and prose simultaneously, represents the eternal present. While, then, there is a parallel progression in temporal perspectives within each of the two hierarchies, the two can also be differentiated on the basis of time. The technical elements are a static manifestation of the cognitive hierarchy, a static manifestation of temporal progression. Persona, verse, prose, and book divisions all remain consistently and unchangingly present from the opening to the close of the *Consolation*; persona, for example, represents the present at the beginning as at the end; prose represents sequential time at the beginning as at the end. The technical elements are, therefore, atemporal. The progression from book 1 to book 5, in contrast, represents sequential time, for as the reader progresses from the opening to the close of the *Consolation*, so the cognitive and temporal perspectives progress. Finally, as will be shown, there is a third manifestation of the cognitive hierarchy, one that subsumes and unifies all previous hierarchies through analogical binding, one that binds but is itself unbound, one that represents simultaneous time, the fullness and perfection of God's eternal present.[23]

The Analogical Binding of the Consolation

The verse that resides at almost the exact spatial center of the *Consolation* and that is unanimously applauded as the finest poem of the work is book 3, verse 9, at once a prayer to discover the ultimate principle of cosmic order and a hymn praising that order. The antecedents of the poem in the first half of Plato's *Timaeus*, which have long been recognized, have great significance in the final structure of the *Consolation*. Lines 6-12 of Boethius's climactic poem speak of the elemental binding of hot and cold, wet and dry, fire and earth — the proportions with which God creates cosmic harmony. These lines are an allusion to *Timaeus* 31C and 32A, the passage in which Plato describes proportion and the nature of the most perfect bond:

> In beginning to construct the body of the All, God was making it of fire and earth. But it is not possible that two things alone should be conjoined without a third; for there must needs be some intermediary bond to connect the two. And the fairest of bonds is that which most perfectly unites into one both itself and the things which it binds together; and to effect this in the fairest manner is the natural property of proportion. For whenever the middle term of any three numbers, cubic or square, is such that as the first term is to it, so is it to the last term, — and again, conversely, as the last term is to the middle, so is the middle to the first, — then the middle term becomes in turn the first and the last, while the first and last become in turn middle terms, and the necessary consequence will be that all the terms are interchangeable, and being interchangeable they all form a unity. Now if the body of the All had had to come into existence as a plane surface, having no depth, one middle term would have sufficed to bind together both itself and its fellow-terms; but now it is otherwise: for it behooved it to be solid of shape, and what brings solids into unison is never one middle term alone but always two. Thus it was that in the midst between fire and earth God set water and air, and having bestowed upon them so far as possible a like ratio one towards another — air being to water as fire to air, and water being to earth as air to water, — he joined together and constructed a Heaven visible and tangible. For these reasons and out of these materials, such in kind and four in number, the body of the Cosmos was harmonized by proportion and brought into existence. These conditions secured for it Amity, so that being united in identity with itself it became

indissoluble by any agent other than Him who had bound it together.[24]

Plato goes on to define the solid shape generated by this perfect binding as that of "a sphere, equidistant in all directions from the center to the extremities, which of all shapes is the most perfect and the most self-similar" (33B). This is the shape that Boethius attributes to Providence.

The creation of an indissoluble bond from four analogical and interchangeable terms is as descriptive of Boethius's *Consolation* as it is of Plato's world-body. Boethius's four analogical terms are not, of course, Plato's earth, water, air, and fire, but the four cognitive faculties, as manifested in the technical elements and in books 1, 2, 4, and 5. It will be helpful to examine the mathematics of this binding[25] — the mathematics through which the work is "harmonized by proportion and brought into existence" — before examining the corresponding analogy of ideas. The total number of prose and verse sections in book 1 is thirteen; in book 2, sixteen; in book 4, fourteen, and in book 5, eleven.[26] These numbers yield the following set

Book 1 : Book 2 : : Book 4 : Book 5
  13   16   14   11

difference of 3   difference of 3

Book 1 : Book 4 : : Book 2 : Book 5
  13   14   16   11

sum of 27   sum of 27

Book 2 : Book 1 : : Book 5 : Book 4
  16   13   11   14

difference of 3   difference of 3

Book 4 : Book 2 : : Book 5 : Book 1
  14   16   11   13

difference of 2   difference of 2

of analogies, each of which can be read forward or backward. Because each of the books can occupy any position in the analogical phrase, the single and fixed reading sequence, 1, 2, 4, 5, is displaced by the indissoluble weave of all possible sequences: 1, 2, 4, 5; 1, 4, 2, 5; 5, 2, 4, 1; 4, 2, 5, 1; 2, 1, 5, 4, and so forth. Books 1, 2, 4, and 5 are interchangeable, and hence the result is not a one-dimensional and one-directional sequential line but a sphere on which these books can occupy all possible points (Figure 8). On this sphere all four books are equidistant from and revolve around their common center, book 3.

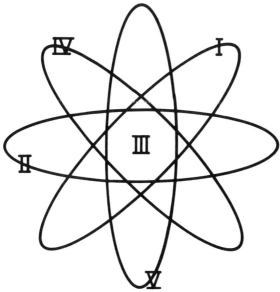

FIG. 8. *Spherical structure of the books of Boethius's* Consolation.

Boethius's inclusion of a fixed and central book conforms to rather than disrupts Plato's conception of creation. After describing the generation of the body of the world, Plato writes:

[According to this plan] He made it smooth and even and

equal on all sides from the centre, a whole and perfect body compounded of perfect bodies. And in the midst thereof He set Soul, which He stretched throughout the whole of it, and therewith He enveloped also the exterior of its body; and as a Circle revolving in a circle He stablished one sole and solitary Heaven, able of itself because of its excellence to company with itself and needing none other beside, sufficing unto itself as acquaintance and friend. And because of all this He generated it [so perfect as] to be a blessed God. [34B]

Book 3, like the world-soul, is fixed in the center of the surrounding books yet simultaneously stretches to their circumference, for, as was shown earlier, book 3 recapitulates and anticipates all that is contained in books 1, 2, 4, and 5. Its relation to the other books is visible in the relation between its own internal numerical structure — its division into two halves, the first half consiting of nine prose and verse sections, the second of three — and the numerical structure binding the other four books.

Book 1: Book 2::Book 3 first half: Book 3 second half :: Book 4 : Book 5
13   16   9   3   14   11
difference of 3   quotient of 3   difference of 3

Book 1 : Book 4 ::Book 3 first half : Book 3 second half :: Book 2 : Book 5
13   14   9   3   16   11
sum of 27   product of 27   sum of 27

Book 2 : Book 1 :: Book 3 first half : Book 3 second half :: Book 5 :Book 4
16   13   9   3   11   14
difference of 3   quotient of 3   difference of 3

Book 4 : Book 2 :: Book 3 first half : Book 3 second half :: Book 5 :Book 1
14   16   9   3   11   13
difference of 2   power of 2   difference of 2

The third book at once participates in the analogical binding and is differentiated from it. In each instance the numerical bond defining the relation between the first and second halves of book 3 is identical with the numerical bond uniting the four books, but those four books achieve their bond through addition and subtraction while book 3 achieves its bond through the higher-order processes of multiplication and division.

The centrality of the third book is again suggested by a second dimension of the analogical binding. While the numerical bonds between books 1, 2, 4, and 5 can be based on the total number of prose and verse sections within each book, they can also be based on the numbers of the books themselves:

Book 1 : Book 2 :: Book 4 : Book 5
difference   of 1   difference   of 1

Book 1 : Book 4 :: Book 2 : Book 5
difference   of 3   difference   of 3

Book 2 : Book 1 :: Book 5 : Book 4
difference   of 1   difference   of 1

Book 4 : Book 2 :: Book 5 : Book 1
sum of 6   sum of 6

When the numerical bonds based on the book numbers are juxtaposed with the numerical bonds based on the prose and verse sections, a new numerical bond is generated. It is always the number three.

| Books 1, 2, 4, and 5: | Bond between | Books 1, 2, 4, and 5: |
| Bonds based on book numbers | two bonds | Bonds based on prose and verse |

$$1 \; : \; 2 \; :: \; 4 \; : \; 5$$
$$\underbrace{}_{\text{diff. 1}} \quad \underbrace{}_{\text{diff. 1}}$$ quotient of 3
$$13 \; : \; 16 :: 14 \; : \; 11$$
$$\underbrace{}_{\text{diff. 3}} \quad \underbrace{}_{\text{diff. 3}}$$

$$1 \; : \; 4 :: \; 2 \; : \; 5$$
$$\underbrace{}_{\text{diff. 3}} \quad \underbrace{}_{\text{diff. 3}}$$ power of 3
$$13 \; : \; 14 :: 16 \; : \; 11$$
$$\underbrace{}_{\text{sum 27}} \quad \underbrace{}_{\text{sum 27}}$$

$$2 \; : \; 1 :: \; 5 \; ; \; 4$$
$$\underbrace{}_{\text{diff. 1}} \quad \underbrace{}_{\text{diff. 1}}$$ quotient of 3
$$16 \; : \; 13 :: 11 \; : \; 14$$
$$\underbrace{}_{\text{diff. 3}} \quad \underbrace{}_{\text{diff. 3}}$$

$$4 \; : \; 2 :: 5 \; : \; 1$$
$$\underbrace{}_{\text{sum 6}} \quad \underbrace{}_{\text{sum 6}}$$ product of 3
$$14 \; : \; 16 :: 11 \; : \; 13$$
$$\underbrace{}_{\text{diff. 2}} \quad \underbrace{}_{\text{diff. 2}}$$

The two modes of analogical binding—that based on the total number of prose and verse sections and that based on the book numbers—generate a single shape, a sphere well rounded on all sides. The bond defining the relation between the two modes of binding, and hence the bond responsible for the conversion of the two into the single and simple shape, is always the number 3. Like Plato's soul, book 3, fixed at the center, simultaneously reveals itself in all surfaces of the All, all surfaces of the sphere formed by books 1, 2, 4, and 5.[27]

The seriousness of Boethius's attitude toward this numerical binding, implicit in his reverence for Plato, Pythagoras, and Euclid, is made explicit in his assertion, in *De Arithmetica*, that *Omnia quaecumque a primaeva rerum natura constructa sunt, numerorum videntur ratione formata* (1.2): All things whatsoever that have been constructed by the primeval nature of things appear to have been formed according to a system of numbers. Far from being an ingenious game, the numerical proportions of the *Consolation* were for the author a reflection of a universe far less wonderful for its "space, firmness, and speedy motion" than for its governing mathematics (*Consolation* 3. pr.8.17-20).

The numerical binding of the work, beautiful in and of itself, simultaneously alerts one to the corresponding and equally beautiful analogy of ideas binding those books, a bin-

ding based on the progressive levels of the cognitive hierarchy.
Just as in the *Timaeus* the hierarchy of elements (earth, water,
air, fire) ultimately makes possible a set of precise analogies in
which the middle terms (water, air) become the outer terms
and the outer (earth, fire) become the inner—

earth	:	water	::	air	:	fire
air	:	water	::	fire	:	air
water	:	earth	::	air	:	water

—so Boethius's hierarchy of cognitive faculties ultimately
makes possible a parallel set of analogies.[28]

sense	:	imagination	::	reason	:	Insight
reason	:	imagination	::	Insight	:	reason
imagination	:	sense	::	reason	:	imagination

This pattern of analogical binding is applicable not only to the
cognitive faculties themselves, but to each part of the *Consolation* where those faculties are present. Since, for example, book
1 is sense, book 2 is imagination, book 4 is reason, and book 5 is
Insight, the single and fixed reading sequence—1, 2, 4, 5—is
displaced by an "indissoluble" weave of sequences.

Book 1	:	Book 2	::	Book 4	:	Book 5
Book 4	:	Book 2	::	Book 5	:	Book 4
Book 2	:	Book 1	::	Book 4	:	Book 2

Again, because the cognitive hierarchy is present in the *Consolation's* persona, verse, prose, and book divisions, what at
first seem to be separate technical elements are actually an inseparable unity.

persona	:	verse	::	prose	:	book divisions
prose	:	verse	::	book div.	:	prose
verse	:	persona	::	prose	:	verse

Again, chance (sense), fortune (imagination), fate (reason), and Providence (Insight) are not discrete realities. They are ultimately all inextricably bound up with Providence.

chance	:	fortune	::	fate	:	Prov.
fate	:	fortune	::	Prov.	:	fate
fortune	:	chance	::	fate	:	fortune

Here, as in each of the earlier sets and in conformity with Plato's description of the world-body, the analogy contains four terms and produces three sequences. The outer and inner terms are interchangeable; the bond is perfect; a sphere is generated.

There is an alternative and condensed way of depicting these analogical patterns. Boethius's emphasis on the cognitive faculties enables us to see that what often appear to be isolated and disparate phenomena are instead a single phenomenon viewed through multiple perspectives.

chance   fortune : : fate   Providence

Providence   *Providence*
(viewed through sense,   *(viewed through reason,*
imagination)   *Insight)*

In this example, the single reality made multiple by four modes of cognition, the common denominator of each pair of terms, is Providence. The weave of analogies can, then, be written in a form that comes close to being an equation, an equation in which Providence equals Providence, one equals one. According to Augustine, equality is the most perfect of all proportions and exists in its absolute form only in God (*De Musica* 6.11).

This process of analogical binding is visible in almost all aspects of the *Consolation*. The following analogies are based on ideas presented in the first two sections of this discussion. In each instance, four apparently unrelated concepts are shown to be in reality a single concept seen from multiple cognitive perspectives. While in each instance only a single arrangement of terms is given, those terms can in every instance be written as a sequence of three interwoven analogies.

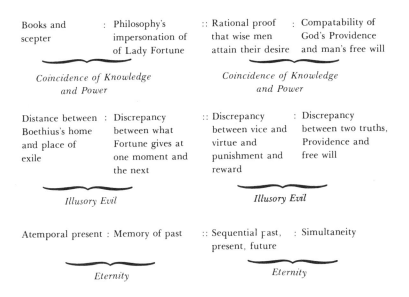

Books and   : Philosophy's   :: Rational proof   : Compatability of
scepter   impersonation of   that wise men   God's Providence
                  of Lady Fortune   attain their desire and man's free will

Coincidence of Knowledge   *Coincidence of Knowledge*
and Power   *and Power*

Distance between : Discrepancy   :: Discrepancy   : Discrepancy
Boethius's home   between what   between vice and   between two truths,
and place of   Fortune gives at   virtue and   Providence and
exile   one moment and   punishment and   free will
                  the next   reward

Illusory Evil   *Illusory Evil*

Atemporal present : Memory of past   :: Sequential past, : Simultaneity
                                        present, future

Eternity   *Eternity*

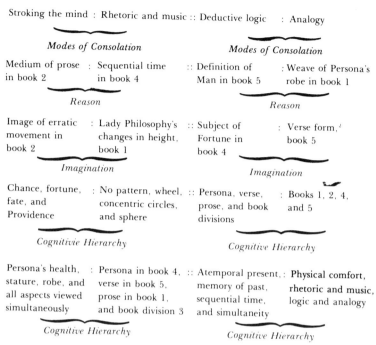

Stroking the mind : Rhetoric and music :: Deductive logic   : Analogy

    Modes of Consolation   *Modes of Consolation*

Medium of prose : Sequential time   :: Definition of   : Weave of Persona's
in book 2   in book 4   Man in book 5   robe in book 1

        Reason   *Reason*

Image of erratic : Lady Philosophy's :: Subject of   : Verse form,[2]
movement in   changes in height,   Fortune in   book 5
book 2   book 1   book 4

     Imagination   *Imagination*

Chance, fortune, : No pattern, wheel, :: Persona, verse, : Books 1, 2, 4,
fate, and   concentric circles,   prose, and book   and 5
Providence   and sphere   divisions

   Cognitivie Hierarchy   *Cognitive Hierarchy*

Persona's health, : Persona in book 4, :: Atemporal present, : Physical comfort,
stature, robe, and   verse in book 5,   memory of past,   rhetoric and music,
all aspects viewed   prose in book 1,   sequential time,   logic and analogy
simultaneously   and book division 3   and simultaneity

   Cognitive Hierarchy   *Cognitive Hierarchy*

These analogies represent rather than exhaust the relentless and omnipresent process of binding through which an image of Aetna's fires in book 2 becomes one with the medium of prose in book 5, through which Philosophy's smile in book 4 becomes one with the whole of book 1, through which the disparate multiplicity of a temporal work achieves the simplicity and simultaneity of divine consciousness. It achieves that simultaneity by affirming not the identity of all things, but the participation of all things in a single unity. In the transition from the multiple cognitive perspectives to the analogical binding made possible by those perspectives, in the transition from the hierarchy to the sphere made possible by that hierarchy, the beneficient intent of that hierarchy begins to emerge. As that which begins by revealing the distinctions among all things goes on to reveal the unity of all things, the ordered ranking of the hierarchical gives way to the absolute uniformity and sameness of the spherical. The final end of the cognitive hierarchy is not exclusion but *inclusion*: its ultimate purpose is not to divide and differentiate Creation into diminishing degrees of divinity, but to assure that no part of Creation will be lost from the immediacy of the divine present.

This essay has shown four manifestations of the cognitive hierarchy in the *Consolation*. The cognitive hierarchy is described in the climactic three prose sections of the final book; it is present in the technical elements, persona, verse, prose, and book divisions; it is again present in the structural progression from the realm of sense in book 1 to the realm of Insight in book 5; and it is once more present in the analogical binding of the work. There is, finally, a fifth manifestation of the hierarchy, a manifestation visible in the first four. Just as man — or evil or knowledge or cosmic order — can be seen through the four cognitive faculties, so the hierarchy itself can be seen through those four faculties. The technical elements represent the sensitive manifestation of the hierarchy; this is a static and atemporal manifestation. The progression through books 1, 2, 4, and 5 represents the imaginative manifestation; just as the imagination mediates between sense and reason, so it is the mediating progression through the four books that leads us from the sensitive manifestation, the introduction of the technical elements in book 1, to the rational manifestation, the explicit analysis of the hierarchy at the end of book 5. That those final prose sections represent the rational manifestation is suggested by three factors: just as the rational is based on the sensitive and the imaginative, so it is only by going through the technical elements and the structural progression that one reaches the concluding prose sections; just as the rational faculty is intimately related to man's capacity for speech,[30] so it is only here that the hierarchy is explicitly articulated; and just as the object of reason is the form of the universal, so the language of the passage is that of abstract universals — for example, when describing the object of the imagination it provides not a specific image but the universal form of specific images apprehensible in the term *immaterial particular*.

Finally, the analogical binding of the work represents the

hierarchy as it manifests itself to Insight. Just as Insight combines all aspects of knowledge simultaneously, so the analogical binding combines the other manifestations of the hierarchy simultaneously. While, then, the hierarchy of cognitive hierarchies contains as its highest term the analogical binding, it is itself contained in that analogical binding. It, too, is part of an analogy—

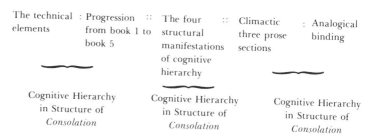

—an analogy in which, once more, all terms are interchangeable. Just as the quintessential fifth element is above yet simultaneously present in earth, water, air, and fire, so the fifth manifestation of the hierarchy, the hierarchy of hierarchies, contains yet is contained in the other four. It becomes a part of the analogical binding that generates the final shape of the *Consolation*, the well-rounded sphere, the sphere that enables one to see, as though with the eye of Insight, the whole of the work in a single glance.

Boethius's achievement of God-likeness reveals itself in three dimensions of the work. First, just as God is the concidence of form and substance, so the *Consolation* achieves a coincidence of form and substance: the idea of the work presented in the closing prose sections is everywhere visible in its structure. Second, just as the final unity of the *Consolation* is achieved through analogical binding, so Boethius's goal is itself an ontological analogy: he does not want to become God; he wants to become God-like (3. pr.10-12). Finally, the shape generated by this analogical binding is, according to the Platonic writings to which Boethius explicitly alludes, a sphere everywhere equidistant from its center, the shape that Philosophy designates as the form of the Divine substance, "in body like a sphere well-rounded on all sides" (3. pr.12.106).

It is regrettable that through the ages so much has been lost from a work whose single purpose was to assure that nothing should be lost. That Fortune's wheel rather than the well-rounded sphere should be the image most often associated with the *Consolation* is symptomatic of our neglect of the work's structure, its aesthetic integrity, its moral beauty. While the foregoing description of the *Consolation* is perhaps imprecise and certainly incomplete, its underlying assumption is correct. It is inconceivable that Boethius, exhilarated by the form residing in mathematics, in astronomy, in music, in human thought, would in that work he knew to be his final work abandon his love of structure. It is inconceivable that the aesthetic rigor he considered a corollary to metaphysical conviction would be diminished by his recognition of his approaching execution. It could be only intensified: he had learned from his beloved Cicero and his more beloved Socrates that "Philosophy is learning how to die." The *Consolation of Philosophy* is an act of learning how to die, an act in which man's death is displaced by his potential divinity. While the outcome of the act is moral and metaphysical, the act itself is essentially aesthetic, for it is in the final and perfect shape of the work, the well-rounded sphere, that the nature of divine consciousness is apprehended. In creating that shape, Boethius intended the work to be, like Plato's perfect cosmos, "able of itself because of its excellence to company with itself and needing none other beside, sufficing unto itself as acquaintance and friend" (*Timaeus* 34). Boethius, Βοηθεια, his name so close to the Greek word for helper, created a work meant to be—even in the most extreme crises of isolation—a consolation, acquaintance, and friend.

Notes

1.   E. K. Rand, *Founders of the Middle Ages* (Cambridge, Mass., 1929), p. 162.

2.   H. F. Stewart and E. K. Rand, eds., *Boethius: The Theological Tractates and The Consolation of Philosophy* (Cambridge, Mass., 1962), p. 32. All further references to the *Tractates* and the *Consolation* will be given in the text and

will refer to these Latin texts. English translations come usually from this edition but sometimes are from *Boethius: The Consolation of Philosophy*, trans. and ed. V. E. Watts (Harmondsworth, England, 1969) and occasionally are collated from these and other translations. References to Boethius's *De Institutione Musica* are to *Patrologia Latina*, vol. 63.

3. Pierre Courcelle, "Le personage de Philosophie dans la littérature latine," *Journal des Savants* (Paris, 1970), pp. 209-52; Joachim Gruber, "Die Erscheinung der Philosophie in der *Consolatio Philosophiae* des Boethius," *Rheinisches Museum für Philologie* 112 (1969): 166-86; Rand, *Founders of the Middle Ages*, pp. 160f.; V. Schmidt-Kohl, *Die neuplatonische Seelelehre in der Consolatio philosophiae des Boethius, Beiträge zur klassiche Philologie*, 16 (Meisenheim am Glan, 1965); E.T. Silk, "Boethius' *Consolatio Philosophiae* as a Sequel to Augustine's *Dialogues* and *Soliloquia*," *Harvard Theological Review* 32 (1939): 19-39.

4. *The Basic Works of Aristotle*, ed. Richard McKeon (New York, 1941), p. 595.

5. Boethius's emphasis on music's mediating power is reflected in the definition of music adopted by the later Middle Ages: "*Musica est de numero relato ad sonos*" (definition cited in Oliver Strunk, *Source Readings in Music History* [New York, 1950], p. 88 n.). Perhaps, too, it was in part Boethius's emphasis on this function that led his student Aquinas to designate sound as the vehicle of revelation.

6. One of these final meters, that in the third book, has often troubled readers for what Rand calls its "somewhat perverted application of the story of Orpheus and Eurydice that no lover. . .would approve" (Rand, *Founders of the Middle Ages*, p. 172). The importance of music's function as a vehicle to a higher sphere should make intelligible, if not wholly forgivable, Boethius's treatment of the myth: the Orpheus story provided the author with excellent material for a cautionary tale since, in attempting to rescue Eurydice from the lower world, Orpheus addresses his music to the lower sphere.

7. Alfred North Whitehead, *Modes of Thought* (New York, 1968), pp. 50, 174.

8. The verb *ratiocinari* as used by Boethius refers both to the power of reasoning and to the power of discoursing (e.g., 5.pr.5.21-24, 36-39; 4.pr.2.25, 26). As one progresses through the *Consolation*, the distinction between mental and verbal acts becomes increasingly small: a truth arrived at by reasoning is repeatedly designated as an act of spoken assertion (e.g., 3.pr.2.10-13; 3.pr.12.42-43; 4.pr.2.19, 20; 5.pr.3.69). This identification between reason and discourse is not necessarily evidence of an identification between reason and prose, since "discourse" in antiquity referred both to prose and to poetry (see E. R. Curtius, *European Literature and the Latin Middle Ages*, trans. W. R. Trask [New York, 1953], p. 147). However, Boethius seems to use "discourse" only in referring to the content of the prose sections. Perhaps he thought of his alternations between prose and meters as alternations between speaking and singing.

9. See, for instance, the *Shorter Oxford English Dictionary*.

10. On the medieval attitude toward the triangle, see Russell Peck's essay in this collection.

11. Other readers have also considered the third book, and in particular 3.m.9, in

some ways a pinnacle. See, for example, Friedrich Klingner, *De Boethii Consolatione Philosophiae*, Philologische Untersuchungen 27 (Berlin, 1921), p. 66.

12. Watts, trans. and ed., *Boethius: The Consolation of Philosophy*, p. 98n.16.

13. That Philosophy's mode of argument in the second book is rhetorical and that rhetoric is intimately related to the imagination are suggested by two additional factors. First, in classical times rhetoric was closely associated with the law courts. Significantly, in book 2 Fortune is put on trial. Second, like the imagination, rhetoric in book 2 is used to examine immaterial particulars, the false forms of happiness, the multiple forms of mortal and material pleasure. The difference between book 2 and book 3, sections 1-9 (which again examines the false forms) is like the difference in the *Phaedrus* between the opening speech of Lysias and Socrates' first speech: while both speeches examine the "false forms" of love, Lysias's speech is a subrational approach to the subject, Socrates' a rational approach.

14. In the fifth book of Euclid's *Elements* (a work translated by Boethius) ratio and proportion are made applicable to incommensurates.

15. Significantly, the imagery of the *Consolation* progresses from the vegetable and nonsentient in book 1 to diminutive animals (worms, flies, mice) in book 2 to higher-order animals (wolves, tiger, swine) in book 4. In book 5 no specific animals other than man are mentioned.

16. To illustrate his concept of necessity, Boethius in prose 3 uses the image of "man sitting." In prose 6 Philosophy, when talking about necessity, changes the example from "man sitting" to "man walking," a change consonant with her insistence on man's capacity for free will.

17. The decreasing emphasis on biography can be seen by examining the references to other philosophers as well as to Boethius. When famous men (e.g., Socrates) are introduced in the early books, it is their biography, the course of events of their personal life, that is the subject. In the higher books it will instead be their ideas that are called forth.

18. This hierarchy of cosmic order is, for example, suggested by the fact that having just discussed the relation between fate and Providence in 4.pr.6, Philosophy at the opening of 4.pr.7 begins, "'Perceivest thou now what followeth of all that we have hitherto said?' 'What?' quoth I. 'That,' quoth she, 'all manner of fortune is good.'"

19. Except for bk. 5, pr.2, which explicitly examines the nature of chance.

20. Philosophy will revise this definition of chance in book 5, prose 1.

21. In examining the cognitive progress from book 1 to book 5, section 2 of this essay focuses on the prose sections and on the changing imagery in the verse. It is possible that a study of the changing meters in the verse would also reveal this progression.

22. The function of verse as a memory aid was frequently emphasized during the Middle Ages, as it was again during the Renaissance (e.g., Sidney, *Apologie for Poetrie*).

23. The concepts of atemporality and eternity (time seen by sense and time seen by Insight) should not be confused. As Lewis S. Ford points out ("Boethius and Whitehead on Time and Eternity," *International Philosophical Quarterly*

8:38-67), Boethius made a very clear and exciting distinction between the two, which Aquinas obliterated, making the two indistinguishable. Whitehead has recovered the distinction for us.

24. R. G. Bury, ed., *Plato* (Cambridge, Mass., 1942), pp. 59 f. All subsequent passages from *Timaeus* are quoted from this edition.

25. The importance of unified numbers is suggested by Boethius's definition of goodness as unity, evil as division (see above; see also Peck's essay in this volume).

26. Boethius's interest in including a predetermined number of prose and verse sections in each book is suggested by the fact that the length of any given prose section does not usually seem to be dictated by the subject matter or by the structure of the argument: that is, he does not end a particular prose section when he has exhausted a topic or worked through an approach. The apparent arbitrariness of some of his divisions is a clue to the crucial importance of the numbers themselves.

In selecting the number of prose and verse sections for each book (13, 16, 14, 11), he could have chosen several alternative groups of numbers and still have successfully created the *first* set of numerical analogies shown here. However, the range of numbers from which he could have selected is much smaller than it at first appears; for in finding numbers of prose and verse sections that he could then play off against the book numbers and against the internal number divisions of book 3, he was considerably more restricted.

27. While this discussion shows that the relation between book 3 and the other four books is a structural parallel to the relation in the *Timaeus* between the world-body and the world-soul, it ignores the further possibility that book 3's own internal division parallels Plato's description of the world-soul. Plato's soul was composed of three terms, one material, one immaterial, and one a combination of the other two. One might find, for example, corresponding divisions in book 3; sections 1 through 8 might represent the material; 10 through 12 the immaterial, and section 9, which contains the conclusion for 1 through 8 and the first premise of 10 through 12, the intermediate third term.

There are also other aspects of the *Consolation*'s numerology that have not been dealt with here. For example, it is entirely possible that the number of lines in each poem was significant to its author: it is probably no more accidental that 3.m.9 has twenty-eight lines, the triple ternary plus one, than that Dante's *Divine Comedy* has 100 cantos, ninety-nine plus one.

28. Significantly, in the *Republic* (6. 508d-511d) Plato talks about four modes of cognition and their analogical relationship.

29. Here I have appended to the terms specific book numbers (4, 5) even though any book number would be valid. The particular book numbers are specified in order to suggest the analogical binding uniting apparently disparate elements of apparently separate books.

30. See n.8 above.

Gawain's Number

Allan Metcalf

As the description of Gawain's arming for his quest of the knight of the Green Chapel[1] builds to a climax, a sign appears that temporarily brings the narrative of the poem known as *Sir Gawain and the Green Knight* to a halt. It is the golden pentangle on Gawain's shield, a sign so potent and important for the narrator that he postpones Gawain's imminent departure for 43 lines, a stanza and a half, in order to give it a leisurely and thorough explanation. "Though it should tarry me," says the narrator, "I intend to tell you why the pentangle pertains to that noble prince" ("And quy þe pentangle apendez to þat prynce noble / I am in tent yow to telle, þof tary hyt me schulde" [ll. 623-24]). The link between pentangle and prince is *number*. The pentangle is an endless knot with 5 points, and it accords with Gawain because of the numbers 5 and 25 (5 times 5). Gawain is known as good in 5 ways and in a 5-fold manner within each of these ways (632). The narrator catalogs them all: 5 faultless wits (640), 5 never-failing fingers (641), trust in Christ's 5 wounds (642-43), fortitude from Mary's 5 joys (645-47), and then a fifth 5, the 5 knightly virtues of generosity, fellowship, cleanness, courtesy, and pity (651-55). Five so thoroughly characterizes Gawain that one might with perfect medieval propriety say that he *is* a 5; he belongs to the category of 5s just as he belongs to the categories of men, Arthur's relatives, and knights of the Round Table.

With the pentangle's pertinence fully and explicitly explained, Gawain finally departs, riding out of Arthur's court so fast that his horse's hoofs strike sparks. The pentagon and its symbolism depart too. The reader catches up with Gawain less

141

than a stanza later, but the 5s and 25s, strangely enough, seem
to have vanished for good. In the entire poem there is only one
subsequent mention of either number. When he reaches the
Green Chapel at the end of his journey, Gawain exclaims:
"Now I feel it is the Fiend, in my five wits, who has made this
appointment to destroy me here" ("Now I fele hit is þe fende,
in my fyue wyttez, / Þat hatz stoken me þis steuen to strye me
here" [2,193-94]). This remark seems to involve an echo of
"First he was found faultless in his five wits" ("Fyrst he watz
funden fautlez in his fyue wyttez" [640]), but it is a faint echo
indeed. It appears as if the poet has puzzlingly underemployed
the symbolism he earlier developed with such insistence. To be
sure, the pentangle passage is unquestionably useful in illuminating Gawain's character and in stating the social,
moral, and religious ideals whose embodiment in Gawain will
soon come to the test. The qualities that make up Gawain's 5 5s
have justly drawn much critical attention.[2] The mention of
generosity, courtesy, and the rest is in no way superfluous.
What seems unnecessary, or underemployed, is the setting of
5s and 25s in which Gawain's virtues appear, a numerical
structure so pointedly brought to the attention of the audience
and then so absolutely ignored.

It might be argued that the sense of underemployment is a
modern one, that for a medieval writer and his audience an excursus on the hero's number would be justified as a simple case
of amplification and digression. Theorists of both the art of
poetry and the art of preaching found positive value in digression. "For the medieval rhetoricians the pressure of narrative
or argument [in poetry] had ceased to be important, and thus
they advocated a constant turning aside from the main path of
a work into descriptive digressions," observes Spearing.[3] But
this practice seems alien to Sir Gawain and the Green Knight.
The poem's narrative appears distinctively purposeful and
economical. As the story unfolds, to be sure, the several
episodes and events at first seem unrelated, but at the end both
reader and Gawain realize, to their edification, that all has
been interconnected: the green man and the host, the old lady
and the young, the hunts and the bedroom interviews, the ex-

changes and the ax blows. Every element of the story seems relevant to the testing of Arthur's court and Gawain's character; every strand comes together to knot up the story at the end. It would be ironic if a passage that stresses interconnectedness — "each one joined to the other, so that it had no end" ("vchone halched in oþer, þat non ende hade" [657]) — should be unconnected with the rest of the poem.

The numbers that knit the structure of the poem do not seem to be 5s and 25s, as the pentangle passage would lead us to expect, but 2s and 3s. Donald R. Howard summarizes the situation: "Everywhere in the poem is balance, contrast, and antithesis. Things are arranged in pairs — there are two New Year's days, two 'beheading' scenes, two courts, two confessions; or in threes — three temptations, three hunts, three kisses, three strokes of the ax."[4] One may also find structural 4s. Modern readers generally accept the fourfold division of the narrative implied by the large capitals in the manuscript,[5] and, as Erzsébet Perényi has observed, the first fitt can be seen as having one part, the second 2, the third 3, and the fourth 4.[6] Such numbers are not hard to account for; they are the stock-in-trade of good storytellers. Twos (and twice 2s) provide contrast; 3s build emphasis and suspense by establishing a pattern that comes to a decisive test the third time. "I have tested you twice and find you faithful. Now 'third time turn out best' think in the morning" ("I haf fraysted þe twys, and faythful I fynde þe. / Now 'þrid tyme þrowe best' þenk on þe morne" [1,679-80]), says Gawain's host on the eve of the last exchange of winnings, stating a proverbial truth. The narrator makes no suggestion that he finds the numbers 2, 3, and 4 symbolic, and, quite properly, neither do the critics.

But the poet himself makes 5s and 25s overtly symbolic. The question remains: how does this symbolism connect with the rest of the poem?

The problem admits of a solution not through closer scrutiny of the matter of the poem, but through attention to its form. The narrative eschews symbolic 5s and 25s in favor of the effective but nonsymbolic 2s and 3s. But the form of the story, the poetic framework, is fundamentally a matter of 5s and 25s.

To begin with, the poem as a whole is neatly enclosed in 25s. A. Kent Hieatt has observed that the last long line of the poem, the line that echoes the opening line and brings the narrative full circle, is the 2,525th.[7] Its number is a duplicated version of 25, a number the poet has explicitly found symbolic. That this appearance of a duplicated 25 at such a structurally significant place is no accident is clear from the parallel occurrence in the companion poem *Pearl*. Like *Sir Gawain and the Green Knight*, *Pearl* has 101 stanzas. It too has a concluding long line that echoes the opening line of the poem, tying the beginning and end together in an endless knot. And in *Pearl*, too, the number of the final echoing line duplicates a number the poet has explicitly found symbolic. Since *Pearl*'s stanzas are uniformly 12 lines long, its ending in line 1,212 would be an automatic and perhaps trivial matter, but in *Sir Gawain* the stanzas have irregularly variable length. Hence the significant position of line 2,525 in that poem must be either "an extraordinary coincidence," as Hieatt puts it (p. 346), or the poet's deliberate choice. To be sure, *Sir Gawain and the Green Knight* does not come to a complete end in line 2,525; only its long lines do. One small group of lines is left over, the final bob and wheel. But this, too, suggests a number-symbolic structure: it is a single group of exactly 5 lines.

Indeed, the (near) end in line 2,525 is a beginning in more ways that one, for it leads to an awareness of the pervasiveness of 5s and 25s in smaller units of the poem as well as in its overall structure. Line 2,525 is especially important for the significant length it implicitly assigns to the stanzas that have come before. *Sir Gawain and the Green Knight* has 101 stanzas and a total of 2,530 lines. Dividing 2,530 by 101 gives 25 as the average length of the stanzas in *Sir Gawain and the Green Knight*, with a remainder of 5. Fives and 25s thus emerge as the fundamental dimensions of the poem's form. Again a parallel with *Pearl* strengthens the conviction that the 5s and 25s in the structure of *Sir Gawain and the Green Knight* are no accident. *Pearl* too has 101 stanzas, and its 1,212 lines apportion themselves exactly 12 per stanza. In *Pearl*, of course, it is this number 12 that emerges as explicitly symbolic during the dreamer's culminating vision of the heavenly Jerusalem, "As deuyses hit þe apostel Jhon," "as the apostle John describes it."[8] The New Jerusalem has 12 courses in its foundation (992-93) marked with 12 different precious stones. It is 12 furlongs in each of its outside dimensions (1,030). Twelve pearly gates lead into the city (1,035). About the river that flows from God's throne are trees that bear 12 fruits of life (1,078) 12 times a year (1,079). The multiplication of 12 times 12 also makes an appearance in the procession of virgins in the heavenly city, who number 144,000 (786, 869-70).

In one important respect, however, the numerical structure of *Sir Gawain and the Green Knight* differs from that of *Pearl*. The normative stanza length of *Pearl* is apparent from the beginning. Each of its stanzas has 12 lines, closely held together with interlocking rhymes, so that the formal division into stanzas is clear and prominent. In *Sir Gawain and the Green Knight*, on the other hand, the stanza length is irregular and unpredictable. The author has made 5 and 25 the foundation of his poem, but he conceals this design from the reader as he conceals the nature of Gawain's test — until the end.

Not without a certain forewarning, however. The 5-line remainder after the echoing line 2,525 at the end of the poem is only the last example of a prominent metrical structure present from the start. At the end of each stanza, distinctively marked off by short lines and 5 interlocking rhyme words, appears the 5-line bob and wheel. Caroline D. Eckhardt has suggested[9] that this rhyming unit might well be considered Gawain's "signature." In the earliest stanzas it serves as an unexplained hint of the identity of the at-first-unspecified protagonist. After the introduction of Gawain and the explanation of his associations with 5 and 25, it becomes a reminder of his important but threatened position.

And at the beginning of the text there occurs, perhaps accidentally, one prominent prefiguration of the importance 25 is to assume later on. Instead of the usual 36 lines, the manuscript page on which the text begins (fol. 91a) shows 25 lines to the reader's eye.[10] It is possible to consider this a sign, from the poet or the scribe, of the symbolic number that is to shape the whole.

Yet not until the very end of the poem is it possible to determine that the average stanza length is, finally, the symbolic 25. From the beginning, stanza length varies so greatly and irregularly that the apt average at the end comes as something of a surprise. But there is one important moment of preparation for the surprise, and it comes at a place of great structural importance. This is a location marked in the manuscript as a major division by means of two horizontal lines and a large capital immediately following: the end of stanza 45, and of what editors have termed fitt 2, at line 1,125. Here, and only here, the average number of lines per stanza becomes exactly 25, with no remainder.

The end of fitt 2 also delineates a delicate and exact division among the long lines of the poem. The last long line of fitt 2 (l. 1,120, counting both long and short) is the 900th long line, the last long line of the poem, the 2,025th. Each of these numbers is a perfect square. They divide the poem in a proportion of 4 parts to 5:

Fitts 1-2:   900 long lines $= 4 \times 15^2 = 30^2$
Fitts 3-4:   1,125 long lines $= 5 \times 15^2 = 30^2 + 15^2$
Total: 2,025 long lines $= 9 \times 15^2 = 30^2 + 15^2 = 45^2$

Since the bob and wheel, omitted in this count, amount to exactly one-fifth of the total number of lines in fitts 1 and 2, a kind of balance results as well: the number of *long* lines in fitts 3-4 (1,125) is exactly equal to the *total* number of lines, long and short, in fitts 1-2. A momentary coming to rest at the exact average of 25 lines per stanza, then, couples with a precise dividing point among the poem's long lines and a major manuscript division to prepare the audience for a possibility of returning to an exact average of 25 at the end—a possibility that is attained, then exceeded by a margin of 5 lines. It is difficult to imagine that such interconnections should be accidental and not part of the poet's deliberate strategy, especially since he has gone to such lengths to state the connection of 5s and 25s with Gawain and his virtues.

What might the poet mean by this structure of 5s and 25s? The obvious and appropriate source of explication is the pentangle passage itself. That passage associates 5s and 25s with perfection of, and trust in, Gawain's physical and mental abilities; with devotion to the Virgin; and with knightly and Christian virtues.[11] But it should be clear from the narrator's statement that Gawain himself is the nexus of the various intertwined 5s. In *Sir Gawain and the Green Knight* the numbers 5 and 25 must stand for Gawain himself. If they imply other virtues and qualities, or the Virgin Mary, it is always through their explicit association with Gawain.

Throughout the poem, of course, one encounters the 5 interlocking rhymed lines of the bob and wheel—Gawain's "signature." Considered in relation to the variable number of alliterating long lines in each stanza, the short rhyming lines of the bob and wheel present a visual and aural analogue of Gawain's courteous, skilled perserverance against the pressure of the larger, threatening, shifting shapes that challenge his perfection. The 5 supernumerary lines that conclude the poem might be seen as Gawain's final signature, an assertion that he has passed his test. But the last bob and wheel may also be an assertion that Gawain has stepped a little beyond the bounds of perfection. One metrical unit of 5 lines beyond the exact average of 25 lines per stanza may indicate here, as one-too-many does elsewhere in number symbolism, a transgression. Eleven, for example, was "a number of transgression, because it goes beyond the 10 Commandments" (Hopper, *Medieval Number Symbolism*, p. 131). In the case of Gawain, the transgression is appropriately minor. The small remainder of 5/101 beyond the average of 25 is an appropriate reminder of the lightness of the Green Knight's judgment and punishment, a mere "nirt in þe nek" (2,498).

A satisfactory explanation for the presence and symbolism of the 5-line bob and wheel, then, is not hard to find. But what about the 25-line average stanza length? If the author intended this average, why should he conceal it so effectively by varying the length of the stanzas unpredictably? One answer suggests itself from the strategy of the narrative, which is to clarify matters only gradually. At first one does not even know what adventure will permit Arthur to sit down to dinner; then one does not know who will respond to the Green Knight's challenge. Only in the second fitt does one become well acquainted with Gawain, his central role, and the numbers with which he is associated. So it accords with the author's initial witholding of information about his hero that he should not immediately display one of the structural analogues of that hero. A related use of the "withholding" strategy would justify the continuation of this pattern of varying numbers of lines in the stanzas even when the hero and his number are known. The irregularly shifting numbers of long lines in each stanza suggest the nature of the forces that are testing Gawain: a shape-shifting green man, a deceitful lady, and behind them a mysterious old woman, Morgan la Faye, to whom at the end the green man attributes the instigation of the entire test. Gawain (and the reader) do not realize who his opponents really are and do not recognize the rules of the game he is playing; likewise, except at two significant locations, the reader cannot recognize the ideal length toward which the stanzas are tending. It is appropriate that the ever-shifting masses of long lines, suggesting the unknown perils Gawain faces, should tower over the modest but invariant and steadfastly recurring 5-line bob-and-wheel unit, suggesting Gawain, throughout the poem. And then, at the end the shifting shapes of the long lines join with the bobs and wheels to settle at a norm of Gawain's other number, 25. He has met the challenge and made the whole his — with just a slight transgression.

Again a comparison with *Pearl* may be helpful. There the structurally symbolic number, 12, stands not for one of the chief characters but for the city of God. The city and the rule of God exist through eternity, of course; the dreamer's problem is one of gaining sufficient spiritual vision to see this fact. *Pearl,* like the source of its vision, is a book of revelation. The dreamer first appears in a state of despair, blind to God's revealed truth that is everywhere about him, even in the shape of the stanzas. As if to attest to his spiritual shortsightedness, the poem surrounds him with 12s from the beginning and he knows it not. Through the intercession of the maiden, the dreamer's vision gradually improves until he can explicitly see the structure of 12s — a structure that, in its poetic analogue, is present for the reader from beginning to end. The poem is for the reader what the New Jerusalem is for the dreamer, a symbolic artifact manifesting God's benevolent rule.[12] Hence the appropriateness of a structure for *Pearl* that plainly manifests the symbolic number throughout, in contrast with one that appropriately conceals it in *Sir Gawain and the Green Knight,* which, as a poem of a different sort of revelation, unfolds its truths to a hero and a reader who are equally (un)comprehending.

As mentioned above, there is one moment midway in *Sir Gawain and the Green Knight* where the structural 25 emerges from concealment, at the end of stanza 45 in line 1,125. The attainment of a perfect average of 25 lines just at this central turning point seems well calculated to provide both a preparation for a return to a nearly perfect average at the end of the poem and also a contrast with it. At line 1,125, Gawain has accepted and met the Green Knight's challenge; he has armed himself physically and spiritually, has sought and found comfortable lodging in the neighborhood of the Green Chapel, has assured himself of a guide to conduct him there to meet his appointment (1,077-78), and, finally, has agreed to a harmless game to while away the time at his jovial host's castle. They make and seal the covenant for this last game in stanza 45. At this point everything seems in order to Gawain and the reader alike, and Gawain seems the exact image of the fivefold perfection ascribed to him. Though concerned about the peril of his appointment, he has not felt the slightest inclination to shrink from it; though the shadow of that meeting falls on his thoughts, he displays flawless courtesy and cheer toward the inhabitants of his host's castle. Above all, Gawain thinks that he knows the game and its rules, and the reader shares Gawain's delusion. It accords with Gawain's confident state of mind that at the end of fitt 2 for a single moment the average stanza length should become exactly 25. This is the height of Gawain's pride, coming before the beginning of his confusion and fall in the temptation scenes that follow in fitt 3. That the entire poem ends in line 2,530, yielding an average stanza length of

25 but with a remainder of 5, provides an appropriate contrast: Gawain relied a little too much on his own abilities and
found himself — through excess — a little beyond the bounds of
what for him would have been perfection.

The movement toward a 25-line average appropriately
enough begins only in the second fitt, where the poet also first
explains the numbers 5 and 25 as analogues of Gawain. The
first fitt shows less inclination toward 25 lines per stanza than
any of the other fitts. *Sir Gawain and the Green Knight* begins
with a stanza just 19 lines long, followed by a 17-line stanza,
the shortest in the entire poem. The 21 stanzas of fitt 1 average
1.7 lines less than 25, while the 24 stanzas of fitt 2 average 1.4
lines more, the 34 stanzas of fitt 3, 0.6 lines more, and the 22
stanzas of fitt 4, 0.8 lines less. The first fitt has only one stanza
of exactly 25 lines (no. 4), while the second fitt has three (nos.
22, 40, and 41), and the third and fourth fitts two each (nos. 65,
72; 91, 92).

It is possible, therefore, to imagine that the poet did not concern himself with bringing his stanzas to a 25-line average until
after he had tarried a while to explain the association of 5s and
25s with his hero in stanzas 27 and 28. Soon thereafter, at the
end of stanza 33, the poem reaches its point of greatest
cumulative deficit, 41 lines short of averaging 25 lines per stanza.[13] The next six stanzas (describing Gawain's entrance into
the castle and introduction to its inhabitants) all exceed 25
lines. They have 26, 31, 33, 26, 27, and finally 42 lines, stanza
39 perhaps reflecting a determination to reach the new norm
quickly. After stanza 39 the poem is only 6 lines short of
averaging exactly 25, and the poet was content to leave it that
way for a while; stanzas 40 and 41 have 25 lines each. A little
further adjustment brings the poem, at the end of stanza 45
and the second fitt, to an average of exactly 25 lines per stanza.
In the remaining two fitts the average again varies, but it never
departs as far from the 25-line norm as it did in the first third
of the poem.

It may be of some relevance that, at the midway point (l.
1,125) when the reader and Gawain are so confident in their
misunderstanding, Gawain is undergoing a change in his

name. Until he enters the castle on Christmas eve, Gawain's
name invariably has just 5 letters: *Gauan* (398, 421, 692);
Gawan (109, 339, 365, 375, 377, 381, 387, 390, 405, 416, 448,
487, 495, 534, 633, 666, 811); *Gawen* (463, 476); or *Wawan*
(343, 559).[14] In all there are two dozen 5-letter occurrences
before the first 6-letter *Gawayn* (838). Five-letter spellings
gradually diminish in frequency, and 6-letter spellings increase
over the next 650 lines. From then on, 6 and occasionally 7 letters always occur in the name (except in line 2,479 near the
end). The spelling *Gawayn* is the most frequent of all, occur-
ring more than 40 times but never once until line 838. One
might argue that adding a $y = i = 1$ to the perfect 5 of the
hero's name parallels the course of temptation that gradually
leads him to his downfall, as 1 added to perfection can symbolize transgression. The lady in the bedroom twice questions
his identity, asking if he be *Gawan* (1,293) and then *Wawen*
(1,481): these are the last times that the hero has a 5-letter
name, with the single exception of line 2,479, which might be a
matter of scribal carelessness.[15] It might be said that the lady's
temptations succeed in altering his name a little as well as in
adding a blemish to his formerly spotless character.

   As the number 5 is associated with Gawain, the mention of
the number 4 always occurs in association with the Green
Knight. Its role is not prominent, but it is consistent. The first
4 occurs in line 1,332, in the description of the lord's servants
breaking the deer caught in the first day's hunt: "Then they
cut off the *four* limbs. . . ." Line 1,425 mentions the hounds,
"*forty* at once," who hasten after the boar in the lord's hunting
party on the second day. The guide who brings Gawain to the
Green Chapel warns him that the Green Knight's body is "big-
ger than the best *four* that are in Arthur's house" (2,101-2).
Finally, when the Green Knight appears for the appointment
with Gawain he is carrying a just-sharpened ax whose blade is
"*four* foot long" (2,225). All four 4s are associated with
violence and peril as well as with the Green Knight in his different guises. Since the *Gawain* poet makes a point of announc-
ing the symbolism of his 5s, in the absence of such testimony
about the 4s it would be unwise to claim with certitude that he

intended them to point to a symbolic definition of the Green
Knight, but the traditional associations of 4 with the earth[16]
would accord well with the often-remarked connection of the
Green Knight with the natural world.[17] And it seems appropriate that the number of divisions in the narrative is the
same as the number associated with the character who directs
the course of events.

Sir Gawain and the Green Knight thus provides a clear example of a work in which both number symbolism and
numerical structure are present and important, and in which
the two interact to reinforce their relevance to the story. The
fundamental structure of the poem is in groups of 5 and of 25
lines; the entire poem spans 2,525 lines, with one 5-line unit
left over. The passage on Gawain's pentangularity teaches one
to interpret this structure as a sign of Gawain's presence,
perseverance, and ultimate near-success. As in so many other
matters, in the use of symbolic 5s and 25s the *Gawain* poet is
both explicit and secretive, seeming to make everything plain
and yet hiding part of the way so that the reader necessarily
stumbles and learns with Gawain.

Notes

1. Line 454. Modernizations of the Middle English text are my own. Citations are from Norman Davis's 2d ed. of the J.R.R. Tolkien and E.V. Gordon text *Sir Gawain and the Green Knight* (Oxford, 1967).

2. See, for example, Richard Hamilton Green, "Gawain's Shield and the Quest for Perfection," *English Literary History*, 29 (1962): 121-39; Robert W. Ackerman, "Gawain's Shield: Penitential Doctrine in *Gawain and the Green Knight*," *Anglia* 76 (1958): 254-65.

3. A. C. Spearing, *Criticism and Medieval Poetry*, 2d ed. (New York, 1972), p. 61.

4. Donald R. Howard, "Structure and Symmetry in *Sir Gawain*," *Speculum* 39 1964): 425. Howard's article has been reprinted in several anthologies and summarized in his *The Three Temptations: Medieval Man in Search of the World* (Princeton, N.J., 1966), pp. 245-48.

5. Manuscript evidence and critical analysis support the structural division of the poem into 4 episodes or fitts. Each fitt ends with something accomplished: Fitt 1, the beheading and appointment; fitt 2, Gawain's journey out; fitt 3, the game at the castle; fitt 4, the meeting and return. A few critics have argued that the 5 small capitals mark equally important divisions; see Laurita Lyttleton Hill, "Madden's Divisions of *Sir Gawain* and the 'Large Initial Capitals' of Cotton Nero A.x.," *Speculum* 21 (1946): 67-71. But there is general agreement that the fourfold division is primary. See Howard, "Structure and Symmetry," and A. Kent Hieatt, "*Sir Gawain:* Pentangle, Luf-Lace, Numerical Structure," *Papers on Language and Literature* 4: (1968): 348-49, who concludes a review of the question with the statement that "the case for four main divisions in *Gawain* seems secure" (p. 349).

6. Erzsébet Perényi, "'Sir Gawain and the Green Knight' and the Traditions of Medieval Art," *Annales Universitatis Scientiarum Budapestiensis de Rolando Eötvös nominatae*, Sectio Philologica Moderna 1 (1969-70): 101-7.

7. See n. 5 above. Hieatt's article was reprinted in *Silent Poetry: Essays in Numerological Analysis*, ed. Alastair Fowler (London, 1970), pp. 116-40. Hieatt also observes (1) parallels between stanzas 10, 20, and 21 of fitt 1 and their counterparts in fitt 4; (2) parallels among stanzas 11, 22, and 33 in fitt 3; (3) multiples of 5 plus 1 (calculated in varying ways), symbolizing transgression, in the numbers of stanzas in each fitt; and (4) extensive references to the birth and cross of Christ in stanza 32, immediately preceding stanza 33, which is the traditional number of years of Christ's life on earth. For a reply see Hans Käsmann, "Numerical Structure in Fitt III of *Sir Gawain and the Green Knight*," pp. 131-39 in *Chaucer and Middle English Studies in Honor of Rossell Hope Robbins*, ed. Beryl Rowland (Kent, Ohio, 1974).

8. The dreamer makes a point of naming his source (ll. 983-84; see also 995-96, 1,007-8, 1,019-20, 1,032, 1,033). I cite *Pearl* from the edition of E. V. Gordon (Oxford, 1953). The prominent and intricate metrical structure of *Pearl* has prompted several numerological studies. See P. M. Kean, "Numerical Composition in 'Pearl,'" *Notes & Queries* 210 (1965): 49-51; Dorothee Metlitzki Finkelstein, "The *Pearl*-Poet as Bezalel," *Mediaeval Studies* 35 (1973): 413-32;

and Russell Peck's essay in this collection. For an application of number symbolism to the question of authorship, see Barbara Nolan, "A Signature and an Anagram in Pearl," *Review of English Studies*, n.s. 22 (1971): 297-300. This study receives a sobering analysis in Edward Wilson, "The Anagrams in 'Pearl' and 'St. Erkenwald,'" *Review of English Studies*, n.s. 26 (1975): 133-43.

9. Personal communication.

10. Fol. 91a of the manuscript (reproduced in Davis's edition facing p. 1) contains metrical ll. 1-26, not ll. 1-25, because the scribe writes the short bobs beside preceding long lines, not on manuscript lines of their own. On this first page the bob, l. 15, is written to the right of l. 12. The 25 lines on fol. 91a are thus 25 *visual* lines. Davis, struck by the redundancy and manuscript placement of the bobs, suggests that they might be "an afterthought of the author's" (p. 152). This would not invalidate the argument that the structure of 5s and 25s is deliberate. If one accepts Davis's suggestion, the "afterthought" would pointedly involve working 5s into the structure: making the bob-and-wheel a 5-line unit, making the average stanza length 25 lines, making the echoing last long line the 2,525th. This presumes that the stanzas had originally averaged 24 lines long, twice the stanza length of *Pearl*. It is certainly possible to imagine the author working first with *Pearl*-sized units, then adapting them to reflect a structure of 5s and 25s. Whether intended from the first or added in revision, 5s and 25s are fundamental to the finished poem.

11. In an extended note, Hieatt ("*Sir Gawain*," p. 354) cites a number of other medieval examples of the association of 5 with the Virgin. Since the narrator of *Sir Gawain and the Green Knight* explicitly associates Mary with Gawain's 5s (ll. 646-50), such examples are unquestionably relevant.

    Vincent Foster Hopper, in his important study, finds the poet's Christian symbolism unsuitable. "Unlike the cross, however, the pentacle appears to have been almost exclusively of magical significance. Its appearance on the shield of Gawain is therefore much more in keeping with the magic of the Green Knight than with the Christian and chivalrous connotations assigned to it" (*Medieval Number Symbolism: Its Sources, Meaning and Influence on Thought and Expression*, Columbia University Studies in English and Comparative Literature 132 [New York, 1938], p. 124). But if there is a conflict between the tradition and the words of the poem, one must certainly, for a proper understanding of the poem, choose the narrator's direct statement. See Green, "Gawain's Shield," n. 2, cited above. The Christianizing of a traditional magical symbol would be of a piece with the poet's making Gawain into an exemplar of chastity where tradition has him ingratiatingly amorous. In that connection see B. J. Whiting, "Gawain: His Reputation, His Courtesy and His Appearance in Chaucer's *Squire's Tale*," *Mediaeval Studies* 9 (1947): 189-234.

12. Compare A. C. Spearing's comment (with no reference to 12s) that the dreamer "must learn that he has failed to understand, or at least to *realize*, the divine framework of human existence. . ." (*The Gawain-Poet: A Critical Study* [Cambridge, 1970], p. 29).

13. Thirty-three, as Hieatt has noted (see n. 7), was the traditional number of the years of Christ's life. Stanzas 32-33 contain the poem's "most extensive references to Christ — both to his birth and to his cross" (Hieatt, "Sir Gawain," p. 357), culminating in Gawain's crossing himself three times at the start of stanza 33. To have the greatest shortcoming in average stanza length at this point invites the reader to contrast Gawain's fallibility with Christ's perfection. The quick reduction thereafter of the deficit in stanza length might be a further indication of the efficacy of Gawain's turning to Christ (and Mary) in prayer. Caroline D. Eckhardt and A. Kent Hieatt pointed out this possible connection (personal communication).

14. *Wawan* in l. 343 is an editor's emendation of MS *Gawan*. For convenient listings of the variant spellings, see Coolidge Otis Chapman, *An Index of Names in Pearl, Purity, Patience, and Gawain*, Cornell Studies in English 38 (Ithaca, N.Y., 1951), p. 22; Barnet Kottler and Alan M. Markman, *A Concordance to Five Middle English Poems* (Pittsburgh, Pa., 1966), pp. 218-20. But neither of these sources gives the MS readings where editors have made emendations; for the original MS readings, see Davis's *Gawain*, p. 231.

15. The systematic variation in the spelling of Gawain's name is certainly not the invention of the scribe of Cotton Nero A.x. This scribe carelessly left off an obviously needed *n* on *Gaway*, l. 1,376, and starting in l. 1,179 he gave a simple *G* for the hero's name nine times. Modern editors expand this abbreviation, reasonably enough, to *Gawayn*.

16. See Hopper, *Medieval Number Symbolism*, p. 8, and the Appendix to Russell Peck's essay in this collection. The earth has, traditionally, 4 directions, 4 winds, and, of course, 4 corners.

17. See Larry D. Benson's extended discussion of the Green Knight's origins in *Art and Tradition in Sir Gawain and the Green Knight* (New Brunswick, N.J., 1965), pp. 58-95, esp. p. 93.

The Number of Chaucer's Pilgrims:
A Review and Reappraisal*

Caroline D. Eckhardt

On that April evening when Chaucer the pilgrim stays overnight at the Tabard Inn, there rides in for lodging a group of
travelers: "Wel nyne and twenty in a compaignye" (A.24).[1] But
when Chaucer enumerates them, there are not twenty-nine but
thirty:

1. Knyght	11. Marchant	21. Shipman
2. Squier	12. Clerk	22. Doctour of Phisik
3. Yeman	13. Sergeant of the Lawe	23. Wif of Bathe
4. Prioresse	14. Frankeleyn	24. Persoun
5. Nonne	15. Haberdasshere	25. Plowman
6. Preest 1	16. Carpenter	26. Millere
7. Preest 2	17. Webbe	27. Maunciple
8. Preest 3	18. Dyere	28. Reve
9. Monk	19. Tapycer	29. Somonour
10. Frere	20. Cook	30. Pardoner

This discrepancy has been many times noted, but, I think, less
explained than explained away. Discussions may be grouped
into three viewpoints: that the "nyne and twenty" of A.24 is
simply an error on a scribe's or Chaucer's part, that A.24 is correct and there are in fact the right number of pilgrims if one
understands the text differently, and that A.24 was once cor-

*This essay first appeared in *Yearbook of English Studies* 5 (1975): 1-18; permission
to reprint has been granted.

rect but now does not appear so because someone else increas-
ed the number of pilgrims in Chaucer's text of the General Prologue. I would like to review these interpretations, all of which
finally render the question insignificant, and suggest one more,
which proposes that the discrepancy between the announced
and the actual number of pilgrims is real, was intentional, and
has symbolic and ironic functions.

The "Nyne and Twenty" of A.24 Is an Error, a Scribe's or Chaucer's

It is not likely that "nyne and twenty" is simply a scribal error. All manuscripts containing this part of the text supply that
number.[2] To regard "nyne and twenty" as a scribe's replacement for Chaucer's "thirty" (the number of pilgrims actually
identified in the General Prologue) causes metrical problems
since difference numbers of syllables are involved. One would
have to assume that Chaucer wrote something like "And they
were thirty in a compaignye," but that the scribe responsible
for the line as it now stands had before him only a fragmentary
line ". . . -ty in a compaignye," and filed it in as "Wel nyne
and twenty." It becomes necessary to assume also that the
scribe was particularly unintelligent or careless, for having
decided to complete the line by specifying the number of
pilgrims, he did not do what elementary good sense would indicate, to count them: if he had, he would have found thirty.
(Arguments that Chaucer's version of the General Prologue did
not contain all thirty pilgrims are discussed below.)

To regard "nyne and twenty" as a scribe's error not for "thirty" but for a number less metrically awkward, specifically
"eighte and twenty," one would have to accept the theory
(discussed below) that two of the present thirty pilgrims are not
Chaucer's, and assume a multiple tampering with the text: the
replacement of Chaucer's correct "eighte" by the incorrect
"nyne" at A.24, and the addition of two pilgrims by an editor
(or one each by two editors) who did not bother to adjust A.24
to agree with the new total thus created.

If "nyne and twenty" is regarded instead as Chaucer's own

error, an oversight that he would have corrected in a final version, the manuscripts' unanimity on that number causes no difficulty, but one does require an explanation of how Chaucer happened to say that there were twenty-nine pilgrims and then enumerate thirty. Such an explanation is provided by Carleton Brown's proposal that one of the thirty pilgrims, specifically the Squire, must have been a later addition on Chaucer's part since the Squire's campaigns do not overlap with those of his father, and since the lines A.101-2 ("A Yeman hadde he and servantz namo / At that tyme, for hym liste ride so"), which follow the Squire's portrait, seem to refer in their pronouns "he" and "hym" to the Knight, whose portrait has preceded.[3] But this couplet's position does not really demonstrate that the Squire is a belated addition. The interrupted sequence (Knight-Squire-Knight-Yeoman) may be one more instance of the apparently inconsequential process of the Narrator, who records details as he seems to observe them rather than in a strictly methodical manner. Thus he may cover the same ground more than once, at intervals, as his attention returns to it (he mentions the Monk's horse or horses at A.168, again at A.203, again at A.207); he may drop in an isolated statement with no very clear connection to what has preceded (of the Doctor, "His studie was but litel on the Bible" [A.438], with "Bible" rhymed incongruously with "digestible" [A.437]); he may begin some portraits with the exterior description and move inward, some the reverse.[4] That the Narrator presents the Knight, moves on to the rather showy Squire, and then returns to the Knight for a final brief observation, is not strong evidence that the Squire did not originally belong in the General Prologue. A natural transition is in fact provided by "fader" (A.100), which also serves as a grammatical antecedent for "he" and "hym" in the next line.

As for the fact that the Squire's campaigns do not coincide with his father's, there is no reason why they should. The Squire is a generation younger, and a knight's son might well be attached to the military entourage of someone other than his father. The different campaigns assigned to father and son help distinguish their characters, for the Knight has fought extensively in wars against the heathens, while the Squire has fought only in a brief expedition against the French.[5] Chaucer implies that the Knight gives the impression of being occupied with distant and holy war, the Squire with more local and profane, and this contrast of course corroborates other factors in their characterizations.

There is thus no adequate reason to regard the Squire as a late addition to the General Prologue, or to see in him the solution to the discrepancy between twenty-nine and thirty.

Alternatively, A. C. Baugh has proposed that both an oversight on Chaucer's part and his own correction of it are involved. This interpretation assumes that two pilgrims are non-Chaucerian additions, so that Chaucer, having indicated at A.24 that the Narrator saw twenty-nine travelers but having actually presented only twenty-eight, found himself at the completion of the General Prologue one pilgrim short. Noticing this, Baugh conjectures, Chaucer supplied the missing pilgrim in fragment G, in the person of the Canon's Yeoman.[6] One difficulty with this argument is that, in addition to relying upon the theory that the text now includes two spurious pilgrims, it does not really explain the discrepancy within the General Prologue. It in no way corrects the Narrator's count at A.24 to add another pilgrim much later. If one grants that the Narrator can count only the people he sees, one must admit that he makes a mistake. Furthermore, the sequence of events in the *Canterbury Tales* (plot) is not necessarily the same as the sequence of Chaucer's intentions (plan). As Kittredge long ago pointed out, the fact that the Canon's Yeoman joins the group belatedly does not mean that Chaucer created him belatedly: Chaucer might well have planned from the first to surprise the pilgrims — and his audience — by adding a final storyteller along the way.[7]

There is no strong reason, then, for regarding the "nyne and twenty" of all relevant manuscripts as an error, either Chaucer's or a scribe's. One can suggest that a well-attested reading is mistaken nevertheless, but this ought to be a last resort.

The Reading of A.24 Is Correct, and Accords with the
Actual Number of Pilgrims in the General Prologue

Let me suppose, now, that the text presents as many
pilgrims as it claims to; rather than emend it, one needs only to
understand it differently. The Narrator describes twenty-two
pilgrims one by one, but the other eight in the tabulation come
from two plural groups: three Priests, and five Gildsmen. It is
conceivable that the number of people in one of these groups
has been misread.

W. P. Lehmann has suggested that in A.163-64, "Another
Nonne with hire hadde she, / That was hir chapeleyne, and
preestes thre," there is a cumulative numeral at the end of a
series; what Chaucer means is that the Prioress, her Nun-
chaplain, and one Priest add up to three.[8] A passage in the
Friar's tale, D.1543-54, is cited as proof that Chaucer knew this
syntactic pattern. D.1554 reads "Bothe hey and cart, and eek
his caples thre," on which Lehmann (p. 321) comments: "The
context leaves no doubt that there were but two horses
. . .We must conclude that Chaucer counted the loaded cart
as one item, the horses ["caples"] as two, and added them." If
this were so, one would indeed have precedent for adding up
the Prioress, the Nun, and one Priest to total three, but, as I
have shown elsewhere, in the Friar's tale there are clearly three
horses, not two, so that the phrase "caples thre" of D.1554 is a
quite normal construction, meaning simply "three
cart-horses," and provides no evidence for Chaucer's
knowledge of an "additive construction."[9]

Lehmann's theory has been sharply criticized by Leo Spitzer
(on the grounds that Lehmann misinterpreted the medieval
French materials cited to show a similar cumulative numeral),
but Spitzer himself suggests that A.164 might indicate the
presence of only one Priest, with "preestes" to be understood as
a genitive singular: "preestes thre" would mean "the priest's
three"; that is, the total of three that is represented by, achieved by, the Priest when he is added to the Prioress and the Nun-
chaplain.[10] As evidence for such a construction, Spitzer cites no
English examples closer than "shank's mare"; that is, the horse

formed by one's legs. This is a metaphoric expression, however, not a normal method of counting, and there is no evidence that a "genitive of shape and arrangement" was normally used for counting in Chaucer's language and would have been recognized as such by his audience. In the absence of such evidence, one must prefer Chaucer's standard usage to the rather distant partial parallels Spitzer offers, and to Lehmann's perhaps nonexistent "additive construction."

One more proposed misreading relates to the "preestes thre": O. F. Emerson has suggested that one is meant to understand the Monk and the Friar as two of the "preestes thre," so that one church group is formed by the Prioress, the Nun-chaplain, and the three Priests who are the Nun's Priest, the Monk, and the Friar.[11] This attractive idea seems to explain why one never again hears of the other two Priests. One does hear of them, if they are the Monk and the Friar, each of whom has a tale and participates in the end-links as well. However, the text itself does not support this theory. Nowhere does Chaucer call a monk or a friar a "priest."[12] While monks and friars might perhaps be considered "priests" in the widest sense of that term, as Emerson indicates, they were quite distinct from (secular) priests in the ways they spent their lives, the places they occupied in ecclesiastical organization and secular society, and even in their appearance. A medieval observer could know from a cleric's costume whether he were priest, monk, or friar, and often to which specific order he belonged. The Narrator recognizes the Canon as such by his garments (G.557-73). This is not the place to review the functions of the various kinds of regular and secular clergy (and the antagonisms among them), but such distinctions were important in Chaucer's time, and he shows his awareness of them. The rivalry between the "possessioners" and the mendicants, for example, is reflected in the Summoner's portrait of a friar discouraging people from giving to "possessioners, that mowen lyve / . . . in wele and habundaunce" (D. 1722).

Furthermore, Chaucer's standard formula of "*Ther was*"[13] for the introduction of new pilgrims in the General Prologue argues against Emerson's reading.

A Kniyght *ther was* . . .	(A.43)
. . . *ther was* . . . a yong Squier	(A.79)
Ther was also a Nonne, a Prioresse	(A.118)
A Marchant *was ther* . . .	(A.270)
A Clerk *ther was* . . .	(A.285)
A Sergeant of the Lawe . . . *Ther was*	(A.309)
A Shipman *was ther* . . .	(A.388)
. . . *ther was* a Doctour of Phisik	(A.411)
A good Wif *was ther* . . .	(A.445)
A good man *was ther* of religioun	(A.477)
. . . *ther was* a Plowman . . .	(A.529)
Ther was also a Reve, and a Millere,	
A Sumnour, and a Pardoner also,	
A Maunciple, and myself—*ther were* namo.	(A.542)
A Gentil Maunciple *was ther* . . .	(A.567)
A Sumnour *was ther* . . .	(A.623)

Compare

A Frankeleyn *was* in his compaignye	(A.311)
. . . *Ther rood* a gentil Pardoner.	(A.669)

The fact that the portraits of the Monk and the Friar both begin with this introductory formula "*ther was*" ("A Monk *ther was* . . ." [A.165]; "A Frere *ther was* . . ." [A.208]) suggests that they too describe new pilgrims. The only exceptions to this pattern occur at A.567 and A.623, where the Manciple and the Summoner, who have been enumerated before as members of a group, reappear with the introductory "*ther was*"—a situation exactly parallel to the one Emerson is proposing for the Monk and the Friar. But here Chaucer is careful to prevent confusion by having individually identified the people in the group as soon as the group appeared (A.542-24), and by having said at that point that "*ther were namo*," in other words that all further portraits would correspond to pilgrims already listed.

Since it is unlikely that Chaucer would have categorized his Monk and Friar as "priests," then, and since he introduces each of their portraits with the formula *"ther was,"* which, in the General Prologue, is virtually a signal for the presentation of a new pilgrim, one should continue to regard the Monk and the Friar as distinct from the "preestes thre" of A.164.

One final argument against reading A.124 as adding only a single new pilgrim, one Nun's Priest, is that nothing is gained by doing so. Despite the repeated statements that counting only one Priest here will provide the announced number of pilgrims,[14] this is not true. The Narrator has said that he sees twenty-nine; to take "preestes thre" as adding one Priest would make the total twenty-eight, so that the Narrator himself must be counted in the group to arrive at the proper twenty-nine. However, it is quite clear from the General Prologue that the Narrator is not one of the "nyne and twenty in a compaignye":

Bifel that in that seson on a day,
In Southwerk at the Tabard as I lay
Redy to wenden on my pilgrymage
To Caunterbury with ful devout corage,
At nyght was come into that hostelrye
Wel nyne and twenty in a compaignye
Of sondry folk, by aventure yfalle
In felaweshipe, and pilgrimes were they alle,
That toward Caunterbury wolden ryde.

(A.19)

In this passage, the Narrator explains (among other things) that he is staying at the Tabard Inn and has arranged overnight lodging there. Then, at the end of the day, there arrive twenty-nine pilgrims in a group. That he regards himself as distinct from the "compaignye of sondry folk" is perfectly clear not only from the reported sequence of events (his arrival, then theirs), but also from the pronoun "they": "pilgrimes were they alle" (A.26). One does not use "they" to refer to a category that includes oneself.[15] (The suggestion of Emerson, "Some Notes on Chaucer," p. 93, that one simply understand "they" as if it were virtually "we" here shows a cavalier disregard for the text.) The point in the General Prologue at which the Narrator joins the group is in fact made explicit: "And shortly, whan the sonne was to reste, / So hadde I spoken with hem everichon / That I was of hir felaweshipe anon" (A.30). Had he originally been one of their fellowship, this remark, explaining that after brief acquaintance he joins them, would be nonsensical. Reading the three Priests as one, then, leaves not the right number but one too few, since the Narrator cannot be included among the "nyne and twenty."

Let me examine the other location at which Chaucer presents pilgrims as a group — the Gildsmen:

An Haberdasshere and a Carpenter,
A Webbe, a Dyere, and a Tapycer.
>   (A.361)

The standard reading of these lines has always been that five people are meant. It is conceivable, however, that there are only four, which would make the number of pilgrims precisely the announced twenty-nine. Grammatically, any two adjacent titles could apply to one person. With varying punctuation, one might read

An Haberdasshere (and a Carpenter),
A Webbe, a Dyere, and a Tapycer

or

An Haberdasshere, and a Carpenter
(A Webbe), a Dyere, and a Tapycer

or

An Haberdasshere, and a Carpenter,
A Webbe (a Dyere), and a Tapycer

or, finally,

An Haberdasshere, and a Carpenter,
A Webbe, a Dyere (and a Tapycer).

Although such readings are possible, they would be defensible
only if external evidence showed that one of these combinations was normally regarded as one occupation in Chaucer's
time. On the contrary, each of the five trades represented had
a separate craft gild in fourteenth-century London; slightly
later, the Brewers' "List of the Crafts of London in 1422"
records no such combinations and in fact suggests further
specialization, for example, in dividing the Weavers into
Weavers of Wool and Weavers of Linen.[16] It is not legitimate
to assert, on the basis of one manuscript variant that deletes
the "a" between "webbe" and "dyer" and so reads "A webbe
dyer," that "there is an occupation that may be referred to as
that of a 'webbe dyer.' "[17] One variant does not an occupation
make. One should remember that Chaucer's Gildsmen are pros-
perous and important people, very conscious of their "image."
Surely each belongs to the gild of his craft as well as to the
parish gild whose livery he is now wearing. Since the craft gild
movement attempted to protect the trades against each other
(as well as against other interests), the argument that one of the
Gildsmen, each "shaply for to been an alderman" (A.372),
represents two of these well-known and separately organized
trades at once, is quite unlikely. And likelihood is important
here, for poetry intended at least partially for oral delivery and
lacking the guidance of modern written punctuation would
have been understood in the most likely, the most self-evident
way. Knowing that the five crafts mentioned were represented
by five distinct and rather powerful London organizations,
Chaucer's audience would naturally have assumed that five
Gildsmen were meant. Therefore the modern reader should do
the same.

One more proposal belongs in this category of possible
misunderstandings of the text: the suggestion that by the expression "Wel nyne and twenty" Chaucer meant to imply
merely a general estimate, so that one might render the phrase

"about twenty-nine" or "some twenty-nine" or even "at least twenty-nine."[18] The function of "wel," in this interpretation, would be to indicate imprecision, to supply the qualifier "approximately," and if this were the case, the discrepancy between twenty-nine and thirty would be permitted by the phrasing of the initial assessment, and therefore negligible. But the objections to this cutting of the Gordian knot are major. The first is logical: one estimates whole entities in round numbers. It would make sense to say "approximately thirty people," but "approximately twenty-nine people" is almost fatuous. The second objection is lexical—and stronger, since there is always a chance that Chaucer intended to make the Narrator say something fatuous. "Wel" does not seem to have meant "approximately." The *OED* does not include this meaning, but does offer precisely its opposite: "clearly, definitely, without any doubt or uncertainty" (14). Here one is interested specifically in what "wel" means when it qualifies a number. For this function *OED* gives "with numerals, or terms of measurement, denoting fulness of the number, distance, etc.," and an example from Mandeville, "Wel a .iiij. quarteres of a furlong ore more" (17). Although in this example as in others the exact force of "wel" may be debated, it evidently indicates "as much as, as many as" but *not* "as much as . . .or more," since "ore more" is supplied also. The selected list of Chaucer's uses of "wel" given in the Tatlock-Kennedy concordance includes several examples of the word qualifying a number:

Hire maistresse clepeth wommen a greete route,
And up they rysen, wel a ten or twelve.
(F.383)

And every tree stood by hymselve
Fro other wel ten foot or twelve.
(The Boke of the Duchess, l. 419)

And wel an hondred tymes gan he syke.
(Troilus and Criseyde, 3. 1,360)

In each case "wel" modifies a number considered large by the

speaker, but does not include the vaguer meaning "that many
or even somewhat more" since where a greater number is intended, it is explicitly supplied. A proper translation for "wel"
in this function would be "even as many as," or, as it is usually
glossed, "fully," with the connotation not of imprecision but of
slight surprise or admiration that the number should be this
large. "Wel nyne and twenty in a compaignye" means, then,
that the Narrator has counted twenty-nine pilgrims in the
group and is reporting both that fact and his somewhat surpris-
ed response at the size of this company. His surprise — which is
perfectly appropriate, since the pilgrimage group is large indeed[19] — is echoed later, where the Narrator says "and
pilgrimes were they alle," with the rhyme-word "alle" emphasized by its position (A.26), and again where he assures us
that "The chambres and the stables weren wyde, / And wel
we weren esed atte beste" (A.28), as if this large a group could
have been accommodated only uncomfortably if the bedrooms
and stables had not been spacious.

Each of these suggestions that one can resolve the apparent
discrepancy by a different understanding of the text is thus to
be rejected: the phrase "preestes thre" does not mean that only
one Priest accompanies the Prioress, or that two of those three
are the Monk and the Friar (and adding only one pilgrim for
that phrase does not give the right number anyway); there are
not four Gildsmen, but five; "wel nyne and twenty" does not
mean "approximately twenty-nine." I return in each case to
the standard interpretation of the text, and therefore to the
fact that the discrepancy between the number of pilgrims announced as arriving "in a compaignye" and the number actually presented in the General Prologue is real.

Not All of the Pilgrims in the General Prologue Are Chaucer's

A number of critics have proposed that one or more of the
pilgrims whom the text now enumerates, and who are counted
in my total of thirty, were added to Chaucer's version of the

General Prologue by another hand. It has been several times suggested that the couplet A.163—64 is spurious, or that Chaucer left A.164 incomplete and someone else, needing a line to follow "Another Nonne with hire hadde she" (A.163), supplied "That was hir chapeleyne, and preestes thre," or at least "and preestes thre" at the end of this line, and so created two more Priests than Chaucer meant to include.[20]

It should be said at once that "and preestes thre" appears in every known manuscript containing this part of the *Canterbury Tales*; A.164 is one of only nine lines in the General Prologue that have no variants (Manly and Rickert, *The Text of the Canterbury Tales*, 5:3-79, my count). The reasons offered for excluding this phrase nevertheless have been the following: a prioress would not plausibly travel with so many priests; Chaucer does not otherwise include more than one pilgrim of any social category; reducing the three priests to one would make the number of pilgrims twenty-nine; and, finally, only one Priest (the one who tells the Nun's Priest's Tale) is ever referred to again. Together these arguments seem formidable, but the first three are demonstrably wrong, and even the last is questionable.

That most prioresses did not travel with so large an entourage as one nun-chaplain and three priests may be true, but it is known that some of Madame Eglentyne's sisters did journey about with what was regarded as an excessive (and excessively expensive) following.[21] Madame Eglentyne was probably the head of a rather large convent capable of supplying her with multiple attendants. It has repeatedly been said that there is no record of more than one priest associated with the convent of St. Leonard's at Stratford-atte-Bowe, to which the Prioress apparently belongs; or that St. Leonard's, which at its founding and in the reign of Henry VIII held only ten nuns, always remained small and would not have needed multiple priests.[22] A papal letter of indulgence of 1354, however, refers to the "thirty nuns of Stratford atte Bowe."[23] The date is particularly important since the membership of many houses had been sharply reduced by the Black Death a few years earlier,[24] so that perhaps before the plague St. Leonard's had been fuller yet.

But even if the thirty nuns of 1354 represent the maximum, it is clear that in Chaucer's time this was not a small foundation. It is not known exactly how many priests were associated with the convent during this period, but at various times the house made appointments to five churches in addition to the parish church of Bromley, which itself may have had more than one priest, and to the Chapel of St. Mary, built within the cloister shortly before 1350.[25] The reference in Elizabeth of Hainault's will to one Geoffrey de Neunton as *capell paroch,* "parish chaplain," need not mean that he was the only priest in the parish, or the only priest associated with the convent of St. Leonard's.[26]

As for the argument that the Prioress ought not to have so many people accompanying her, if one were to hold her strictly to what she ought to have done, one would have to remove her from the *Canterbury Tales* altogether, for nuns were not supposed to go on pilgrimages.[27] In many other ways Madame Eglentyne conducts herself with a magnificent disregard of the rules—one has only to recall the pet dogs she should not have, or the fashionable high forehead that should not be bare for the Narrator to admire. The final touch to this portrait of femininity quietly rebelling against the conventual "thou shalt not's" is that she likes to surround herself with more male companions than she should.[28] They are, of course, priests, and this charming lady who elicits courtesies from even Harry Bailly harbors no intentions productive of fabliau plots in her "tendre herte," but to say that her riding along with three priests is "absurd"[29] is to be guided by an ideal of what a nun should be, and to ignore the reality of what Chaucer says Madame Eglentyne, Prioress of a substantial convent, actually was. The argument from plausibility is really all on her side.[30]

The viewpoint that Chaucer's principle of construction permitted only one representative of each social category fails to consider the presence of two Yeomen on the pilgrimage (one serving the Knight, the other the Canon), and of two clergymen called Priests even if one regards the Prioress as accompanied by only one (the Parson is the other, I.22). There are also two pilgrims introduced as Nuns, although subsequently differentiated: "Ther was also a Nonne" (A.118), and "Another Nonne with hire hadde she" (A.163). There is no reason to assume that Chaucer would not have individualized the Prioress's three Priests had he completed the work. The predominating principle in the General Prologue is certainly extension — the representation of many different social groups by one pilgrim each — but too rigorous and mechanical an application of this principle would be unlike Chaucer, who is bound by no rules, not even those of his own making.

The claim that reducing the three Priests to one yields the right number has been dealt with above.

The only remaining reason for discarding "preestes thre" is that Chaucer elsewhere writes as if only one Nun's Priest were present: at B.3999 the Host addresses "the Nonnes Preest," while if more than one were there, presumably he would address *one* of the Nun's Priests. This is the strongest argument against supposing, with A.164, that the Prioress has three Priests with her. However, A.164 does not say that there are three Nun's Priests, but only that there are three Priests traveling with the Nun. One of these may be her confessor (the Nun's Priest in a narrow sense), while the others may be two Priests not normally assigned to duties specifically at the nunnery, and therefore not necessarily called "Nun's Priests," although they are accompanying the Nuns now.

Furthermore, there may indeed be one reference in the *Canterbury Tales* to the second and third Priests. At C.371 the Pardoner, detailing his disreputable devices, claims that well water into which a certain sheep's bone has been dipped will cure the jealousy of a cuckold even if there is proof that his wife has "taken prestes two or thre." This little jibe gains point if one pictures the Prioress riding along with her three Priests, and if one remembers that nuns were at times accused and convicted of improper relations with the priests associated with them; the priest who served as chaplain to a nunnery was an object of some suspicion.[31] The Host calls attention to the evident virility of the Priest who tells the Tale of Chanticler (B.4645-9), and the Pardoner, acquainted both professionally and personally with sinful tendencies, sees an opportunity here to discomfit not only priests, whom he has already attacked once (C.339), but also nuns. Remarking, but not charmed by, the Prioress's femininity, he may refer to the woman who has "taken prestes two or thre" with the Prioress, her three male companions, and the scandals about nuns and priests, in mind.

None of the reasons for rejecting the phrase "and preestes thre" is adequate to justify exclusion of a reading attested by all manuscripts. It is not necessary, in terms of plausibility, to reduce the number of Priests traveling with the Prioress from three to one; it is not accurate to say that a one-of-each-category principle is strictly applied to the pilgrims; it is not true that reducing the Priests to one yields the right number, twenty-nine; it is questionable that only one Priest is referred to again since the Pardoner's insult at C.371 may be aimed at the Prioress's three Priests. One responds most legitimately to the text if one accepts what it says, then, rather than ignoring or emending "and preestes thre."

Another pilgrim whose authenticity has been questioned is the Second Nun, who appears only in two lines at the close of the Prioress's portrait: "Another Nonne with hire hadde she, / That was hir chapeleyne" (A.163). Norman E. Eliason has proposed that the Second Nun is a non-Chaucerian addition owing her existence to an ambiguity in the rubric for the Tale of St. Cecilia. This rubric originally read, he conjectures, "The Second Nun's Tale," a phrase by which Chaucer meant "the second tale of the Nun," that is, of the Prioress, but which an early editor interpreted as "the tale of the Second Nun." Since there was then no second nun, according to Eliason, the editor added A.163 − 64 to create the pilgrim required by his misunderstanding of the rubric. The number of pilgrims in Chaucer's own General Prologue would have been twenty-nine.[32]

The difficulties with this ingenious theory are multiple. The first is, again, the absolute manuscript authority of at least the second line of the couplet A.163 − 64. Second, if the couplet is discarded as spurious, there remains no reference in the General Prologue to the pilgrim who tells the Nun's Priest's Tale and responds to Harry Bailly's remarks at B.4,000. Third, one should hesitate to make the Prioress go traveling without a female companion. Madame Eglentyne breaks many rules, but desires always to appear both attractive and decorous — to invite and to discourage male attention, to affirm and to deny her sexuality — and this parallel between the limitations of her worldliness and the limitations of her holiness would be destroyed if she were seen as journeying without one of her sisters. The point is not simply that regulations required a prioress to take along another member of her convent if she had to travel,[33] but that the essential ambivalence of the Prioress's characterization is lost if one deletes her "chapeleyne." She becomes a woman conspicuously lacking the female companion she should have had, a woman available. The Prioress's faults are more subtle ones.

Finally, and most decisively, the rubrics for the Tale of St. Cecilia do not really give evidence of ambiguity. Eliason divides the rubrics, English and Latin, into three types: those which clearly designate a "Second Nun" (twenty-four manuscripts), those which call the tale "the Second Nun's Tale" or its equivalent (thirteen manuscripts), and those which designate simply "the Nun" (thirteen manuscripts).[34] Actually, since nine manuscripts of the third category attribute the Prioress's tale uniformly to the "Prioress," never to the "Nun," their scribes clearly distinguished between these two pilgrims, and the number of manuscripts whose rubrics unarguably assume the presence of the Second Nun is therefore thirty-three. But the important question is whether the rubrics of the type "Second Nun's Tale" are actually ambiguous. Two facts suggest not: first, Eliason's failure to demonstrate that Chaucer ever used the construction *ordinal plus genitive plus noun* with the ordinal modifying the noun, the usage required for "the Second Nun's Tale" to mean "the second tale of the Nun";[35] second, the presence in certain manuscripts classified in the first type of a number of significant pairs:

> the prologe of the Seconde Nonne
> the Seconde Nonnes tale (En²; cf. Gl, Ha², Lc, Mg, Pw, Ph³)

the Second Nonnes tale
Here endeth the Seconde Nonne hir tale (Ha⁴)

In each of these manuscripts the construction allegedly ambiguous is paired with a version in which no ambiguity is possible, and in every case the meaning is the same: "the Second
Nun's Tale," which follows upon "the prologue of the Second
Nun" or is followed by the statement that the "Second Nun"
has ended her tale, is obviously understood by the scribes as
meaning "the tale of the Second Nun."

Surely if the phrase "Second Nun's Tale" were ambiguous,
so that the meaning "second tale of the Nun" were plausible,
indeed the correct and original meaning, as Eliason thinks, one
would find this rendering somewhere among the quite various
manuscript rubrics.   Its complete absence suggests that
Chaucer's contemporaries did not understand the phrase in
that way; the pairs cited above show that they did regard the
phrase as altogether consistent with the presence of a second
nun.

All of these factors support the traditional attribution of St.
Cecilia's Tale to a second nun, the Nun-chaplain of A.163-64,
who should continue to be accepted as a genuinely Chaucerian
character.

Where does this leave us? In every case, with the text of the
General Prologue as we have received it, and usually as it has
normally been understood. To recapitulate: there is no warrant for regarding the "nyne and twenty" of A.24 as either a
scribe's or Chaucer's error; there is no justification for reading
the stated number of Priests as other than three, of Gildsmen
as other than five, or of pilgrims as other than exactly twenty-
nine; there is no adequate reason for rejecting either two of the
Priests or the Second Nun as non-Chaucerian additions. In
every case, one can simply accept what is there, which is surely
preferable to emendation, deletion, or unusual interpretation.
Therefore, one must also accept the fact that when the Narrator reports the arrival of twenty-nine pilgrims, he makes a

mistake, for the group actually consists of thirty.
To these thirty are added a few more as the pilgrimage company continues the process of accumulation that is nearly, but
not quite, complete when the General Prologue opens. The
thirty-first pilgrim is the Narrator, who joins at A.32; the
thirty-second is the Host, who offers to join at A.803-4 and is
welcomed at A.810-18. There will be two more: the thirty-
third pilgrim, an apostate,[36] joins and defects between G.583
and G.702; the thirty-fourth, who arrives with him, remains.
The net number of pilgrims who travel to Canterbury is 33 — a
number that has inescapable symbolic significance.

In medieval literature, any number is a potential
metaphor.[37] This literary fact derives from the scientific and
religious assumption that God created the universe in
mathematical terms, assigning to its shape, structure, motion,
parts, creatures, and history such numbers as expressed His
divine intention: "thou hast ordered all things in number and
measure and weight" (Wisdom 11.20). The concept of
mathematics as a means of comprehending the universal
design antedates Christianity, which accepted, with modifica-
tions, a basically Pythagorean system of access to the particular
meanings that individual numbers were assumed to contain.
Medieval commentators developed a fairly consistent set of interpretations for the primary numbers 1-12; numbers beyond
12 could easily be analyzed also, by such techniques as adding
up their component integers, and many acquired specific symbolic values from their use in Scripture. In literature such
numbers, far from serving only as rhetorical decorations, could
be used to express a poet's most serious intentions. When
Dante identifies the Beatrice of the *Vita Nuova* with the
number 9, he is evoking the conventional significance of 9 as a
holy number representing a miracle, a demonstration of divine
perfection; for the *Commedia* he devises an intricate
mathematical structure whose most obvious factors are the
division of the whole into one hundred cantos (100, like 10, is a
perfect number) presented in 3 parts (3 is the number of the
Trinity).[38]

That Chaucer participates in this medieval tradition, and

that the numbers central to the design of the *Canterbury Tales* may have a symbolic function, has been pointed out several times before. The usual interpretations are that Chaucer assembles an initial company of 29, a number indicating imperfection, or alternatively the approach toward perfection; that this group becomes, with the addition of the Narrator, 30, indicating "the active life and the married state"; and that these 30 pilgrims are to tell 4 tales each in order to produce 120 tales in all, a "long hundred," a number representative of religious perfection.[39]

But the initial company does not in fact number 29, the total company exceeds 30, and one does not really know that Chaucer ever planned for each pilgrim to tell 4 tales. That is Harry Bailly's plan. It is in his voice that the audience hears of it, and his voice is not the same as that of Chaucer. There is no need here for a general discussion of Chaucerian irony, but one reference to the author's ironic distance from his characters may be made: the most familiar case pertains to the Narrator himself, who is, and is not, the voice of the author.[40] The Host is a fictional character in exactly this sense also, and Chaucer sometimes pokes fun at him, makes him show ignorance or insensitivity, and, most important for this purpose, has the course of events demonstrate that the Host is not really the successful manager of men ("gyde" [A.804]; "governour" [A.813]) he would like to be. He makes plans, but things do not turn out precisely that way. At A.3118 he calls on the Monk but is unable to prevent the Miller from intruding, he is afraid of his wife — and so forth.[41] The characterization of the Host is a study in comic diminution, the reduction of the self-pronounced authority figure whose pretensions, even in the General Prologue, are slyly mocked by the rooster comparison:

Up roos oure Hoost, and was oure aller cok,
And gadrede us togidre alle in a flok,
                                        (A.823)

which makes him an antecedent colleague of Chanticler the mock hero. It is one more aspect of the Host's diminution that

his original grand plan for each pilgrim to tell four tales has
shrunk by at least half in the Prologue to the Parson's tale
(I.16,25). Chaucer uses the Host to suggest, among other
things, the overambitious designer of literary projects, the
would-be artistic creator who establishes a pattern that external circumstances and his own deficiencies somehow prevent
him from fulfilling. Surely Chaucer, who some ten times em-
barked upon a writing project that (to our knowledge) he did
not complete, enjoyed making this small joke at himself and at
others like him.

We do not know, then, how many tales Chaucer planned to
write. We do know that when Harry Bailly says "ech of
you . . . / . . . shall telle tales tweye / To Caunterbury-
ward . . . / And homeward he shal tellen othere two"
(A.791), he has before him a group of thirty-one pilgrims.
Since he does not know that the Canon's Yeoman will join them
later, he must be understood as proposing a total of 124 tales.
By implication, the Host is playing God, is planning to direct
an entire Creation, since the sum of the integers of 124 is seven,
the number of universality or of Creation itself.[42]

What we know of Chaucer's own intentions is that the company of travelers consists, finally, of thirty-three. Chaucer uses
this number both structurally and symbolically. Edmund Reiss
has pointed out that some modern critics, in their interest in
Zahlenkomposition (structuring a literary work according to
arithmetic principles), have concentrated on the purely formal
value of such structure, discussing the total number of lines or
other units, the proportion of this total devoted to different
parts, the recurrence of individual structural numbers or sequences of numbers, and so on. This kind of study can il-
luminate basic matters of literary form, but, as Reiss shows, is
unlikely to be sufficient for the medieval period, where
numbers traditionally have symbolic function as well: for example, the perception that a lyric is constructed in terms of 5s
helps make its form apparent, but the structural use of this
number makes full sense only when considered along with the
symbolic value of 5, which is the number associated with the
Virgin, the "mayden" about whom the poet sings.[43]

Structurally, Chaucer's 33 implies 33 divisions for the (completed) *Canterbury Tales,* one part or performance for the Knight, one for the Squire, and so forth, including one for the Narrator.[44] (Whether each pilgrim's "part" consists of one or of several narratives does not matter here.) An indebtedness to Dante's triple use of 33 divisions is possible; like Dante's cantos, Chaucer's parts are of variable length. What proportional relationships were intended among these parts is not known, since the work is not complete, but it might be pointed out that the Miller and the Reeve together do not suffice, numerically, to balance the Knight, but the Parson does; the weightiest parts of the *Canterbury Tales* are the Knight's, the Parson's, and that of Chaucer the pilgrim, who in some ways represents Everyman, and this might suggest that by these three kinds of strength the rest of Chaucer's fictional world is supported. It is surely significant that, within the Narrator's frame, the last part in many ways balances the first — the Knight is the company's secular model, the Parson its religious — but in view of the uncertain ordering of the fragments in between, it is unwise to speculate much further on Chaucer's possible use of numbers in structural patterning, although it would be of great interest to know whether, following Dante, he perhaps meant to place particular significance on the numerical center of the work.[45] In terms of length, specifying the numerical center would be difficult in view of the prose passages. In terms of the 33 performances rather than length, the numerical center would belong to the seventeenth pilgrim, who in Robinson's sequence is Chaucer himself if one begins the count with the Knight (Chaucer's continuing performance as Narrator cannot be assigned one location in the sequence) and includes the Cook. It is curious to note that at the center of the *Commedia* Dante located what Singleton sees as a "conversion, a great turning about," and that in the central performance of Chaucer the pilgrim the foolishness of "Sir Thopas" is set aside in favor of the moral earnestness of "Melibee," as if in preparation for the culminating earnestness of the company's mood at the end. But it is not really known where the center was to lie.

Apart from whatever structural patterns Chaucer would

have developed among his 33 parts, the symbolic value of the number functions to reinforce the religious aspect of the work. Thirty-three is a holy number, according to medieval systems of numerical analysis, because it is composed of two 3s, because the sum of its integers is 6 (the number of earthly perfection), and because it may be analysed as 30 (fulfilment) plus 3 (the Trinity). But its primary symbolic value is as a reflection of the life of Christ, who is said to have died without completing his thirty-fourth year. This detail, not in Scripture itself, was inferred by early commentators on New Testament chronology and became firmly established as part of the medieval understanding of the life of Christ. The numbers 33 and 34 (sometimes also 32) were used as a means of suggesting some relationship between a literary work and Christian idealism, a relationship ranging from a simple biographical parallelism between a character's experiences and Christ's (in the *Vie de Saint Alexis* the saint, imitating his master, lives 34 years in holiness),[46] to a fundamental formal parallelism between the entire work and the life of Christ (Dante's assignment of 33 or 34 parts to each of the three major sections of the *Commedia* is again the best-known example; Curtius, *European Literature*, p. 505, lists a dozen others). The number could also contribute to a localized religious intensity; in *Sir Gawain and the Green Knight* references to Christ are most extensive in stanzas 32 and 33.[47] In the medieval period, numerical composition necessarily implies an analogy between the human artist and that Artist who created all things in measure, number, and weight, and to compose in the particular numbers associated with the life of Christ is to specify one's awareness of Christian tradition and to affirm one's desire to be read in the context of that tradition.

Certainly Chaucer is not as devotional a poet as Dante. The quality "Chaucerian" suggests above all multiplicity, comprehensiveness, a refusal to be or to mean one thing alone, a refusal to arbitrate between the sacred and the profane. The act of devotion implied by the structural and symbolic use of 33, which in the completed work would have permitted 33 narrative voices to be heard, does not outweigh the many aspects of the *Canterbury Tales* that are clearly secular, sometimes emphatically so. The presence of the number does, however, corroborate many other matters of artistic choice — the most obvious is, of course, the pilgrimage setting itself — which demonstrate that Chaucer intended the *Canterbury Tales* to be read in a traditional religious context. This does not exclude the probability that he intended the *Tales* to be read in other contexts too.

To be sure, the number 33 remains unobtrusive. One has to look for it to find it, and perhaps in an oral delivery of the work it would escape notice altogether. But Chaucer does not write solely for the level of comprehension likely in a single oral experience of his work. There is little that would impede that first level of comprehension, but there is often much beyond it, as has been shown by the progress of modern critical studies, many of which point out subtle relationships among parts of the *Canterbury Tales*, ironic repetitions of words or characters or situations, a wealth of literary echoes, and other complexities that can be appreciated only by close acquaintance with, presumably, a written text. That the *Canterbury Tales* were written for oral delivery does not mean they were written for oral delivery *only*.

Even if one must assume that most of Chaucer's audience was a listening audience that would probably have remained unaware of the number 33 with its religious associations, one should keep in mind the medieval aesthetic principle that a work of art is intended for the eye of God as well as of man: as Singleton points out in discussing Dante's "hidden" patterns of symbolic numbers, which perhaps no ordinary reader of the *Commedia* ever perceived, many details of medieval art, for example the carvings on the roofs of cathedrals, were designed and executed without apparent consideration of whether they would ever be noticed by human audiences. If no one else saw a devotional detail, God did. Chaucer's number symbolism certainly does not approach that degree of exclusivity, but the point is that the content of the work should not be seen as limited to what an ordinary listener would be likely to receive.

Why—to return to the beginning of this discussion—should Chaucer have made the Narrator miscount? I would suggest that this mistake is part of Chaucer's ironic attitude toward the Narrator, who characteristically overestimates his ability to judge his fellow men and puts forth quick verdicts that later need to be modified. Thus the Narrator, having stopped for the night at the Tabard, sees a large group of travelers arrive, and at once takes their measure:

At nyght was come into that hostelrye
Wel nyne and twenty in a compaignye.

Were the total given toward the end of the General Prologue, *after* the list of pilgrims, the effect would have been completely different. We would then have had, as it were, the logical conclusion to an argument: there was a Knight, a Squire, a Yeoman, . . .and so twenty-nine in all. Chaucer's reversed sequence makes the Narrator judge before he fully knows. There is no pause in the verse; one is given the impression that the Narrator makes the quickest count of noses (which one he fails to see will never be known) and immediately announces his assessment, which, as one is then gradually allowed to recognize, is not quite accurate. The reader can come to this recognition, but the Narrator apparently does not, for the error is permitted to remain.

A small irony, to be sure, but an important one, partly because it appears early in the *Canterbury Tales,* partly because it is related to larger aspects of structure and implication, partly because it is accessible only if one is willing to take into account everything—everyone—Chaucer included in that April "compaignye."

Notes

1. Citations are from *The Works of Geoffrey Chaucer,* ed. F. N. Robinson, 2d ed. (London, 1957).
2. John M. Manly and Edith Rickert, *The Text of the Canterbury Tales,* 8 vols. (Chicago, 1940), 5:4.
3. Carleton Brown, "The Squire and the Number of the Canterbury Pilgrims,"

Modern Language Notes 49 (1934):216-22.

4. Among recent studies of the Narrator's method in the portraits are: Ralph Baldwin, *The Unity of the Canterbury Tales*, Anglistica, no. 5 (Copenhagen, 1955), pp. 35-54; R. M. Lumiansky, *Of Sondry Folk* (Austin, Tex., 1955), pp. 20-23; Paull F. Baum, *Chaucer: A Critical Appreciation* (Durham, N.C., 1958), pp. 61-69; D. W. Robertson, Jr., *A Preface to Chaucer* (Princeton, N.J., 1962), pp. 242-56; and Thomas A. Kirby, "The General Prologue," in *Companion to Chaucer Studies*, ed. Beryl Rowland (London, 1968), pp. 218-22.

5. John M. Manly, "A Knight Ther Was," *Transactions of the American Philological Association* 38 (1907):89-104; J. S. P. Tatlock, *The Development and Chronology of Chaucer's Works*, Chaucer Society, 2d Ser., no. 37 (London, 1907), pp. 147-48.

6. A. C. Baugh, ed., *Chaucer's Major Poetry* (New York, 1963), pp. 233, 237.

7. George Lyman Kittredge, "That Canon's Yeoman's Prologue and Tale," *Transactions of the Royal Society of Literature*, 2d ser. 30 (1910):87-88.

8. W. P. Lehmann, "A Rare Use of Numerals in Chaucer," *Modern Language Notes* 67 (1952):317 21

9. Caroline D. Eckhardt, "*Canterbury Tales* D.1554: *caples thre*," *Notes & Queries*, new ser. 20 (1973):283-84.

10. Leo Spitzer, "And Prestes Three," *Modern Language Notes* 67 (1952):502-4.

11. O. F. Emerson, "Some Notes on Chaucer and Some Conjectures, Part V," *Philological Quarterly* 2 (1923):89-96. A similar proposal by Peter M. Farina suggests that the "preestes thre" are meant to be the Monk, the Friar, and the Parson; an emendation of the text and a masculine interpretation of the feminine term *chapeleyne* are necessary ("The Twenty-Nine Again: Another Count of Chaucer's Pilgrims," *Language Quarterly* 9 [1971]:29-32).

12. There are more than a hundred occurrences of "priest" in Chaucer (see J. S. P. Tatlock and Arthur G. Kennedy, *A Concordance to the Complete Works of Geoffrey Chaucer* [Washington, D.C., 1927]). In none of these is "priest" applied to a person previously or subsequently identified as a monk or friar; some cases clearly show that Chaucer does not combine those categories, for example: "I trowe thou hast some frere or preest with thee" (D.1583); "al be he monk or frere, / Preest or chanoun" (G.839); compare "the preest sholde be enterdited that dide swiche a vileynye; to terme of his lif he sholde namoore synge masse" (I.965), where the class "priest" is limited to those authorized to celebrate Mass.

13. Baldwin links this phrase to the "rubric of classical biography," *erat* or *fuit autem* (*The Unity of the Canterbury Tales*, p. 48).

14. For example, *The Complete Works of Geoffrey Chaucer*, ed. W. W. Skeat, 2d ed., 7 vols. (Oxford, 1900), 5:19; J. M Manly, *Some New Light on Chaucer* (New York, 1926), pp. 223-24; Robinson, ed., *The Works of Geoffrey Chaucer*, p. 655; Muriel Bowden, *A Commentary on the General Prologue to the Canterbury Tales*, 2d ed. (New York, 1967), p. 104.

15. See Brown, "The Squire and the Number," pp. 216-17.

16. Ann B. Fullerton, "The Five Craftsmen," *Modern Language Notes* 61 (1946): 515-23, esp. p. 516; George Unwin, *The Gilds and Companies of London* (Lon-

don, 1963), pp. 167, 370-71.

17. Norman Nathan, "The Number of the Canterbury Pilgrims," *Modern Language Notes* 67 (1952):533-34. Besides, a "webbe dyer" would seem to mean "one who dyes weavers."

18. Skeat, ed., *The Complete Works of Geoffrey Chaucer*, 5:19; Eleanor P. Hammond, *Chaucer: A Bibliographical Manual* (New York, 1908), p. 255; Marie P. Hamilton, "The Convent of Chaucer's Prioress and Her Priests," *Philologica: The Malone Anniversary Studies*, ed. Thomas A. Kirby and Henry B. Woolf (Baltimore, Md., 1949), p. 182; Lumiansky, *Of Sondry Folk*, p. 19; E. Talbot Donaldson, "The Masculine Narrator and Four Women of Style," in his *Speaking of Chaucer* (New York, 1970), p. 63.

19. Hammond, *Chaucer: A Bibliographical Manual*, p. 255; it would be impossible to specify a "normal" size, since expeditions ranged from a single pilgrim's to a king's, but it is clear that Chaucer's company had initially consisted of groups no larger than six (the Gildsmen and their Cook) and of individuals traveling alone (for example, the Narrator).

20. For example, Tyrwhitt, Introductory Discourse to *The Canterbury Tales*, 2d ed., 2 vols. (Oxford, 1798), 1:77-79; *The Canterbury Tales*, ed. J. M. Manly (New York, 1928), p. 508; Manly, *Some New Light on Chaucer*, pp. 223-24; Manly and Rickert, *The Text of the Canterbury Tales*, 2:95, 3:422-23; Bowden, *Commentary on the General Prologue*, p. 104; Robinson, ed., *The Works of Geoffrey Chaucer*, p. 655; Baugh, ed., *Chaucer's Major Poetry*, p. 241.

21. Eileen Power, *Medieval English Nunneries* (1922; reprint ed., New York, 1964), pp. 77-78.

22. Manly, *Some New Light on Chaucer*, pp. 222-23; Bowden, *Commentary on the General Prologue*, p. 104; Baugh, ed., *Chaucer's Major Poetry*, p. 240.

23. Hamilton, "The Convent. . . ," p. 184. Chaucer may have visted St. Leonard's in 1356 (Manly, *Some New Light on Chaucer*, pp. 204-5), when it presumably held about the same number of nuns as the thirty of 1354.

24. Power, *Medieval English Nunneries*, pp. 177-83; Hamilton, "The Convent . . . ," p. 184.

25. Hamilton, "The Convent. . . ," pp. 185, 188.

26. See ibid., p. 186; the will is translated in Manly, *Some New Light on Chaucer*, pp. 206-8. Arthur Sherbo points out that if the Prioress were head of a convent associated with only the single priest of the parish, both convent and parish would have been left without a priest since the priest is on the pilgrimage ("Chaucer's Nun's Priest Again," *PMLA* 64 [1949]:240-41).

27. Power, *Medieval English Nunneries*, pp. 344, 371-75.

28. See Donaldson, "The Masculine Narrator," p. 63. Sherbo argues that she needs the three Priests as bodyguards ("Chaucer's Nun's Priest Again," pp. 245-46), but the willingness of the Wife, who welcomes male attention but surely not molestation, to travel quite alone discourages this interpretation.

29. Manly, ed., *The Canterbury Tales*, p. 508; compare Manly and Rickert, *The Text of the Canterbury Tales*, 2:95, and Robinson, ed. ("altogether improbable"), *The Works of Geoffrey Chaucer*, p. 655.

30. The three Priests are accepted, more or less explicitly, by, among others, F. J. Furnivall, *Temporary Preface*, Chaucer Society, 2d ser., no. 3 (London, 1868), pp. 92-93; Nevill Coghill, *The Poet Chaucer* (London, 1949), p. 117; Sherbo, "Chaucer's Nun's Priest Again," passim; William W. Lawrence, *Chaucer and the Canterbury Tales* (New York, 1950), p. 45; Kemp Malone, *Chapters on Chaucer* (Baltimore, Md., 1951), pp. 150-51, 165-66; Donaldson, "The Masculine Narrator," pp. 62-64. The argument most similar to mine is Hamilton's in "the Convent. . . ." passim.

31. Power, *Medieval English Nunneries*, pp. 466-68.

32. Norman E. Eliason, "Chaucer's Second Nun?" *Modern Language Quarterly* 3 (1942):9-16. Eliason's count of twenty-nine involves not only excluding the Second Nun, but also excluding two of the Priests and then including the Narrator and even the Host—who obviously does *not* arrive as a member of the "compaignye" of twenty-nine.

33. Eileen Power shows that "it was invariably ordered that a nun was on no account to leave her house, without another nun of mature age and good reputation who would be a constant witness to her behaviour" (*Medieval English Nunneries*, p. 359).

34. Eliason, "Chaucer's Second Nun?" p. 14. The remaining manuscripts have no useful rubrics. The rubrics are in William McCormick, with Janet E. Heseltine, *The Manuscripts of Chaucer's Canterbury Tales* (Oxford, 1933); I use McCormick's abbreviations.

35. Although Eliason expects the construction to be "fairly common" ("Chaucer's Second Nun?" p. 13), there is no parallel phrase in Chaucer's use of at least the ordinals 1-20 (Tatlock and Kennedy, *A Concordance*). When Chaucer does want the ordinal to modify the noun, apparently he changes the sequence to *ordinal plus noun plus genitive*; for example, "sixte morwe of May" (F.906); compare "an hooly Jewes sheep" (C.351) where "hooly" must modify "Jewes," not "sheep."

36. From his order perhaps (Marie P. Hamilton, "The Clerical Status of Chaucer's Alchemist," *Speculum* 16 [1941]:107); from "the human congregation" certainly (Charles Muscatine, *Chaucer and the French Tradition* [Berkeley and Los Angeles, Calif., 1957], p. 221).

37. I am following Vincent F. Hopper, *Medieval Number Symbolism* (New York, 1938). On the literary use of number symbolism, see also Ernst R. Curtius, *European Literature and the Latin Middle Ages*, trans. Willard R. Trask (London, 1953), pp. 504-9; Edmund Reiss, "Number Symbolism and Medieval Literature," *Medievalia et Humanistica*, n.s. 1 (1970):161-74; Christopher Butler, "Numerological Thought," in *Silent Poetry: Essays in Numerological Analysis*, ed. Alastair Fowler (London, 1970), pp. 1-31; idem, *Number Symbolism* (London, 1970), esp. chaps. 1, 2, 5, and 6.

38. Hopper, *Medieval Number Symbolism*, pp. 138-40, 147-49; Curtius, *European Literature. . .*, p. 509; Charles S. Singleton, "The Poet's Number at the Center," in this volume.

39. Russell A. Peck, "Number Symbolism and the Idea of Order in the Works of Geoffrey Chaucer" (Ph.D. diss., Indiana University, 1962), pp. 200-201; idem,

"Number Symbolism in the Prologue to Chaucer's *Parson's Tale*," *English Studies* 48 (1967):206-9; Edmund Reiss, "The Pilgrimage Narrative and *The Canterbury Tales*," *Studies in Philology* 67 (1970):304-5; John M. Steadman, "Chaucer's Thirty Pilgrims and Activa Vita," *Neophilologus* 45 (1961):224-30, esp. pp. 227, 230. On the number symbolism of the *Book of the Duchess*, see Russell A. Peck, "Theme and Number in Chaucer's *Book of the Duchess*," in *Silent Poetry*, ed. Fowler, pp. 73-115.

40. An excessive identification of the Narrator with the author leads some critics to accept, as a principle of criticism, the idea that whatever the Narrator says must be right. Thus Farina, discussing the number of the pilgrims, remarks "The point is how to get twenty-nine" ("The Twenty-Nine Again," p. 29). On the contrary, the point is to read the General Prologue, and without the prior conviction that the Narrator will be proven right.

41. On the Host, see R. M. Lumiansky, "The Meaning of Chaucer's Prologue to 'Sir Thopas,' " *Philological Quarterly* 26 (1947):313-20; idem, "The Nun's Priest in *The Canterbury Tales*," *PMLA* 68 (1953):896-906; Barbara Page, "Concerning the Host," *Chaucer Review* 4 (1970):1-13; Cynthia C. Richardson, "The Function of the Host in *The Canterbury Tales*," *Texas Studies in Literature and Language* 12 (1970):325-44.

42. Hopper, *Medieval Number Symbolism*, pp. 95-96; Singleton, "The Poet's Number."

43. Reiss, "Number Symbolism," pp. 164-65.

44. One might assign a fractional thirty-fourth part, reflective of Christ's unfinished thirty-fourth year, to the Canon, who speaks eight lines (G.583-86, 693-96).

45. Singleton demonstrates ("The Poet's Number" passim) that Dante arranged a particular pattern of numbers around the center of the *Commedia*, and concentrated crucial statements there.

46. Eleanor W. Bulatkin, "The Arithmetic Structure of the Old-French *Vie de Saint Alexis*," *PMLA* 74 (1959):498-99.

47. A. Kent Hieatt, "*Sir Gawain*: Pentangle, *luf-lace*, Numerical Structure," in *Silent Poetry*, ed. Fowler, pp. 116-40 (esp. pp. 133-34).

Tectonic Methodology and an Application to *Beowulf*

Thomas Elwood Hart

One of the more engaging and demanding topics of study for the cultural historian is Western man's enduring quest for the principles of beauty. If one were to attempt a history of this quest from Greek antiquity to the present, an important (perhaps the crucial) chapter might well be called "Our Love Affair with Number." It would be a chapter of considerable scope because our artists and poets have so often sought models in nature's own quantitative designs, translating into their various media not only the timeless rhythms of life but also patterns of mathematics and geometry reflecting the structure of their world. Even a survey limited to the uses of number by poets alone would be much more extensive than could have been foreseen a mere generation ago, for it has become apparent only during the past few decades just how seminal a role number has played throughout the history of Western literary aesthetics. In fact, the numerical aspects of poetic structure have now become a topic of broad interdisciplinary research, which not only cuts across the traditional academic borders separating the national languages but also engages (and is increasingly contributing to) such other disciplines as the history of art, philosophy, religion, music, mathematics, and astronomy.

Much remains to be done before a comprehensive chapter on number in art could even be outlined, since so much of the evidence needed resides in the artworks themselves rather than in theoretical treatises and must therefore be compiled through the patient inductive analysis of individual works. This fact, no less true for poetry than for the other art forms, explains why much of the current interest within this branch of literary scholarship is grouped around concrete issues of fact and method, especially the issues of how numbers have been (and are still being) used by poets for aesthetic purposes in specific works, and which analytical techniques are proving successful in identifying both the mathematical characteristics and the literary functions of such uses.[1] Given the nature of the evidence—as well as the modern lack of empathy for the almost mystical appeal that number seems to have had for our ancestors—our quest for the poets' own principles of beauty will presumably remain focused on structural analyses of individual poems for some time. For only when we have detailed knowledge about the kinds and extent of numerical structuring in poetry can we confidently take up the broader humanistic questions concerning its historical relevance, psychological motivation, and aesthetic achievement.

However ambitious the larger humanistic context of the discipline may seem at present, my goals in this essay are of course much more modest, as my rather positivistic title indicates. As part of an effort to encourage the serious inductive study of this element in the structure of individual literary works—and ultimately, it is hoped, as a contribution toward treatment of the larger implications—I will focus here on two of the more concrete features of my recent work in this field. The first feature involves some of the conclusions about methodology to which I have been led both by the published findings of others and by my own grappling with numerical designs during the past dozen or so years. The second feature concerns one specific pattern-complex, illustrating how numbers were used in what is probably the oldest extant major poem in a European vernacular, *Beowulf*, and thus a rather early representative of the art. In conclusion, I will comment briefly on what I see as the promising implications of such findings, but these comments, necessarily tentative, are meant only to suggest the potential humanistic significance of research in this area.

Let me begin with a brief look at the background of the present situation. It is, I think, fairly clear from the past twenty-five years of pioneer work on what Ernst Robert Curtius called *Zahlenkomposition* — numerical composition or, perhaps more conveniently, tectonics — that there is, strictly speaking, no common method.[2] Some studies are primarily concerned with number symbolism,[3] others with the structural uses of number. Some begin with manuscript data and work toward numerically controlled units of meaning; others take the opposite course, beginning with what they perceive as units of meaning and then seeking to discern numerical patterns based on these units. Some indulge in unbridled numerological speculation. Others — unfortunately, still too few — are well-documented and convincing studies that have contributed measurably to our understanding of the poems concerned. The only common factor among these various approaches is an interest in the literary uses of number. And this surface resemblance has had the lamentable result that studies of quite different quality and widely diverging goals and methods have been assigned a common public image: lumped together uncritically, they often have been either praised or scorned as a group. It is small wonder, then, that many scholars working on tectonic analyses today feel constrained, in preemptive self-defense, to begin by disavowing any connection with the dubious conclusions and inadquate methods of some earlier studies.

Understandable as this attitude may be, one would do well to remember that pioneer work can be valuable for its false starts as well as for its successes. By attending to the kinds of deficiencies that have marred earlier efforts, scholars can perhaps find ways of avoiding similar mistakes in the future. In two earlier papers I have addressed methodological problems associated with the analysis of tectonic structure in the Old High German *Ludwigslied* and in the Middle High German courtly epics of Hartman von Ouwe.[4] Those essays and this one are concerned primarily with the structural uses of number rather than with their possible symbolic meanings, and all three share the premises that basic aspects of methodology in this field can be fruitfully generalized and that inter-disciplinary cooperation is advisable if not indispensable. Here I will attempt to present and illustrate my present conclusions in a somewhat more interdisciplinary context than in the earlier studies.

What has disturbed me most about the less convincing earlier tectonic studies can ultimately be reduced to one underlying methodological flaw — an uncritical reliance on on-ly *partial evidence.* One form this mistake has taken is a disregard of the structural markers in the manuscripts. Another is the divorce of thematic from numerical features, resulting in an overemphasis on one or the other. A third is the ignoring of formal textual patterns that a poet may have used to support his numerical design, especially verbal repetition, rhyme patterns, and similar kinds of word play.

Before proposing a general procedural framework that can help reduce, if not eliminate, many of these shortcomings, let me emphasize that I am not advocating any one method. Each literary work is unique and therefore makes its own kinds of demands on the reader. What I am advocating is that the various methods employed in tectonic research meet common standards of verifiability and thoroughness in the presentation and evaluation of the evidence available.

Perhaps the simplest way to assure comprehensive treatment of all the evidence is to ask at the start of the analysis what kinds of structuring devices were available to the poet. My ex-perience with works in Latin, Old English, Old Saxon, Old Norse, Old High German, and Middle High German, as well as my acquaintance with the published results of others, in-dicates that there are at least four kinds of evidence that must be considered. This is the case because the medieval poet who was inclined by nature or tradition to structure his poem tec-tonically had basically four means of indicating his patterns: (1) graphic, such as manuscript punctuation marking relevant divisions; (2) formal or textural, such as numerically controlled patterns of wording, rhyme, or other textual features within structural divisions; (3) numerical[5], especially precision and consistency among parts and whole (what may be termed the *aesthetics* of the chosen arithmetic relationships themselves); and (4) thematic, such as change of person, place, time, or action, coincident with numerical junctures and parallels among resulting structural units.

From these theoretical considerations about the nature of the evidence, in my view, three methodological corollaries follow. Tectonic research should (a) examine texts for all four kinds of evidence — graphic, formal, numerical, and thematic; (b) explain rather than ignore any discrepancies among these kinds of evidence; and (c) proceed — with constant reticulation among the four types of evidence — in the approximate order of increasing abstraction, namely graphic, formal, numerical, thematic.[6]

These recommendations are simply stated and probably will not inspire much controversy. But in practice they are often quite demanding, since to give comprehensive attention to different kinds of evidence can require time-consuming systematic collection and analysis of data — for example, the evaluation of punctuation and paragraphing where many manuscripts are involved. In the present context I can attempt only to suggest the kind of reticulating, probe-and-correct-by-comparison approach that seems to yield reliable tectonic findings. The pattern that I have selected from the marvelously intricate tectonic structure of *Beowulf* should provide some insight into how one poet used the numerical potential of his text for structural purposes. And although it incorporates rather elaborate patterns of wording and number, it is nevertheless striking enough in its thematic component to be accessible in verse translations as well as in the original.

Graphic evidence. The pattern involves four passages that are symmetrically contraposed within the poem's 3,182-line text. Paragraphing is not an issue in the pattern; the only features of manuscript layout or punctuation affecting it are the line-sum of the total text and the position of the relevant lines of verse within that text. All four recent major critical editions of the unique manuscript are agreed on both these points, and their agreement is based on a substantial corpus of textual research that has shown the manuscript to be generally reliable on nontectonic grounds. Moreover, because subtle tectonic structuring like that in *Beowulf* required the poet to be rigorously precise in his use of numbers and text intervals, each tectonic discovery based on the 3,182-line count adds to the cumulative evidence of its accuracy. Thus tectonic patterns themselves furnish an additional and independent corroboration for the evidence of textual scholarship. Some tectonic findings relevant to this issue have been published, and those presented below provide still further proof for the line-sum 3,182. Given this consistency between the unanimous judgment of recent editors and all my findings published to date, the textual basis of my present analysis would be controversial and require further documentation here only if I were to deviate from the accepted text.[7]

Formal or textural evidence. The first item of formal evidence that draws attention to the pattern is prosodic. There are some dozen lines in the poem that are generally considered to be hypermetric; that is, either the first half of the verse line or the last or both contain an additional metrical lift.[8] Two of the lines associated with hypermetric passages are remarkably similar not only in wording, but also in metric and syntactic shape:

1,162   win of *wunder*fatum. Ða cwom *Wealhþeo* ford
        (wine from wondrous vessels. Then **Wealhtheow**
        came forth)

2,173   wrǣtlicne   *wundur*maddum, done þe him
        Wealhdeo g̈eaf (ornamented wondrous jewel,
        which **Wealhtheow had given to him**)

The name Wealhtheow occurs four more times in the poem (lines 612, 629, 664, and 1,215), but it is collocated with *wundor* or its compounds only in lines 1,162 and 2,173.

Numerical evidence. These two lines are disposed in such a way within the poem's 3,182-line text that the interval between them and the interval from the second of them to the end of the poem are the same, each spanning 1,010 verse lines (Figure 9).

FIG. 9. Relative position of lines 1,162 and 2,173 in Beowulf.

Given both the uniqueness of the verbal collocations in these two lines and the fact that many other tectonic patterns have been found in this poem,[9] one suspects that this conjunction of lexical, metric, and numerical similarities is the result of conscious design by the poet. But at this point the pattern seems incomplete, at least by comparison with other typical tectonic relationships in this poem. I will return to the question of completeness later. First, other aspects of the passages around lines 1,162 and 2,173 must be considered.

Thematic evidence. Is there some feature of the thematic organization of the narrative to which attention is called or that is supported by the linguistic and numerical conjunction of the two lines diagramed in Figure 9? Line 1,162 (*wunder-. . . . Wealhþeo*) announces the entrance of queen Wealhtheow, the wife of the Danish king Hrothgar, at the banquet celebrating Beowulf's victory over Grendel. The lines immediately preceding tell of hall joy and the serving of wine. The lines immediately following describe how Wealhtheow, wearing a piece of gold jewelry ("under gyldnum beage" [1,163a], perhaps a crown, perhaps a necklace), approaches the place where Hrothgar and his nephew Hrothulf are sitting. The narrator comments: "Their familial relationship was still intact, each was true to the other" ("þa gyt wæs hiera sib ætgædere, / æghwylc oðrum trywe" [1,164b-1,165a]).

The corresponding line (*wunder-. . .Wealhðeo*), line 2,173, is part of the passage in which Beowulf, upon returning home from Denmark, reports to his uncle, the Geatish king Hygelac, about his victory over Grendel and how it was

celebrated at Hrothgar's hall. The immediate context of line
2,173 is Beowulf's gift of a necklace to Hygd, the wife of his
uncle-king, Hygelac. The Danish queen Wealhtheow is mentioned in line 2,173 because it was she who had given the
necklace to Beowulf during the earlier celebration in Denmark. (Indeed, the *beah* referred to in line 2,172 is very
possibly the same one mentioned for the first time in line
1,163; cf. lines 1,195, 1,211, 1,216.) The lines preceding 2,173
describe the close relationship between Hygelac and his
nephew, Beowulf, and the language used echoes that of the
lines immediately after 1,162 with which the relationship between Hrothgar and his nephew Hrothulf had been portrayed:
"Hygelac's nephew (Beowulf) was completely loyal to
him . . . and each was intent upon the good of the other"
("Hygelace wæs / niða heardum nefa swyde hold, / ond
gehwæder odrum hroþra gemyndig" [2,169b-2,171]).

It would perhaps be helpful at this point to present the two
passages in the original and then summarize the lexical and
thematic connections between them. The verbal correspondences to be abstracted in the diagram (Figure 10) are
italicized in the citation below.

1,160	Gamen eft astah,
1,161	*beorht*ode bencsweg, byrelas *sealdon*
1,162	win of *wunder*fatum. Þa cwom *Wealhþeo* ford
1,163	*gan under gyldnum beage* þær þa godan twegen
1,164	sæton suhtergefæderan; þa gyt wæs hiera sib ætgædere,
1,165	æghwylc *odrum* trywe.

2,169	Hygelace wæs
2,170	niða heardum nefa swyde hold,
2,171	ond gehwæder *odrum* hroþra gemyndig.
2,172	Hyrde ic þæt he done heals*beah* Hygde *gesealde*,
2,173	*wrætlicne wunder*maddum, done þe him *Wealhdeo* geaf,
2,174	deodnes dohtor, þrio wicg somod
2,175	swancor ond sadol*beorht*;

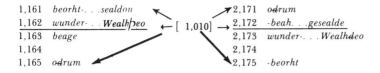

FIG. 10. Wording pattern, lines 1,161-65 and 2,171-75 in Beowulf.

The themes around line 1,162 are: the banquet in Denmark, the appearance of Wealhtheow, and the fragile loyalty between uncle-king (Hrothgar) and nephew (Hrothulf); the themes around line 2,173 are: the banquet in Geatland, with allusion to the earlier celebration in Denmark and to Wealhtheow, and the firm loyalty between uncle-king (Hygelac) and nephew (Beowulf).

Numerical evidence: an analogue. As noted earlier, the numerical aspects of the relationships diagramed in Figure 9 above seem purposeful, but taken alone lack the completeness typical of other tectonic patterns in the poem. The thematic evidence just considered shows that the passages around 1,162 and 2,173 (2,020 and 1,010 lines from the end of the poem) are closely related in meaning. This fact lends further confirmation to the conjunction of lexical, metric, and numerical connections between the two passages (Figures 9 and 10). But in comparison with the standards of numerical intricacy evident in the poem's other tectonic patterns, the connections between the passages still do not seem sufficiently self-contained.

Fortunately, however, enough is known about the kinds of tectonic patterning used in this poem to facilitate the search for the larger pattern of which lines 1,162 and 2,173 are a part. It has, for example, been shown that the two episodes about Finn and Ingeld, which are very closely related in meaning and in wording, are *symmetrically* opposite one another in the poem.[10] One variational feature of the symmetry of these two episodes is a chiasmic pattern of verbal repetitions connecting the opening lines of both and the concluding lines of both. The pattern involved there may be diagramed as follows (Figures 11 and 12; a number in parentheses indicates a line's position relative to the *end* of the poem):

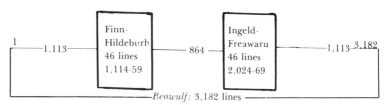

FIG. 11. *Symmetrical disposition of the Finn and Ingeld episodes in* Beowulf.

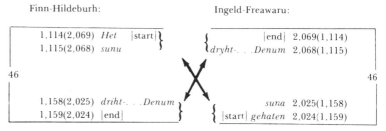

FIG. 12. *Chiasmic pattern of verbal repetitions (Finn and Ingeld episodes) in* Beowulf.

Note in Figure 12 that it is not the lines symmetrically opposite one another in a center-plus-wings structure[11] (these would be the *stȧrt* of one account, line 1,114, and the *end* of the other, line 2,069, the 1,114th line from the end of the poem) that are connected. Rather, the pattern is more intricate, so that the correspondence of, for example, lines 1,158 and 2,068 is not apparent unless (a) the symmetry of the two 46-line accounts is noticed and (b) the correspondence of lines 1,115 (2,068) and 2,025 (1,158) is seen to balance the correspondence of lines 1,158 (2,025) and 2,068 (1,115).

The important feature of this tectonic pattern (Figures 11 and 12) for present purposes is the chiasmic character of the variation on the overall symmetry (indicated by the crossing lines in Figure 12). Lines 1,162 and 2,173 — to return to the passages with *wundor* and *Wealhþeo* that form two intervals with 1,010 lines each — are not poem-symmetrical (symmetrically opposite one another, at equal distances from beginning and end of the poem), but they are connected. If the poet wished to complete a pattern involving lines 1,162 and 2,173, one way he could have done so would have been to establish similar connections between the passages 1,162 and 2,173 lines from the *end* of the poem. The result would be a self-contained symmetrical and chiasmic pattern among four passages, comparable to that summarized in Figure 12.

Before proceeding, I might mention that there were of course other possibilities open to the poet, to judge from the kinds of patterns he used elsewhere. Among these are the use of the same intervals within major sections; of sequences of multiples of the intervals; of positional correspondence within two equivalent structural units (e.g., fitt groups); and of symmetry within major structural units. But I have yet to find a kind of pattern for lines 1,162 and 2,173 other than the one based on chiasmic symmetry as described below. Once the analogue (chiasmic symmetry in the Finn and Ingeld episodes and elsewhere) had been seen, examination of the passages in question quickly revealed further correspondences in wording and sense to complement those in lines 1,162 and 2,173 and complete the pattern.

Thematic evidence. Line 1,010 (line 2,173 from the end of the poem) occurs near the start of the banquet celebrating Beowulf's victory over Grendel. The two lines immediately preceding announce the arrival of the Danish king to begin the celebration. The lines immediately following describe the excellence of the assemblage and the distribution of the mead cups. Lines 1,017-19 refer explicitly to the present (but fragile) loyalty between Hrothgar and his nephew Hrothulf. Line 2020 (line 1,163 from the end of the poem) occurs in a passage in which Beowulf begins to report to his uncle Hygelac about the earlier celebration in the Danish hall. The lines immediately preceding 2,020 describe the hall joy and how the Danish queen Wealhtheow provided for drinks and gifts. The lines immediately following show her daughter Freawaru carrying the cups and gifts to the men in the hall. The two passages read as follows (again the important verbal correspondences near lines 1,010 and 2,020 are italicized; the line distance to the end is indicated in parentheses):

1,008(2,175)   þa wæs sæl ond mæl,
1,009(2,174)   þæt *to* healle *gang* Healfdenes sunu;

1,010(2,173)	wolde self cyning symbel þicgan.
1,011(2,172)	Ne gefraegen *ic þa* maegþe maran weorode
1,012(2,171)	ymb hyra sincgyfan sel *gebaeran.*
1,013(2,170)	Bugon þa to bence blaedagande,
1,014(2,169)	fylle gefaegon; faegere geþaegon
1,015(2,168)	medoful manig magas þara
1,016(2,167)	swidhicgende on sele þam hean,
1,017(2,166)	Hrodgar ond Hroþulf. Heorot innan waes
1,018(2,165)	freondum afylled; nalles facenstafas
1,019(2,164)	Þeod-Scyldingas þenden fremedon.

2,014(1,169)	Weorod waes on wynne; ne seah ic widan feorh
2,015(1,168)	under heofones hwealf healsittendra
2,016(1,167)	medudream maran. Hwilum maeru cwen,
2,017(1,166)	fridusibb folca flet eall geondhwearf,
2,018(1,165)	baedde byre geonge; oft hio beahwridan
2,019(1,164)	secge (sealde), aer hie *to* setle *geong.*
2,020(1,163)	Hwilum for dugude dohtor Hrodgares
2,021(1,162)	eorlum on ende ealuwaege baer,
2,022(1,161)	þa *ic* Freaware fletsittende
2,023(1,160)	nemnan hyrde, þaer hio naegled sinc
2,024(1,159)	haeledum sealde.

To summarize the themes connecting the two passages, the themes around line 1,010 (2,173 lines from the end) are: the start of the banquet in Denmark, the entrance of the Danish king Hrothgar to his hall, and hall joy; the themes around line 2,020 (1,163) are: Beowulf reports on the banquet in Denmark, hall joy there, before and after the Danish queen Wealhtheow went to her seat.

Formal evidence. The verbal correspondences in the immediate vicinity of lines 1,010 and 2,020, as underscored in the quotations above, are shown in Figure 13.

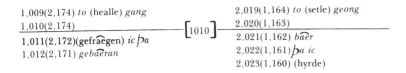

FIG. 13. Wording pattern, lines 1,009-12 and 2,019-23 in Beowulf.

For convenience in the remainder of the analysis I will label these two passages around lines 1,010 and 2,020 and those around 1,163(2,020) and 2,173(1,010) with the letters A, B, C, and D respectively. Their positions relative to one another and to the beginning and end of the poem may be diagramed as in Figure 14.

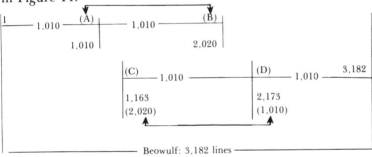

FIG. 14. Paired positions of four passages in Beowulf.

This manner of diagraming the intervals as overlapping sequences highlights the numerical and lexical conjunction of A and B with one another and of C and D with one another, as the arrows reinforce. But the pattern would have a somewhat different appearance if viewed in terms of poem-symmetry, since A is poem-symmetrical with D positionally, while C is poem-symmetrical with B. This may be seen from the following diagram (Figure 15) of the relative positions of the same four passages.

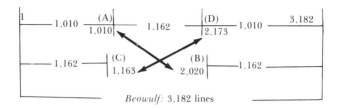

FIG. 15. Poem-symmetrical positions of four passages in Beowulf.

Here the arrows indicating the lexical and thematic correspondences (the same arrows as in Figure 14) reveal that the
symmetry of the four passages is chiasmic. The similarity of
this pattern to the chiasmic relationships shown in Figure 12
(the Finn-Ingeld passages) can perhaps be better seen from a
juxtaposition of the poem-symmetrical lines in the four
passages, A, B, C, and D (Figure 16).

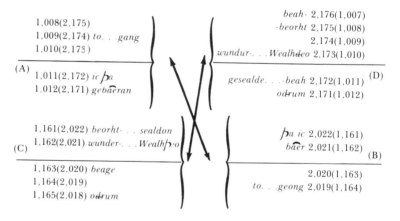

FIG. 16. Chiasmic pattern of verbal repetitions in four passages in
Beowulf.

Thematic evidence. The chiasmic connections among the
four passages established by the numerical and lexical relationships just examined are confirmed by the thematic correspondences that were pointed out earlier. Again the principal vectors connect A with B and C with D, as a schematic
presentation (Figure 17) shows.

(A) around 1,010(2,173):	(D) around 2,173(1,010):
Start of banquet in Denmark; Danish King Hrothgar goes to the hall; hall-joy.	Banquet in Geatland, with allusion to earlier banquet in Denmark and to Wealhtheow's gift; firm loyalty between uncle (Hygelac) and nephew (Beowulf).

(C) around 1,163(2,020):	(B) around 2,020(1,163):
Banquet in Denmark continues; Wealhtheow appears; fragile loyalty between uncle (Hrothgar) and nephew (Hrothulf).	Beowulf reports on banquet in Denmark; hall-joy; Danish queen Wealhtheow goes to her seat.

FIG. 17. Thematic correspondences (A, B, C, D): chiasmic symmetry.

Although the connections in wording, theme, and number among the four points in the text are thus chiasmic, it should nevertheless be stressed that all four passages are related: A and C are part of the description of the banquet festivities in the Danish royal hall, B and D part of the account of the celebration in the Geatish royal hall during which Beowulf reports on, among other things, the earlier banquet in Denmark. What the poet has done here, then, is to introduce a subtle (chiasmic) variation into the symmetry in a section of his text where there is a rather prominent bilateral symmetry in the organization of the narrative material. Thus in this part of the text there are two kinds of symmetry. One is a direct type in which the lines symmetrically opposite one another in the poem contain close correspondences in wording and sense. A good example of this type is the precise poem-symmetry of the Finn-Hildeburh and Ingeld-Freawaru episodes referred to earlier and diagramed in Figure 11. The second type of symmetry is more intricate. It builds on the underlying symmetry of the narrative material by introducing variations. The two variations noted here are chiasmic. One is the chiasmic pattern of wording *within* the episodes about Finn and Ingeld (see Figure 12). The other is the chiasmic pattern of correspondences *among* the symmetrical passages at lines 1,010(2,173), 1,163(2,020), 2,020(1,163), and 2,173(1,010).

It will be observed that the chiasmic pattern among these four passages and the symmetrical contraposition of the Finn and Ingeld episodes are very close together in the text. The conclusion of the Finn episode in line 1,159 is only three lines from the appearance of the Danish queen Wealhtheow in 1,162, the beginning of the sequence of hypermetric lines with which this analysis began. Similarly, Beowulf's reference to Wealhtheow and her daughter Freawaru around line 2,020(1,163) provides the framework for the narration of the Ingeld-Freawaru episode beginning in line 2,024.

The question naturally arises here as to why the poet introduced such subtle variations into the symmetry of the narrative at these points. One can only speculate about answers to such questions. For the present let me mention two. One possible explanation may be found in the principle of *idem in aliter* to which A. Kent and Constance Hieatt have appealed in comparing variation in poetic structure with variation in pictorial and musical art.[12] Another possible explanation (compatible with the first) may be derived from the "web of words" metaphor so popular in Anglo-Saxon poetry and so well motivated in the typical patterns of contemporary metalwork and manuscript illumination. And indeed the diagrammatic representations of the numerical positioning of the four passages within the text's 3,182-line continuum (Figure 18) seem to suggest an intertwining and weaving.[13]

To summarize, then, I have examined formal, numerical, and thematic evidence (graphic evidence did not apply directly to this structure) to show that four passages in the *Beowulf* text are interrelated in a tectonic pattern. The analysis of each type of evidence contributed its own kind of support for the cumulative case. For example, symmetry is largely a numerical (positional) matter, whereas the chiasmic aspects of the pattern turned up as a function of wording and thematic correspondences. To determine the value of one kind of evidence it was necessary to consider the others at each step in the procedure. In this case all the evidence proved corroborative.

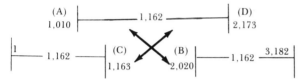

FIG. 18. Alternative conceptions of four symmetrical passages in *Beowulf*.

However, the actual process of research on which this essay is based entailed the time-consuming investigation of many alternative possibilities that did not pan out. In fact, although I had noted the suggestive intervals established by the rather pronounced similarites between lines 1,162 and 2,173 several years ago (and duly filed the observation away in my "hypermetric" folder), it was not until recently — during a discussion with Kenneth Lundgren — that even the outlines of this intricate chiasmic pattern began to reveal themselves. Moreover, it should be at least mentioned that there is yet more to this pattern than need be considered here. Though in a sense self-contained as a symmetrical grouping, these four passages are also tied in with yet other aspects of the poem's tectonic structure — numerically, lexically, prosodically, and thematically.[14]

A final few words are perhaps in order on the subject of interpretation. This essay has been devoted to aspects of methodology and to some tectonic features of the structure of *Beowulf*. It is not my purpose here to interpret this tectonic evidence in support of one or another reading of the poem. But tectonic patterns, like all other aspects of the poem's structure, have interpretative significance. One highly suggestive feature of this pattern, for example, is the explicit comparison it makes between the two uncle-nephew relationships (Hrothgar-Hrothulf and Hygelac-Beowulf). These relationships are very important for a full understanding of the foreground narrative (Beowulf's exploits and future kingship) and also of the background of feuds among individuals and entire peoples against which that foreground is set. Yet the critical methodological point to be observed here is that the tectonic patterns do not of themselves yield or guarantee any one interpretation. They only provide the critic with opportunities (and guidance) by placing more evidence at his disposal. That is, even though tectonic phenomena, because of their numerical properties, may be more accessible to objective scrutiny than some other aspects of literary structure, one cannot on that account claim that tectonic patterns are *a priori* more valuable than others as interpretive tools. Those of us who study this kind of literary patterning would do well not to make claims for the hermeneutic usefulness of our discoveries that we cannot ourselves document. Conversely, however, well-documented tectonic data are *a priori* no less valuable as interpretive tools than are the traditionally accepted aspects of poetry and should not be overlooked by the critic. For wherever tectonic patterning plays a significant role in the organization of a literary work, it seems reasonable to assume that a knowledge of such patterning will help to expose new paths of interpretation—if only because the decision to use such structural devices presumably made demands upon the poet, which influenced the way he arranged his narrative and lexical materials.

My final methodological observation, accordingly, is that the analysis and description of tectonic patterns in a work of poetry should be considered to be procedurally separate from the interpretation of what the tectonic patterns may mean for the understanding of the work. I am, of course, aware that all description entails some interpretation. But if there is any lesson to be learned from the defects of some past research in this field, it is that especially in studying tectonic patterns one must strive to be as objective as possible. Indeed, it is this goal that informs all the methodological recommendations I ventured at the outset. Stated summarily: tectonic research should consider all available textual evidence so that the analysis and presentation of proposed tectonic findings will depend as little as possible on subjective factors and as much as possible on objectively verifiable features of the literary text itself.

In conclusion, let me return briefly to some implications of the topic for the larger humanistic context mentioned at this essay's beginning. Perhaps because the subject and methods of tectonic research to date have seemed to some humanists so different from traditional literary scholarship—*quid ars mathematica cum poetica?*—the potential contribution of tectonic discoveries to other humanistic concerns has not been duly credited. Two areas of larger relevance stand out, partially interrelated: the historical and the aesthetic. As to the first, even the present rudimentary state of our knowledge about specific works suggests that the apparently widespread use of numerical structuring by some of the foremost authors (artists, composers, etc.) of our Western heritage will alter our picture of such basic humanistic issues as (Western) man's sense of self, sense of world, and sense of beauty.[15] For even in the unlikely event that future scholars were to find no causal link between tectonic designs and aesthetic impact, could we lightly dismiss the historical fact that many literary artists in our tradition apparently did? The historical evidence that poets experimented with number as one principle of poetic shape does not by itself prove that number has aesthetic value. But it shows that in their quest for the principles of beauty some of our major poets *thought* that number had aesthetic value (or at the very least did not disagree with a tradition that did). This historical insight must affect at least our intellectual assessment of their achievements in poetry.

This brings me to the second area of implication, aesthetics.

Because questions about the apparent aesthetic appeal of
number for *poets* are akin to deeper questions about the nature
of aesthetic response in *readers*, it seems almost inevitable that
historical evidence of structural techniques such as those considered here will eventually inspire controlled psychological ex-
periments on whether or not—to quote Peterson's paren-
thetical, but provocative question—"the esthetic emotion is affected . . . by unapprehended 'technical procedures.' "[16] I am
not, of course, advocating either mathematical or psychological reductionism; poetry for me is more than calculations
and the chemistry of the occipito-parietal cortex. But can
one ignore the aesthetic implications of the discovery that
premeditated number-based designs inform works of poetry
(art, music, etc.) that we have valued all along? Given what
we know about man as an experience-structuring and struc-
ture-seeking being, can we reasonably dismiss evidence of
his possible capacity to respond intuitively to (perhaps even
rather intricate) regularities of structure he does not quite con-
sciously perceive?[17] Clearly, then, the implications of symmetries and proportions such as those examined in the *Beowulf*
text have an aesthetic as well as a historical dimension. But I
am not suggesting that tectonic research attempt to answer
psychological questions about subconscious responses when
such questions are quite beyond its competence. What I am
urging is that students of literature devote more attention to
regularities of tectonic design so that modern readers of earlier
poetry can, if they wish, respond to these aspects of poetic
structure in the way that the poets who created them
presumably did: with *conscious* delight.

Notes

1. See on both points most recently R. G. Peterson, "Critical Calculations:
    Measure and Symmetry in Literature," *PMLA* 91 (May 1976): 367-75, and my
    comments and Peterson's reply, *PMLA* 92 (January 1977): 126-29.
2. Ernst Robert Curtius, *Europäische Literatur und lateinisches Mittelalter* (Bern,
    1948), Excursus 15, "Zahlenkomposition." Of the selective bibliographies on
    research on this topic since 1948, the most comprehensive is now Ernst
    Hellgardt, *Zum Problem symbolbestimmter und formalästhetischer Zahlen-*

*komposition in mittelalterlicher Literatur: mit Studien zum Quadrivium und
zur Vorgeschichte des mittelalterlichen Zahlendenkens* (Munich, 1973), esp. the
bibliography, pp. 303-51, in the following categories: "Zur Geschichte der
Mathematik," "Zur Ontologie und Asthetik der Zahl," "Zur Zahlenexegese und
Zahlensymbolik," "Zur bildenden Kunst," "Zur symbolbestimmten und
formalästhetischen Zahlenkomposition in mittelalterlicher deutscher Literatur,"
"Anhang: Abhandlungen zur literarischen Zahlenkomposition im Altertum und
in nichtdeutscher mittelalterlicher Literatur." The earlier bibliographies by
Michael S. Batts (1969), Alastair Fowler (1964), Gunnar Qvarnström (1966),
and Horst Schümann (1968) are listed by Hellgardt (see his author index).
Coverage for German literature is quite complete to 1972; coverage for non-
German literature since (and before) Fowler and Qvarnström remains a
desideratum.

3. Or, by A. Kent Hieatt's definition, these studies are "numerological." See the
    recent survey by Christopher Butler, *Number Symbolism* (London, 1970).

4. Thomas Elwood Hart, "Tectonic Research: A Critical Survey (with Illustrations
    from the 'Ludwigslied')" (Paper delivered at the Annual MLA convention,
    German 1, Chicago, December 30, 1971); and idem, "Symmetry in the Structure
    of Hartmann's *Iwein*" (Paper delivered at the Twenty-fourth Annual Kentucky
    Foreign Language Conference, April 23, 1973), a considerably expanded
    version of which has appeared in *Colloquia Germanica* 10 (1976-77). 97-120,
    entitled: "The Structure of *Iwein* and Tectonic Research: What Evidence,
    Which Methods?"

5. Since *tectonic* may be defined as referring to those structural features of
    poetic texts which result from the poet's deliberate use of number in shaping his
    linguistic materials, all aspects of tectonic patterning are in a sense *numerical,*
    just as all poetic materials are in a sense *linguistic.* However, it is possible to
    to distinguish, at least for analytical purposes, components or levels within
    tectonic patterns that are mainly formal, mainly numerical, mainly thematic,
    etc., and to isolate them for discussion as such. It is in this narrower sense of
    numerical that I speak here of "numerical means." For example, a design of
    numerically harmonious relationships that was constructed by a poet in the
    abstract before a word of the text was actually penned, and was then used by
    him as a principle of text structure, has become a component of the work's
    tectonic structure and is thus no longer a mere abstraction. Yet, as one step in
    a tectonic analysis, its numerical harmonies per se may be considered in the
    abstract. Because such numerical means contribute their own characteristic
    (arithmetic) qualities, their internal consistency is crucial for both the poet and
    the critic. Tectonic patterns do not of course live by numerical harmonies
    alone (such harmonies must have demonstrable relevance to text structure),
    but without them text structures are not tectonic.

6. Peterson's representation of my view on this matter is inaccurate. It is decidedly
    not my recommendation, in his words, "that analysis begin with number"
    (*PMLA* 92 [January 1977]: 128). Rather, I suggested two priorities: first, that
    analysis of possible numerical *structure* should precede interpretation of possible
    number *symbolism* (ibid., p. 127) and, second, that the *formal* divisions of

text structure (lines, stanzas, cantos, books, etc.) — at least at the start of the analysis — would typically promise the critic more reliable access to the poet's tectonic design than the (more abstract) *content* groupings of plot and theme that the critic happens to perceive (pp. 127 f.). In both cases, of course, these judgments represent priorities of method, not necessarily hierarchies of aesthetic value.

7. In addition to the standard editions by Dobbie, Klaeber, von Schaubert, and Wrenn-Bolton, cf. most recently Robert D. Stevick, ed., *Beowulf: An Edition with Manuscript Spacing Notation and Graphotactic Analyses* (New York, 1975). On the reliability of the line count, see also my "Tectonic Design, Formulaic Craft, and Literary Execution; the Episodes of Finn and Ingeld in *Beowulf*," *Amsterdamer Beiträge zur älteren Germanistik* 2 (1972): 1-61, esp. n. 17 and pp. 32-33. A detailed reanalysis of the manuscript divisions and several hitherto unexplained punctuational features relevant to the poem's tectonic design is in preparation. But since these features relate almost solely to the fitts and fitt groups and are therefore only indirectly relevant to the poem's line sum, truly conclusive proof for the number 3,182 is to be expected not from the manuscript evidence itself, but from the *numerical* properties of the tectonic design based on that evidence. In other words, validation of the basic graphic criterion in this instance (as perhaps in many other works) is only to a point a matter of (paleo) graphic evidence. Beyond that point verification must come from the hermeneutic circle. An exemplary instance of this situation is the cogently reasoned argument calculating the totals of missing lines in the MS lacunae of *Andreas* by Robert D. Stevick, "Arithmetical Design of the Old English *Andreas*," in *Anglo-Saxon Poetry: Essays in Appreciation for John C. McGalliard*, ed. Lewis E. Nicholson and Dolores Warwick Frese (South Bend, Ind., 1975), pp. 99-115. In *Beowulf*, by comparison, the case is much simpler. One pattern system, which I described in a paper before the English 1 group at the 1974 MLA convention in New York, may be summarized here as a preliminary illustration of this (hermeneutically circular) evidence. The sum 3,182 is the product of twice two large prime numbers, 37 and 43. The poet deliberately reflected this equation in his design by establishing two fitt sequences with 370 lines each (lines 1-370 and 189-558) at the beginning and two with 430 lines each at the end of the poem (lines 2,391-820 and 2,752-3,182, including the supernumerary unit, line 3,182), labeled in order of occurrence 370A, 370B, 430A, and 430'B. These fitt groups are disposed in such a way within the 3,182-line text that the intervening fitt groups (lines 371-2,751 and 559-2,390) have line totals with precisely the same digits as the poem total 3,182: 2,381Z and 1,832Z respectively, one the digit inversion of the other (Z signifies that no other fitt sequence has this line total). Thus the overlapping patterns 370A + 2,381Z + 430'B and 370B + 1,832Z + 430A, based on fitt junctures all clearly marked in the MS, numerically reflect the total 3,182 and its prime factors: $(37 \times 43) + (37 \times 43) = 3,182$. For a different kind of numerical corroboration of the poem's line sum, see also the proportions cited in n. 14 below.

8. According to John Collins Pope, *The Rhythm of Beowulf* (1942; 2d ed., New

Haven, Conn., 1966), p. 231: lines 1,163-68, 1,705-7, 2,995-96; according to Fr. Klaeber, *Beowulf and the Fight at Finnsburg*, 3d ed. (Boston, 1950), p. lxx: lines 1,163-68, 1,705-7, and 2,995-96 (perhaps 2,173a and 2,367a); according to A. J. Bliss, *The Metre of Beowulf* (Oxford, 1962), p. 162: lines 1,163-68 (except 1,167a), 1705-7, 2,173a, 2297a, 2995-96. At one point Klaeber termed the hypermetric character of 2,173a "very doubtful" (p. lxx, n. 1), but later, citing Sievers and Richter, conceded that it was "possibly hypermetrical" (p. 279). Bliss concluded, however, that 2,173a was a "perfect hypermetric" verse (p. 94). Line 1,162, on the other hand, is not considered hypermetric but is contiguous with the poem's first and most extensive group of hypermetric verses, 1,163-68. Klaeber's reading of the manuscript is the basis for quotations throughout, although his diacritics have been omitted; the translations are intentionally literal.

9. See Hart, "Tectonic Design" (cited in n. 7 above); idem, "A Tectonic Consideration of the *eotenas* in *Beowulf*," *Thoth* (Festschrift issue for Professor Sanford B. Meech) 10 (1969):4-17; and idem, "Ellen: Some Tectonic Relationships in *Beowulf* and their Formal Resemblance to Anglo-Saxon Art," *Papers on Language and Literature*, 6 (1970): 263-90. See also for *Andreas* the findings by Stevick, "Arithmetical Design" (cited in n. 7 above).

10. Cf. Hart, "Tectonic Design," esp. pp. 9 ff.

11. The triptych principle of many medieval (particularly Gothic) altars has frequently been cited as an analogue of bilateral symmetry in literature of the period. See, for example, A. Kent Hieatt and Constance B. Hieatt, " 'The Bird with Four Feathers': Numerical Analysis of a Fourteenth-Century Poem," *Papers on Language and Literature*, 6 (1970): 18-38, esp. pp. 25 and 28 and the facing plate. The authors cite (cf. also A. Kent Hieatt in this vol.) similar findings by Johannes A. Huisman, *Neue Wege zur dichterischen und musikalischen Technik Walthers von der Vogelweide, mit einem Exkurs über die symmetrische Zahlenkomposition im Mittelalter* (Utrecht, 1950 = Studia Litteraria Rheno-Traiectina 1), esp. concerning Walther's *Leich* (3,1 ff.), pp. 53-65. This part of Huisman's study is now more readily available in the anthology *Walther von der Vogelweide*, ed. Siegfried Beyschlag (Darmstadt, 1971 = Wege der Forschung 112), pp. 275-88. A detailed analysis of the *Leich's* structure and of Huisman's theory of symmetry constitutes part of a dissertation in progress by Ingeborg Klemperer (doctoral candidate, Syracuse University). For something resembling the triptych analogue in the Carolingian period see Johannes Rathofer, *Der Heliand: theologischer Sinn als tektonische Form* (Köln, 1962), esp. pp. 505 ff., 330 ff., 534, and plates 5 ff. and 18. For the earlier Middle Ages, however, the concept *symmetria* appears to have had more to do with proportionality than with bilateral symmetry; cf. Wolfgang Haubrichs, *Ordo als Form: Strukturstudien zur Zahlenkomposition bei Otfrid von Weissenburg und in karolingischer Literatur* (Tübingen, 1969), pp. 37 ff.

12. Hieatt and Hieatt, " 'The Bird with Four Feathers,' " pp. 28 f.

13. For an early comparison of similar weaving patterns in manuscript illuminations and courtly romance see Eugène Vinaver, *Form and Meaning in Medieval Romance* (Cambridge, 1966) and his *The Rise of Romance* (Oxford, 1971); the

interlace metaphor was first applied to *Beowulf* by John Leyerle, "The Interlace Structure of *Beowulf*," *University of Toronto Quarterly*, 37 (1967): 1-17. If the question of how the *Beowulf* poet "pictured" his tectonic patterns proves at all answerable as the numerical design unfolds, any proposed "shape" will probably have to remain to some extent an approximation. Although I agree with the general reservations expressed by Constance B. Hieatt concerning Leyerle's application of the interlace metaphor to *Beowulf* — see her "Envelope Patterns and the Structure of *Beowulf*," *English Studies in Canada* 1 (1975): 250-65, p. 259 — it seems reasonable to expect that analogues such as those Leyerle cited from Hiberno-Saxon art will warrant increasing scrutiny, not only because of the contemporary prevalence of the interlace formula, but also because tectonic techniques provided the poet with the means of translating this formula to the literary medium with precision if he chose to do so. As Prof. Hieatt has pointed out (p. 259), evidence like the formal rhetorical groupings she described suggests that he did. But a methodological caveat deserves mention here. While noting the compatibility of the interlace analogue with some of my data (e.g. Fig. 18), I do not, in Prof. Hieatt's words (p. 259), "regard the Leyerle thesis as at the base" of my theory. The first task, it seems to me, is to unravel the complexities of the poem's structure. Pointing out its general or specific resemblance to analogues in other art forms — like interpretation of possible number symbolism — I consider methodologically posterior to that task and rather independent of it. In calling attention to that resemblance, both here and elsewhere (e.g., my paper on *ellen* compounds), I have not intended to make my findings in any way dependent on the Leyerle thesis or vice versa. This methodological distinction notwithstanding, my work of the past few years especially leads me to conclude that my hypothesis concerning the poet's tectonic design is more compatible with some of Prof. Leyerle's structural conclusions (e.g., on the importance of the episodes intersecting the narrative, pp. 9 ff.) and more involved with the kinds of content and formal rhetorical groupings Prof. Hieatt analyzed (but not only in bilateral symmetry as envelope patterns) than my earlier papers taken alone have perhaps suggested.

14. Russell A. Peck (see his essay in this vol.), like Haubrichs, *Ordo als Form* (cf. n. 11 above), has stressed the importance of proportionality in medieval art theory. Proportion is a basic feature of the tectonic design of *Beowulf*. Since to my knowledge no evidence of this proportionality has yet been presented, it will be illustrated in a preliminary way by two examples here to suggest the richness of the design within which these symmetrical patterns function. Both examples concern the disposition of the hypermetric lines. As indicated in n. 8 above, most of the hypermetric lines are concentrated in three places: 1,163-68, 1,705-7, and 2,995-96. I will call these clusters HM1, HM2, and HM3 respectively. The lines beginning and ending the first and last of these three clusters, line 1,163(2,020 from the end) and line 2,996, are the *first* and *last* hypermetric lines in the poem. The interval between them spans 1,832 lines. The ratio between this interval and the poem's line sum (note also the play on digits as in the fitt groups 2,381Z and 1,832Z referred to in n. 7 above) is the same as the ratio of the segments defined by the position of line 1,163 within the poem:

1,832/3,182 = 1,163/2,020. This proportion is very precise, the difference between the two ratios being merely 0.000004. The precision is all the more remarkable because the proportion involves no multiples; 1,163 is a prime number. Of course this proportion may also be expressed, by corollary, in terms of sequential intervals: 1,163/1,832 = 2,020/3,182, that is, from the start of the poem to HM1 (1,163) then on to HM3 (another 1,832 lines), and from the end of the poem back to HM1 (inclusively 2,020 lines), then on to the start for a total of 3,182. The crucial ingredient — whatever corollary formulation is preferred — is the proportionality determining the relative placement of the first and last hypermetric clusters within the total text.

The second example of proportionality also begins with line 1,163 and involves the two passages with which the analysis of our symmetrical patterns began, 1,162-63 and 2,172-73, the lines with the repetitions of *wundor*, *Wealhþeo*, and *beag* (cf. Fig. 9 and 10 above). The ratio expressing the relative position of these (partially) hypermetric passages is equal to the ratio between the number of lines preceding the other hypermetric cluster, HM2 (1,704 lines), and the line sum 3,182: 1,163/2,172 = 1,704/3,182 (the difference here being 0.00006). By corollary this proportion too may be expressed in terms of sequential intervals: from the start of HM1 in 1,163 to the last line before HM2 (1,704) is 541 lines; from line 3,182 back to 2,172 is 1,010 lines; 541/1,163 = 1,010/3,182. (My numerical formulation of this proportional placement here is an expedient; the poet himself may well have conceived these proportions in some quasi-spatial manner, and readers interested in appreciating the pattern's "shape" may wish to sketch it out in diagram.)

In sum, then, the relative placement of all three hypermetric clusters and the (partially) hypermetric *Wealhþeo*-passage in 2,172-73 within the poem's 3,182-line continuum is governed by two precisely coupled proportions. These examples of proportion are consistent with other principles controlling the poet's tectonic design. In both textual salience and numerical precision they are representative of many others I have observed in this work. Although such proportionality required considerably more mathematical sophistication on the poet's part than simple symmetries, these proportional relationships appear to be too numerous, too clearly marked by textual features, too precise numerically, and too consistent with the rest of the poem's structure to be accidental. For a representative instance involving lexical (rather than chiefly prosodic) features, compare lines 196-97 and 789-90, the only two passages in the poem containing repetitions of two entire verse lines in sequence ("se wæs moncynnes mægenes strengest / on þæm dæge þysses lifes" and "se þe manna wæs mægene strengest / on þæm dæge þysses lifes") and their striking proportional placement: 196(= exactly 195.6)/789 = 789/3,182.

15. As Georg Lukács expressed it in the section of his *Ästhetik* dealing with "Symmetrie und Proportion": "Da aber alle Formen Widerspiegelungen der Wirklichkeit sind, stecken hinter allen Proportionalitätsfragen der Komposition Probleme der Weltanschauung: die des Schaffenden und die der Gesellschaft, in welcher und für welche seine Werke entstehen." Cf. his *Ästhetik Teil I: Die Eigenart des Ästhetischen* (Berlin, 1963), 1. Halbband, pp. 284-311, esp. p. 307.

16. Peterson, "Critical Calculations," p. 370.
17. I have broached this question elsewhere in connection with a much shorter text, eight lines, where the possibility of subconscious aesthetic impact from tectonic features is more palpable than in so long a text as *Beowulf*; cf. Hart, "Linguistic Patterns, Literary Structure, and the Genesis of C. F. Meyer's 'Der römische Brunnen,' " *Language and Style*, 4 (1971): 83-115, esp. pp. 114 f. Others have also begun to explore the related issues of aesthetic impact that have arisen from the (nontectonic but cognate) findings of structuralists and formalists; cf. Daniel Laferrière, "Automorphic Structures in the Poem's Grammatical Space," *Semiotica* 10 (1974): 333-50, and the scholarship embraced by his bibliography. The studies on proportionality by major painters such as Leonardo and Dürer are well known and of self-evident relevance to both the compositional requirements and the essentially nondiscursive character of their art form. The relevance of proportionality to the aesthetic impact of poetry will always be more difficult to assess because of the discursive nature of reading. Appreciation of a tectonic design — at least in a long poem — presupposes a kind of mental conversion of the discursive text into a nondiscursive mode in which all sequential parts are "pictured" as simultaneously present to one another. For most of us, one expects, to make this conversion will always require conscious attention to the proportionality, an effort hardly comparable to the unconscious enjoyment of the proportions in a painting.

Patterns of Arithmetical Proportion in the *Nibelungenlied*

In recent scholarship the term *numerical structure* is used with two meanings, which are sometimes rendered by the more specific terms *number symbolism* and *arithmetical proportion*. The former is applied to cases in which a specific number is used in a text in a conspicuous way to evoke certain associations that derive from the significance of that number in another context. The numbers 3 and 12, for example, have a special meaning within a Christian frame of reference because of their associations with the Trinity and the Twelve Apostles, respectively. In a given text, these numbers may be mentioned explicitly or referred to indirectly. It is also possible to arrange the text in such a way that groups of like structural features — verses, chapters, strophes, and the like — recur at regular intervals. When such structures are distributed in balanced or symmetrical patterns, one may speak of arithmetical proportion. For example, the two halves of a poem may be correlated with the two most important parts of the content, and structure thus serves to underscore or emphasize the division of the subject matter. It is also possible to combine these devices, as in Dante's *Divine Comedy*, which contains 100 cantos: a 1-canto introduction and 3 sections of 33 cantos each. The 3 sections of equal numbers of cantos show arithmetical proportion, while the number 3 itself makes symbolic reference to the threefold division of the world beyond this one — the subject of the work — into Hell, Purgatory, and

Heaven. This feature of the structure of Dante's poem thus combines arithmetical proportion with number symbolism. To be sure, not all works of medieval literature contain both kinds of numerical structure: some display the one, but not the other. It is the thesis of this study that patterns of arithmetical proportion may be detected in the great medieval German epic, the *Nibelungenlied*.

The notion that arithmetically defined patterns are to be found in the *Nibelungenlied* is by no means new. As early as 1836, one of that poem's first editors, Karl Lachmann, expressed the belief that the epic was composed of groups of strophes, and that the number of strophes in each group was always divisible by 7; thus, on Lachmann's theory, the poem could be analyzed as a series of "Heptaden." Toward the end of the century, Emil Kettner advanced the view that the *Nibelungenlied* was composed of 5 books, each subdivided into "Lieder." Both of these theories collide with the inescapable fact that the work contains 39 separate divisions or *aventiuren* that are clearly attested throughout the manuscript tradition.[1]

These early attempts were without notable consequence. Perhaps the most powerful stimulus to the study of patterns of arithmetically defined structure in medieval literature has come from the well-known essay by Ernst Robert Curtius entitled "Zahlenkomposition."[2] In the wake of this work, a number of scholars have again tried to establish comparable patterns of arithmetical regularity in a variety of works, among them the *Nibelungenlied*.[3] Their research has proceeded in two general directions. In one group are those who seek to identify patterns of regularity in blocks of strophes within a single aventiure: Maurer, for example, views aventiure 37 as consisting of 3 groups of 29 strophes each.[4] The results produced by this approach have not been wholly convincing; I will examine some of its strengths and weaknesses later in this paper in connection with aventiure 20. Those in the second group have tried to find patterns of arithmetical proportion in various aggregations of aventiuren: Mergell, for example, believes that the basic structure of the *Nibelungenlied* consists of a series of 8 groups of 5 aventiuren each, falling into 2 blocks of 4 pentads each, which share aventiure 20 as a common element.[5]

In any attempt to demonstrate a "structure" among the elements that constitute a larger work, one must be able to point to some feature of the poem by which the structure is, in effect, defined. This defining factor may be some aspect of the content of the poem. Wachinger, for example, divides the *Nibelungenlied* into an introduction followed by 4 phases, using as his criterion the inner chronology of the poem: the divisions between his phases coincide with the longer pauses and intervals between the clusters of events that comprise the subject matter of the work. Like many scholars, he regards the first two aventiuren as the introduction. The division between the first and second phases lies between aventiuren 11 and 12, and coincides with the interval of 11 years that Sîfrid and Kriemhild spend happily in Xanten. Further divisions lie between aventiuren 18 and 19 and between 19 and 20. In the former case, 3 to 4 years elapse between Sîfrid's death and the events of aventiure 19; in the latter, 9 years pass before the appearance of Rüedegêr of Bechelâren, Etzel's ambassador, to ask for Kriemhilt's hand in marriage in behalf of his liege lord. The division between the two final phases falls between aventiuren 22 and 23 — it coincides with the period of 12 years between Kriemhilt's marriage and the invitation to her brothers to visit her in Hungary. Thus, Wachinger conceives the structure of the *Nibelungenlied* as follows:

Av.   1-2:   Introduction (2 avn.)
Av.   3-11: Phase A (9 avn.)
             (approx. 11 years)
Av.   12-18: Phase B (6 avn.)
             (3-4 years)
Av.   19:   "Zwischenglied" (1 av.)
             (approx. 9 years)
Av.   20-22: Phase C (3 avn.)
             (approx. 12 years)
Av.   23-39: Phase D (17 avn.)[6]

It should be stated that these divisions are completely justified as larger interruptions in the flow of time in the period represented in the poem. Indeed, as has been pointed out elsewhere, the treatment of time is a distinctive characteristic of the *Nibelungenlied*, compared with other works of medieval German literature.[7] Nevertheless, one may well ask, in light of the numerous studies that have demonstrated the existence of numerical structure in other literary works of the Middle Ages, whether patterns of regularity—defined arithmetically—are not to be found here as well.

If one is prepared to accept this direction of inquiry, then the conclusions about the *Nibelungenlied* reached by McCarthy should occasion no surprise.[8] She sees the poem as a symmetrically structured unity. First, in her view the 39 aventiuren constituting the work fall into two sections of 19 aventiuren each, separated by a central pivotal segment, aventiure 20 (pp. 158-59). Each of the 2 sections of 19 aventiuren may be analyzed in like fashion as containing 2 sections of 9 aventiuren each, with a separating central aventiure (p. 160). Moreover, each of these 4 sections of 9 aventiuren each is held to contain 2 sections of 4 aventiuren each, on either side of a central, pivotal aventiure.[9] One may summarize McCarthy's findings concerning the structure of the *Nibelungenlied* in the following diagram (Figure 19).

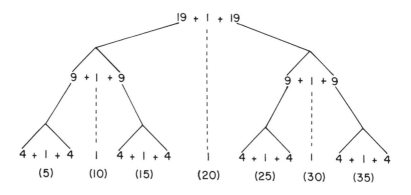

FIG. 19. *The K-structure of the* Nibelungenlied *(after McCarthy).*

Not only do the pivotal strophes give the impression of mathematical regularity, but they also deal with events that are "pivotal" in the metaphorical sense as well. The central function of aventiure 20 is apparent to any reader of the *Nibelungenlied*—it is the bridge between the two great geographical areas where the events of the poem take place, that is, the Rhine around Worms and Xanten, and the Danube in Hungary, presumably near Gran. (Because of its importance, I will return to this section of the poem below for a more detailed study of its content.) As McCarthy points out, the two large sections preceding and following aventiure 20 contain the pivotal aventiuren 10 and 30. In the former, Sîfrid helps Gunther on his wedding night to make Brünhilt his wife; in the latter, there is the first overt conflict between the Burgundians and Kriemhilt's allies, when these latter make a sneak attack on the hall where Volkêr and Hagen are standing watch; the tenth and the thirtieth aventiuren have the additional features in common that they involve deception, and that they take place under cover of night. The pivotal aventiuren in the small groups of 9 also stand out by reason of their significance for the movement of the plot. The fifth and the fifteenth are both important in connection with Kriemhilt's relation to Sîfrid: in aventiure 5, she sees him for the first time, during the celebration upon his return from the Saxon wars; in aventiure 15 he returns from the campaign occasioned by the false report of hostilities on the part of the Saxons and is betrayed, however unwittingly, by Kriemhilt. Aventiuren 25 and 35 show a similar relation of anticipation and fulfillment: in the former the Rhine-maidens make their prediction to Hagen that only the kings' chaplain will return to Worms alive; in the latter Kriemhilt fails in her last attempt to wreak revenge on Hagen without drawing her kinsmen into the general destruction. It is in aventiure 35 that *Kriemhilts rache* is finally transformed into *der Nibelunge nôt* (p. 164). This series of interrelationships—the division of the work into 8 groups of 4 aventiuren each, separated by 7 pivotal aventiuren—will in this essay be called the "K-structure" because of its close connection with the figure of Kriemhilt.

The close correlation between the pivotal aventiuren and various events in the poem supports the contention that it was the purpose of the author of the *Nibelungenlied* to use arithmetical proportion as a way of underscoring certain aspects of the work. And yet McCarthy observes, as have others before her, that other aventiuren are of almost equal importance when judged by the same criteria. She points out, for example, that aventiuren 14, 15, and 16 "vie for position" (p. 161). Similarly, aventiure 26 — not an aventiure made prominent in any way by the arithmetical patterns of the K-structure — is noteworthy as the culmination of Kriemhilt's plan to lure Hagen and the Nibelung kings to Etzel's land (p. 164). One's feeling that these aventiuren are also of some special importance suggests that the K-structure may not be the only pattern of mathematical regularity in the *Nibelungenlied*. Moreover, the fact that important aventiuren such as the fourteenth and the twenty-sixth have to do not with Kriemhilt alone but also with the Burgundian kings leads one to look for another structure, the component elements of which would emphasize those aventiuren in which the Nibelung kings play a dominant role.

If one surveys the work as a whole from this perspective, one sees that the *Nibelungenlied* may again be divided into three sections: the first, in which the coming catastrophe lies concealed beneath the surface; the second, which covers the transition from Sîfrid's death to the departure of the Nibelungs for the east; and the third, which includes the events that take place after the arrival of the Nibelungs in Etzel's land. Each of these parts consists of exactly 13 aventiuren. The first section takes the reader from the beginning of the epic through aventiure 13, in which Gunther, at Brünhilt's suggestion, arranges a grand celebration in Worms. The next group of 13, that is, aventiuren 14-26, carries the reader from the disastrous confrontation before the cathedral door, through the slaying of Sîfrid and Kriemhilt's marriage to Etzel, to the Nibelungs' departure from their land for the last time to make their fateful visit to Etzel's court. The last 13 aventiuren, 26-39, relate the events in Etzel's country from the welcome by

Margrave Rüedegêr in Bechelâren to the final destruction of the Burgundians at the hands of Etzel's warriors. I will call these three groups of 13 aventiuren each the "N-structure" because of their close correlation with events involving the Nibelungs.

Just as in the case of the K-structure, the N-structure also contains certain pivotal aventiuren: the seventh in each group, precisely at the midpoint of the section. As to aventiure 7, it is here that Sifrid, with the help of the *tarnkappe*, aids Gunther in the contests with Brünhilt; in the seventh aventiure in the third group of 13, aventiure 33, Hagen slays Etzel's son Ortlieb after learning of the attack on the Burgundians by Etzel's warriors — an act that makes it impossible for Etzel to stay out of the conflict. The seventh aventiure of the second group of 13, aventiure 20, is also the pivotal aventiure of the K-structure; it is of such importance that I will examine it separately below. The relationship between the K-structure and the N-structure is presented in the following diagram (Figure 20, p. 218).

From this diagram, it is not difficult to see why certain groups of aventiuren seem to be of superordinate importance — 13, 14, and 15, for example, or 25, 26, and 27: these are either pivotal aventiuren, or they are terminal aventiuren in the N-structure. The two systems, the K-structure and the N-structure, operate dialectically throughout the poem, representing in the form of patterns of arithmetical proportion the conflicts between Kriemhilt and the Nibelungs. The systems are in harmony at only three points: aventiure 1, aventiure 39, and aventiure 20, the last being the pivotal aventiure of the K-structure as well as the pivotal aventiure of the N2 section. The significance of the first and last aventiuren quite obviously lies in their initial and final positions; the importance of aventiure 20 can be revealed only by a careful analysis of its structure. But before undertaking this investigation, it will be necessary to digress to anticipate an objection to the conclusions about the K- and N-structures reached above.

The question has been raised, in connection with the presence of arithmetical proportion in medieval literature, as to whether the mathematical patterns could not be

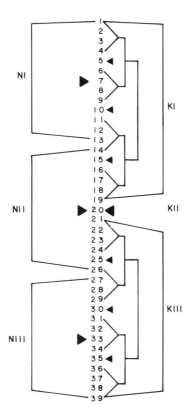

FIG. 20. The correlation of the K- and N-structures of the Nibelungenlied.

accidental.[10] This challenge cannot be brushed aside or
refuted by a modern variant of the cosmological proof, an
argument for the existence of arithmetical proportion from the
principle of order. In every case when one adverts to patterns
of mathematical regularity in literature, one implies that these
patterns are the product of the author's intention and hence
represent the visible signs of his artistic conception. But what if
the author in fact held no such intention, or, in the present

case, what if the division of the *Nibelungenlied* into 39 aventiuren "just happened"? If this be the case, then the segmentation of the poem into two groups of 19 aventiuren each, plus one (the K-structure), in conjunction with a second division into 3 groups of 13 aventiuren each (the N-structure), may not flow from the author's creative impulse, but may be merely the accidental consequence of the mathematical properties of the number 39, which "just happens" to be the sum of 19 + 1 + 19, as well as the sum of 13 + 13 + 13.[11] To be sure, scholars have attempted to correlate certain regularly recurring arithmetical patterns with coherent segments of the poem itself. Despite some degree of correspondence, one could be more confident that these patterns in fact reflected the intent of the author if further evidence could be found that would independently corroborate the conclusions reached above.

One can find additional support in the number of strophes in each of the various sections of the K- and N-structures identified above. But if one resorts to the absolute length of the poem and its constituent sections in terms of the number of strophes, one strikes against yet another difficulty. As is well known, the *Nibelungenlied* is not a work that has been preserved in its original form. For this reason, one must first consider the complicated and not altogether transparent textual history of the work. It is noteworthy that it was quite popular in the Middle Ages: an unusually large number of manuscripts, and of fragments of manuscripts, has been preserved — 34 altogether. This being so, it is not surprising that scholars who have studied the manuscript tradition are not in complete accord on every point. Nevertheless, the current view is that the three main manuscripts, labeled "A" (the Hohenems-München manuscript, *cgm.* 34 in the Bayerische Staatsbibliothek in Munich), "B" (MS 857 in the library of the monastery of Sankt Gallen in Switzerland), and "C" (the Hohenems-Lassberg manuscript, MS. 63 in the Fürstlich Fürstenbergische Hofbibliothek in Donaueschingen) represent the three chief strands in the tradition. The following stemma (Figure 21), constructed by Wilhelm Braune in 1900, is still widely accepted, and even its critics have only modified it.[12]

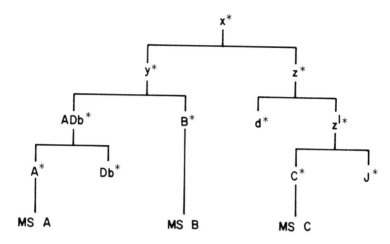

FIG. 21. The manuscript tradition of the Nibelungenlied (after Braune).

As the stemma suggests, the text of MS B is closer to the original by one generation, so to speak, and is hence usually taken as the basis for scholarly studies where the question of manuscript filiation is not crucial. But because of this uncertainty in the matter of the text, I will, in the analysis below, refer to all three of these manuscripts when the question of the absolute number of strophes in a given section is raised.

The two patterns of arithmetical proportions, one for the K-structure and one for the N-structure, are presented in Table 1.

TABLE 1

THE K AND N STRUCTURES

Section	K-Structure Avs.	No. Avs.	Section	N-Structure Avs.	No. Avs.
K1	1-19	19	N1	1-13	13
K2	20	1	N2	14-26	13
K3	21-39	19	N3	27-39	13
		39			39

When one turns to the actual number of strophes in the various sections of the K- and N-structures, one finds a remarkable similarity. In the table below, figures are given for each of the three manuscripts.[13]

TABLE 2

NUMBER OF STROPHES IN THE SECTIONS
OF THE KRIEMHILT-STRUCTURE

Section	MS A (2,316 str.)	MS B (2,376 str.)	MS C (2,439 str.)
K1 (Av. 1-19)	1,082 (46.71%)	1,139 (47.93%)	1,165 (47.76%)
K2 (Av. 20)	147 (6.34%)	147 (6.18%)	150 (6.15%)
K3 (Av. 21-39)	1,087 (46.93%)	1,090 (45.87%)	1,124 (46.08%)

Table 2 shows, first, that the K1 and K3 sections are almost equal in length: the difference between the larger and the smaller sections is only slightly more than two percent in MS B, and less in the other MSS. The number of strophes in the middle section, K2, is almost the same in each manuscript and constitutes approximately the same percentage of strophes of the poem as a whole in each manuscript—slightly more than six percent. These figures convey the impression that the length of the K1 and K3 sections might well have been equal in the original.

As to the N-structure, one finds a similar correspondence there; the figures for the three sections are presented in Table 3.

TABLE 3

NUMBER OF STROPHES IN THE SECTIONS OF THE
NIBELUNGEN STRUCTURE

Section	MS A (2,316 str.)	MS B (2,376 str.)	MS C (2,439 str.)
N1 (Av. 1-13)	756 (32.64%)	810 (34.09%)	822 (33.70%)
N2 (Av. 14-26)	833 (35.96%)	836 (35.18%)	867 (35.54%)
N3 (Av. 27-39)	727 (31.39%)	730 (30.72%)	750 (30.75%)

Each of the three sections contains roughly one-third the number of strophes in each manuscript; the difference between the largest and the smallest is in no case greater than five percent.

While not in themselves conclusive, these statistics suggest that arithmetical proportion was indeed a structural principle employed in the composition of the *Nibelungenlied*, and that this principle was carried through, not only to the number of aventiuren in the various sections, but also to the total number of strophes in each section. This observation, in turn, corroborates the view that these patterns of arithmetical proportion do reflect the artistic purpose of the author of the work—indeed, they support the contention that the poem, in its present form, is the work of a single author.

At several points I have alluded to the twentieth aventiure and to its importance in both of the two structures. In the N-structure it is the pivotal aventiure in section N2; in the K-structure it stands alone as section K2, the central segment of the poem. Because both structures point toward this aventiure, it may behoove one to examine it further to see whether evidence of arithmetical proportion can be detected within it. It is striking, to begin with, that the twentieth is the largest aventiure in the entire work: whereas the average aventiure is about 60 strophes in length, the twentieth contains 147 strophes in MSS A and B and 150 in MS C. Its length as well as its position suggests that it is of superordinate importance.

When one turns to its content, one notes that it is of particular significance within the frame of reference of the Kriemhilt-structure. The first 19 aventiuren, section K1, recount the main events in Sifrid's and Kriemhilt's lives on the Rhine, their meeting and marriage, his death, and finally her withdrawal to a widow's seclusion in the monastery of Lorsch. So complete is this section in itself that it would be quite possible to break off the poem at this point with no sacrifice of internal consistency. The twentieth aventiure shifts the scene to Etzel's court at Etzelnburc in Hungary. The events there, the political desirability of finding a new queen for the ruler of the land, all coincide both with Kriemhilt's widowed state and, as the reader comes to learn, with her desire for revenge. In this aventiure, Etzel's ambassador, Margrave Rüedegêr, succeeds in obtaining her consent to a marriage with Etzel, which in turn gives her the opportunity to wreak her revenge on those responsible for Sîfrid's murder, chiefly Hagen. Thus, on internal evidence, it is Rüedegêr's suit that is the central event in aventiure 20. It comes as no surprise, then, that the marriage proposal is presented to Kriemhilt for the first time — to be sure, at this point not by Rüedegêr — precisely at the midpoint of the aventiure. Thus the journey to Worms, the proposal, and her initial refusal constitute the first half of the aventiure; her reconsideration, her subsequent acceptance, and the preparations for departure, the second half.

In contrast to this two-element structure relating to Kriemhilt, one again detects a three-element structure related to Rüedegêr. The first section of about 45 strophes has to do with his preparations for departure from Etzel's land, the last section (which is of equal length), with his winning of Kriemhilt's hand for his monarch and with the preparations for the return to Hungary. The central section, longer than the other two, portrays his activities and efforts as ambassador at the Burgundian court. The following diagram (Figure 22) — which ignores a small number of inconsistencies to be examined presently — illuminates the dialectical character of the Rüedegêr- and Kriemhilt-substructures as they appear in aventiure 20.

It is apparent that the principle of arithmetical proportion has been carried through to the composition of the twentieth aventiure. And yet I have not reached the limits to which this literary device has been extended.

If one examines the various segments of these substructures, one finds that these, too, reveal patterns of mathematical symmetry. In the first of the Rüedegêr-substructures, R1, one notes that the discussion at Etzel's court, Rüedegêr's return to Bechelâren, and his subsequent journey to the Burgundian court take about 15 strophes each. Similarly, the three events in the last of these three substructures, R3 — that is, Rüedegêr's successful attempt to persuade Kriemhilt to accept Etzel's offer, her effort to secure the treasure of the Nibelungs, and the preparations for departure — also occupy about 15 strophes

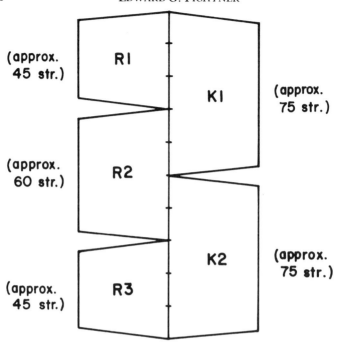

FIG. 22. Structural outline of the Nibelungenlied's *aventiure 20.*

each. As to the larger middle section, R2, it is cut into two
parts by virtue of the intersection with the Kriemhilt-
substructure, so that R2 may be divided into two segments of
30 strophes each. Each of these 30-strophe segments is in turn
subdivided into segments that are mirror images of one
another. The first 10 strophes contain Rüedegêr's address to
the Burgundian kings, in which he states the purpose of his
journey; during the next 15 strophes, the kings deliberate; in
the following 5 strophes, Margrave Gêre rushes to Kriemhilt to
relay to her the proposal just presented by Rüedegêr. At this
point, the sequence is reversed. In the first 5 strophes,
Kriemhilt states her refusal, but agrees to listen to Rüedegêr's
presentation, which takes place during the next 15 strophes; in
the following 10, Kriemhilt considers the offer.[14] These patterns may be represented, in somewhat oversimplified form, as
in Figure 23.

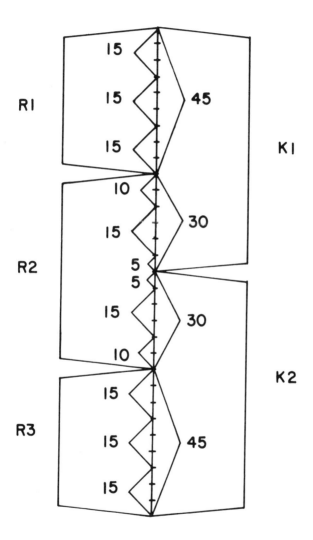

FIG. 23. Detailed structural outline of the Nibelungenlied's *aventiure 20.*

This diagram represents the structure of the twentieth aventiure as being completely symmetrical in design. But, as I have observed, structures of this kind are not always reflected quite so precisely in the manuscripts themselves, which are at several removes from the hypothetical original. Nevertheless, the patterns are clear enough to show that the structures of arithmetical proportion have not been simply read into the text. To permit reference to any or all of the three versions of the *Nibelungenlied* that have been preserved, Table 4 shows the number of strophes in each segment in each manuscript and identifies (in parentheses) the particular strophes in each

TABLE 4

ARITHMETICAL PROPORTION IN AVENTIURE 20 IN MSS A, B, AND C

Substruc-ture	Hypothe-tical No. of Strophes	MS A	MS B	MS C
R1	15	17 (1,083-99)	17 (1,140-56)	17 (1,166-82)
	15	14 (1,100-13)	14 (1,157-70)	14 (1,183-96)
	15	17 (1,114-30)	17 (1,171-87)	18 (1,197-1214)
	45	48 (1,083-1130)	48 (1,140-87	49 (1,166-1214)
R2	10	9 (1,131-39)	9 (1,188-96)	9 (1,215-23)
	15	16 (1,140-55)	16 (1,197-1212)	16 (1,224-39)
	5	5 (1,156-60)	5 (1,213-17)	5 (1,240-44)
	30	30 (1,131-60)	30 (1,188-1217)	30 (1,215-44)
	5	5 (1,161-65)	5 (1,218-22)	5 (1,245-49)
	15	16 (1,166-81)	16 (1,223-38)	16 (1,250-65)
	10	9 (1,182-90)	9 (1,239-47)	9 (1,266-74)
	30	30 (1,161-90)	30 (1,218-47)	30 (1,245-74)
R3	15	17 (1,191-1207)	17 (1,248-64)	16 (1,275-90)
	15	14 (1,208-21)	14 (1,265-78)	14 (1,291-1304)
	15	8 (1,222-29)	8 (1,279-86)	11 (1,305-15)
	45	39 (1,191-1229)	39 (1,248-86)	41(1,275-1315)
	150	147	147	150

segment in each manuscript.

The figures in Table 4 show that the actual number of strophes in each section in some cases departs slightly from the patterns that were described above and represented in the various tables and diagrams. In section R1 the number of strophes actually present in the manuscripts exceeds by 3 or 4 the number expected on the basis of my assumptions about arithmetical proportion; on the other hand, in section R3 the number of strophes present falls short by 4 to 6. Taken together, these discrepancies may reflect a condition that can be observed elsewhere in the manuscripts of the *Nibelungenlied*, that is, the tendency to expand the early parts of a section, coupled with a countervailing tendency to lose strophes toward the end of that section. Tables 2 and 3 are illustrative in this connection. Whether this situation represents the collective errors of copyists and scribes, or the literary intentions of an intervenient redactor, is a matter for future research. Variation again appears in the two sections of R2, which, to be sure, contain the expected 30 strophes each but in sections of 5, 9, and 16 strophes instead of the hypothesized 5, 10 and 15. These disparities notwithstanding, the presence of arithmetical proportion seems probable on the basis of the close correlation between these arithmetical patterns and the lines of cleavage identified in the text itself.

In conclusion, the evidence appears to support the claim that arithmetical proportion is a structural feature of the *Nibelungenlied*. Arithmetical proportion is seen in the poem as a whole, where this principle is used to bring out the twin lines of action: that connected with the Burgundian court—that is, the Nibelungen-structure; and that revolving around the figure of Kriemhilt—that is, the Kriemhilt-structure. At the point of intersection between these two structures lies the twentieth aventiure, within which one is also able to discern comparable patterns of arithmetical proportion. These patterns, too, serve as a formal device by which certain priorities can be unobtrusively expressed, specifically as a way of drawing the attention of the careful reader both to the importance of Kriemhilt's decision within the context of aventiure 20 and to

228   EDWARD G. FICHTNER

its larger significance for the work as a whole.

Notes

1. Karl Lachmann, *Zu den Nibelungen und zur Klage: Anmerkungen* (Berlin, 1836) and Emil Kettner, *Die österreichische Nibelungendichtung* (Berlin, 1897); this account is based on the description given by Bert Nagel, *Das Nibelungenlied: Stoff—Form—Ethos* (Frankfurt, 1965), p. 97.

2. Excursus 15 in Ernst Robert Curtius, *Europäische Literatur und lateinisches Mittelalter*, 2d ed. (Bern, 1954), pp. 491-98.

3. Recent scholarship on the *Nibelungenlied* is surveyed in: Siegfried Beyschlag, "Das Nibelungenlied in gegenwärtiger Sicht," in *Zur germanisch-deutschen Heldensage*, ed. Karl Hauck, Wege der Forschung, Bd. 14 (Darmstadt, 1965), pp. 214-47, which is an updating of Beyschlag's earlier article in *Wirkendes Wort* 3 (1953): 193-200; Werner Hoffmann, "Zur Situation der gegenwärtigen Nibelungenforschung," *Wirkendes Wort* 12 (1962): 79-91 Gottfried Weber, *Nibelungenlied*, 2d ed., Sammlung Metzler, M7 (Stuttgart, 1964); and Willy Krogmann and Ulrich Pretzel, *Bibliographie zum Nibelungenlied und zur Klage*, 4th ed., Bibliographien zur deutschen Literatur des Mittelalters, Heft 1 (Berlin, 1966). Cf. also Nagel, *Das Nibelungenlied* passim.

4. Friedrich Maurer, "Über den Bau der Aventiuren des Nibelungenlieds," in *Festschrift für Dietrich Kralik* (Horn, NÖ., 1954), pp. 93-98. Other works in which this approach is represented include Maurer's "Über die Formkunst des Dichters unseres Nibelungenliedes," *Der Deutschunterricht* 6, no. 5 (1954): 77-83, and a number of publications by Michael S. Batts: *Die Form der Aventiuren im Nibelungenlied*, Beiträge zur deutschen Philologie, Bd. 29 (Giessen, 1961), which is based on his Freiburg/Br. dissertation of 1957; "Poetic Form as a Criterion in Manuscript Criticism," *Modern Language Review* 55 (1960): 543-52; "Numerical Structure in German Literature," in *Formal Aspects of Medieval German Poetry*, ed. Stanley Werbow (Austin, Tex., 1969), pp. 93-119.

5. Bodo Mergell, "Nibelungenlied und höfischer Roman," *Euphorion* 45 (1950): 305-6. Others who propose comparable interpretations of the poem are: Jean Fourquet, "Zum Aufbau des Nibelungenlieds und des Kudrunlieds," *Zeitschrift für deutsches Altertum* 85 (1954/55): 137-49; Burghart Wachinger, *Studien zum Nibelungenlied: Vorausdeutung, Aufbau, Motivierung* (Tübingen, 1960); and Sister Mary Frances McCarthy, S.N.D., "Architectonic Symmetry as a Principle of Structure in the *Nibelungenlied*," *Germanic Review* 41 (1966): 157-69. The last-named article is the point of departure for the present study, and I will have occasion below to examine the author's findings in detail. Other important studies that apply this principle to medieval German works other than the *Nibelungenlied* include Hans Eggers, *Symmetrie und Proportion epischen Erzählens: Studien zur Kunstform Hartmanns von Aue* (Stuttgart, 1956) and the same author's article "Der Goldene Schnitt im Aufbau alt- und mittelhochdeutscher Epen," *Wirkendes Wort* 10 (1960): 193-203. The same phenom-

enon has been identified in medieval French literature by C. A. Robson, "The Technique of Symmetrical Composition in Medieval Narrative Poetry," in *Studies in Medieval French presented to Alfred Ewert. . .* , ed. E. A. Francis (Oxford, 1961), pp. 26-75. More recently, a complex system of arithmetical proportion has been posited for the Oxford version of the *Chanson de Roland* by Eleanor Webster Bulatkin in her *Structural Arithmetic Metaphor in the Oxford "Roland"* (Columbus, Ohio, 1972); see A. Kent Hieatt's comments in this volume. I am indebted to Professor Thomas Elwood Hart of Syracuse University for drawing my attention to several works on this subject, including the important book by Ernst Hellgardt, *Zum Problem symbolbestimmter und formalästhetischer Zahlenkomposition in mittelalterlicher Literatur*, Münchener Texte and Untersuchungen zur deutschen Literatur des Mittelalters, Bd. 45 (Munich, 1973).

6. Wachinger, *Studien*, pp. 82 ff.

7. Nagel, *Das Nibelungenlied*, pp. 92 f.

8. McCarthy, "Architectonic Symmetry." Page references in the discussion to follow are to this article.

9. McCarthy seems to be unaware that these segments of 4 aventiuren plus a pivotal aventiure correspond closely to Mergell's "Pentaden"; cf. the latter's article, cited above.

    McCarthy's structure, and the N-structure to be discussed below, show the bilaterally symmetrical design of two "wings" surrounding a center that has been proposed for certain examples of lyric poetry. See J. A. Huisman, *Neue Wege zur dichterischen und musikalischen Technik Walthers von der Vogelweide*, Studia Litteraria Rheno-Traiectina 1 (Utrecht, 1950), and Constance Hieatt and A. Kent Hieatt, " 'The Bird with Four Feathers': Numerical Analysis of a Fourteenth-Century Poem," *Papers on Language and Literature* 6 (1970): 18-38.

10. Cf. Batts, "Numerical Structure," pp. 101 ff. I am also indebted to Professor A. Kent Hieatt for some stimulating thoughts on this point.

11. Peter Wiehl, "Über den Aufbau des Nibelungenlieds," *Wirkendes Wort* 16 (1966): 309-23 raises this argument implicitly when he states that for MS B four different structural patterns can be found that display arithmetical proportion. Wiehl's claim (p. 320) that this can be accomplished "ohne Zwang" is not, however, borne out by what he does in his article; in several cases he adjusts his figures in an arbitrary manner to make his categories proportional. Moreover, his entire approach exemplifies a confusion of priorities: he has, in effect, converted the search for mathematical properties corresponding to divisions of content into a search for lines of cleavage in the content of the poem that correspond to arbitrarily chosen patterns of arithmetical proportion. The principle underlying the present investigation is that arithmetical proportion underscores structure as determined by literary analysis, and not vice versa.

12. Convenient summaries of current scholarship may be found in Weber, *Nibelungenlied*, cited above, and in the article by Friedrich Neumann, "Handschriftenkritik am Nibelungenlied," *Germanisch-romanische Monatsschrift* 46 (1965): 225-44.

13. References to the *Nibelungenlied*, including strophe numbers, are taken from the diplomatic edition of Michael S. Batts, *Das Nibelungenlied: Paralleldruck der Handschriften A, B, und C nebst Lesarten der übrigen Handschriften* (Tübingen, 1971).

14. Batts, *Die Form der Aventiuren*, pp. 64-65, in his analysis of the structure of this aventiure, overlooks the fact that the event at its very center is the first presentation of the offer of marriage to Kriemhilt by her kinsman Margrave Gêre (and not by Rüedegêr!) in str. 1,217. Gêre's words are meant seriously, but they have a double meaning for Kriemhilt: "ir muget mich gerne grüezen und geben botenbrôt. / iuch wil gelücke scheiden vil schiere ûz aller iwer nôt" (str. 1,216, 11. 3-4, in *Das Nibelungenlied*, ed. Bartsch-de Boor, 14th ed., Deutsche Klassiker des Mittelalters [Wiesbaden, 1957]). His use of the word *nôt* here anticipates the last word in the poem.

Bibliographical Note

The published literature on medieval number theory and practice has become large and diverse. It ranges from broad investigations into the aesthetics of number to close studies of single texts. No complete bibliography of all of this material exists. However, there are excellent introductions to the subject, important recent syntheses, and a variety of bibliographic guides. Many of these works have been cited in the notes to the essays in this collection. The purpose of this Bibliographical Note is to group a few of the major sources together as a brief guide to further reading and research.

I know of no better relatively short treatment of the general principles of medieval number theory than Russell A. Peck's essay, with its Appendix, in this volume. Vincent Hopper's book *Medieval Number Symbolism: Its Sources, Meaning, and Influence on Thought and Expression* (New York, 1938) is still basic and has recently been reprinted (Norwood, Pa., 1977). Ernst Robert Curtius's influential remarks on numerical composition are conveniently available as Excursus 15 in his book *Europäische Literatur und lateinisches Mittelalter* (*European Literature and the Latin Middle Ages*; Bern, 1948, in German; London, 1953, in English; and subsequent editions). These three solid and lucid studies can be read as introductions and can be usefully supplemented, in that category, by others. A few in English are Charles Alan Robson's "The Technique of Symmetrical Composition in Medieval Narrative Poetry," in *Studies in Medieval French Presented to Alfred Ewert*, ed. E. A. Francis (Oxford, 1961), pp. 26-75; Michael Stanley Batts's "Numerical Structure in Medieval Literature, with a Bibliography," in *Formal Aspects of Medieval German Poetry*, ed. S. N. Werbow (Austin, Tex., 1969), pp. 93-119; and Edmund Reiss's "Number Symbolism and Medieval Literature," *Medievalia et Humanistica*, new ser. 1 (1970):161-74.

Two recent collections of critical studies — somewhat akin to this book — deserve mention. One is *Number Symbolism*, ed. Christopher Butler (London, 1970). The other is *Silent Poetry: Essays in Numerological Analysis*, ed. Alastair Fowler (London, 1970); to it

Christopher Butler has contributed a chapter on "Numerological Thought" (pp. 1-31), a good general treatment that might be added to those listed above. Many other critical studies are scattered throughout the journal literature (see bibliographies, just below). The best full-length comprehensive treatments of the subject since Hopper are now two books in German: Ernst Hellgardt, *Zum Problem symbolbestimmter und formalästhetischer Zahlenkomposition in mittelalterlicher Literatur* (Munich, 1973), and Heinz Meyer, *Die Zahlenallegorese im Mittelalter: Methode und Gebrauch* (Munich, 1975). These synthetic works treat the importance of numbers to related fields, such as architecture, as well as discussing their values in medieval literature.

As for locating studies on particular texts, in the absence of a complete bibliography one must consult the lists in several studies not primarily bibliographical. Useful lists are to be found in Batts's "Numerical Structure," cited above; Eleanor Webster Bulatkin's *Structural Arithmetic Metaphor in the Oxford "Roland"* (Columbus, Ohio, 1972); and Hellgardt's and Meyer's books just mentioned, especially Hellgardt's, where the *Literaturverzeichnis*, in several sections, runs to nearly fifty pages (pp. 303-51). Hellgardt's bibliography ends with August 1972. For works published since then, or earlier works not included in his list, which emphasizes German literature, one should check the standard bibliographies that cover medieval literature, such as the annual *MLA Bibliography, The Year's Work in Modern Language Studies, The Year's Work in English Studies, BBSIA (Bulletin Bibliographique de la Société Internationale Arthurienne)*, and the International Medieval Bibliography. Since much of the work in this field continues to be published in German, one must use bibliographies with good continental coverage. Finally, the recent article by R. G. Peterson, "Critical Calculations: Measure and Symmetry in Literature," *PMLA* 91 (1976):367-75, ranges from classical to modern literature and cites several interesting studies of post-Renaissance works: for example, Douglas Brooks's interpretation of the use of number in eighteenth-century novels, Stuart Gilbert's proposal for structural symmetry in James Joyce's *Ulysses*, and Oskar Seidlin's analysis of the numbers in Thomas Mann's *Der Zauberberg*. Perhaps eventually a comprehensive work on all of the literary uses of number will be written.

C. D. E.

Notes on Contributors

RUSSELL A. PECK is Professor of English at the University of Rochester. His major research interests are Middle English literature, medieval poetics and aesthetics, and the history of the English language; his publications include the book *Confessio Amantis* (1968) and articles in such journals as *Mosaic, English Literary History,* and *PMLA*.

A. KENT HIEATT is Professor of English at the University of Western Ontario. His specialties are English and Comparative Literature of the fourteenth through seventeenth centuries; his books include *Short Time's Endless Monument* (1960) and *Selections from the Poetry of Edmund Spenser* (1968).

CHARLES S. SINGLETON is Professor of Humanistic Studies and Director of the Humanities Center at John Hopkins University. He is known for his work on Italian literature (particularly on Dante), literary criticism, and Florence during the Renaissance; his publications on Dante include *Journey to Beatrice* (1958), an annotated edition of the *Commedia* (1972), and a translation of the *Commedia* with commentary (1970-75).

ELAINE SCARRY is Associate Professor of English at the University of Pennsylvania. She is the author of a monograph *Henry Esmond: the Rookery at Castlewood* (1975) and of an article on Beckett (*James Joyce Quarterly* 8); she has also worked on Plato and is currently studying the capacity of language to communicate physical pain.

ALLAN METCALF is Associate Professor of English at MacMurray College in Jacksonville, Illinois. He is the author of *Poetic Diction in the Old English Meters of Boethius* (1973) and of several articles on the poems of the *Gawain* manuscript; a bibliography of studies of the poems is in preparation.

CAROLINE D. ECKHARDT is Associate Professor of English and Comparative Literature at the Pennsylvania State University. She has published articles on Chaucer, Provençal poetry, and the Middle English romance *Sir Perceval of Galles*, and is currently editing a fifteenth-century *Prophetia Merlini* commentary.

THOMAS ELWOOD HART is Associate Professor of Germanic Philology at Syracuse University. He has held post-doctoral research grants from the Fulbright-Hays Commission and the National Endowment for the Humanities; his research and publications have dealt chiefly with problems of structure and literary aesthetics in medieval literature.

EDWARD G. FICHTNER is Associate Professor of German and Scandinavian at Queens College and a member of the Doctoral Faculty of the CUNY Graduate School. His research interests include medieval German and Scandinavian literature and the structure of the German language.

Index

DATE DUE

GAYLORD

PRINTED IN U.S.A.